Keith Ward is an Anglican priest and was a Canon of Christ Church, Oxford. He has been F. D. Maurice Professor of Moral Theology in the University of London, Professor of the History and Philosophy of Religion at the University of London, and Regius Professor of Divinity at the University of Oxford. He is a Fellow of the British Academy. SPCK published *Comparative Theology: Essays for Keith Ward* in 2003.

D0264034

What the Bible Really Teaches

A challenge for fundamentalists

Keith Ward

First published in Great Britain in 2004 by
Society for Promoting Christian Knowledge
Holy Trinity Church
Marylebone Road
London NW1 4DU

Scripture quotations taken from the HOLY BIBLE,
NEW INTERNATIONAL VERSION
Copyright © 1973, 1978, 1984 by International Bible Society
Used by permission of Hodder & Stoughton,
a member of the Hodder Headline Group.

British Library Cataloguing-in-Publication Data

A catalogue record for this book is available from the British Library

ISBN 0–281–05680–3

1 3 5 7 9 10 8 6 4 2

Typeset by Avocet Typeset, Chilton, Aylesbury, Bucks
Printed in Great Britain by Ashford Colour Press

Contents

♦ 1 ♦

Fundamentalism and the Bible

I am a born-again Christian. I can give a precise day when Christ came to me and began to transform my life with his power and his love. He did not make me a saint. But he did make me a forgiven sinner, liberated and renewed, touched by divine power and given the immense gift of an intimate sense of the personal presence of God. I have no difficulty in saying that I wholeheartedly accept Jesus as my personal Lord and Saviour.

But I do not believe what born-again Christians are supposed to believe, or at least what the other born-again Christians I knew said that I was supposed to believe. At first I thought I was the odd one out. I thought that perhaps I was failing to read the Bible carefully enough, or be obedient to its message. But, like thousands of other Christians, I have come to think that it is my old friends who were not reading the Bible properly. They were in fact being very selective in picking out a few favourite texts which they repeated over and over, while ignoring many other equally important texts altogether. They often distorted or gave a very implausible meaning to many of the passages they liked, in order to fit a set of beliefs that they already had.

My friends would not like to be called 'fundamentalists' because that word is so often misunderstood. But there is nothing wrong with the word 'fundamentalist'. At the Bible Conference of Conservative Christians at Niagara in 1895 a statement defending five fundamental points of Christian belief was issued, which was later taken up and amplified in a series of pamphlets issued between 1910 and 1915 called *The Fundamentals*. The five points are: the verbal inerrancy of Scripture, the divinity of Jesus, the virgin birth, the substitutionary theory of the atonement, and the physical, bodily return of Jesus.

It seems very odd to make these the fundamental items of Christian belief. My list of fundamental beliefs would be the existence of a creator God, the revelation of the unlimited love of God shown in the life and death of Jesus, and the hope that all might share in the redemption of the world that is accomplished by God in and through Jesus Christ and in the power of the Spirit. The virgin birth does not seem a very important issue, the substitutionary theory of atonement is only one of four or five ancient and widely accepted models of how God reconciles the world to the divine being in Christ, and I think a literal reading of New Testament statements about the coming of Christ in glory can be shown to be pretty unbiblical! In addition, fundamentalists often have very one-sided readings of the biblical teaching about resurrection and life after death. They are extremely selective about which biblical moral teachings they choose to obey. Most oddly of all, their belief in the verbal inerrancy of the Bible is not itself based on biblical teaching.

My friends prefer to say that they are conservative evangelical Christians, or 'Bible-based Christians'. That is just where I have to disagree with them. I have come to see that there are great differences between evangelicals and fundamentalists. Evangelicals are Bible-based, but they do not necessarily share the distinctive doctrines of fundamentalism. There are millions of Christians who do have some or all of the beliefs I am calling fundamentalist – this is not just a category I have invented because it is easy for me to knock it down. But evangelicals do not have to be fundamentalists at all. Some of my friends, however, are fundamentalist – they hold the beliefs I am going to criticize. I would like to persuade them that they can be properly evangelical and Bible-based without being fundamentalist.

That is because I do not think that fundamentalists are Bible-based at all. I think they have a very selective, restrictive and exclusive view of what the Bible teaches. Their view is selective, because it accepts only some biblical teachings, and it interprets them in an implausibly literalistic sense. It is restrictive, because it does not permit alternative interpretations, not even interpretations that have existed in the Church for hundreds of years, and it has to ignore a lot of biblical material altogether. And it is exclusive, because it seems to interpret the Bible in a way that excludes most people from the saving love of God, and often even excludes people who sincerely try to love God, but just have a different interpretation of some basic Christian beliefs. For example, some of my friends would exclude Catholics from salvation, just because Catholics disagree with some of my friends' beliefs. The fact is that mainstream Christian faith, whether Catholic or evangelical, is more biblical than the allegedly 'Bible-based' beliefs of my friends.

When I was converted to an evangelical form of Christian belief, many of my friends tried to convince me that fundamentalist beliefs were somehow essential to faith. They tried to convince me that, as a result, evolutionary science (and that is almost the whole of modern science) was mistaken, that most of the people I had known until then, including my own family, were destined for endless hellfire, and that Jesus might appear in the sky at any moment. I always had great difficulty with those beliefs. From the first I could not see how they were connected with my experience of renewal in Christ. I could not see that they were biblical beliefs in any case. For forty years since then my professional work has been the study of religion, theology and the Bible. I ended my professional career as the Regius Professor of Divinity (the senior Chair in theology) at Oxford University. That does not make me an expert on everything in the Bible. But it does mean that I have had access to the best biblical scholars in the world, and from them I have gained a better idea of what the Bible actually does say.

The time has come for me to set out what I think the Bible does say – about itself, about the coming of Christ in glory, about who is saved and how, about Christ's saving death on the cross, about eternal life, and about the moral law. On all these matters, the fundamentalists seem to me, and to most Christians, to have it wrong. At the very best, they have just one highly debatable reading of what the Bible really teaches. It is not a very ancient one, and it is not one that most Christians accept. I still respect my fundamentalist friends, and am grateful to them for the vital experience of Christ to which they introduced me. But they do not, as they seem to assume, have privileged access to what the Bible really means. There are many other interpretations, more ancient and widespread than theirs. And on quite a few very important matters they seem just to have got it wrong.

What the Bible says about itself

I will start with the Bible, and with what the Bible says about itself. The Bible is written in Hebrew, Aramaic and Greek, and there are many translations of it, which are sometimes quite different from one another. I will quote from the New International Version, the 1984 edition, because it is the version most widely used by evangelicals and fundamentalists. Roman Catholic translations are slightly different, but these differences are not of major importance – though Catholic Bibles include those Books called the Apocrypha, which the New International Version does not.

Does the Bible, then, anywhere say that it is to be taken literally – even when it is talking about Jonah being swallowed by a fish, about the six days of creation, or about the end of the world – and that it is inerrant in every detail? No, it does not. The Bible is, of course, enormously important to Christians. It is the only remaining witness to the life of Jesus. It is a record of the history, teachings and laws of the Jewish people among whom Jesus was born and among whom his early life and beliefs were shaped. It provides an inside view of some of the beliefs of the very first Christians. The Bible is absolutely essential for every Christian, and it is very reasonable to think that in it God does teach truths that God wills to reveal through Christ. Through it God speaks to inspire men and women of every age to new spiritual insights.

A text often quoted by fundamentalists is from 2 Timothy 3.16. It reads, 'All Scripture is God-breathed and is useful for teaching, rebuking, correcting and training in righteousness'. The Greek word the writer uses is *Theopneustos*, and it does indeed mean 'breathed by or from God'. It does not, however, say, 'All Scripture is written or spoken by God'.

The writer of the letter to Timothy has in mind what Christians now call the Old Testament since, of course, the New Testament had not yet been compiled when he wrote. The Old Testament was written mostly in Hebrew, but it was written over many centuries by many different human authors. The different books of the Old Testament are written in many different styles, and even though orthodox Jews believe that God did dictate the Torah (the Jewish Law) to Moses, they do not often think that God dictated all the Psalms, the Proverbs, the prophetic books and the histories that go to make up the Hebrew Bible.

When we come to the New Testament, there is no question of the writers just putting down what God dictates to them. Jesus probably spoke Aramaic, and since the Gospels are written in Greek, we have almost none of the actual words of Jesus. Even if Jesus was divine, he did not write down or dictate his teachings to his hearers, and those teachings were passed down by word of mouth, translated and then put into four different Gospels many years later. That does not mean they are inaccurate. But it does mean that it is not the exact words, exactly as at first spoken, which are of primary importance.

The letters to early Christians which form a large part of the New Testament do not claim to be dictated by God, and contain many personal opinions which changed at various times (see Paul's attitudes to women speaking in church, which will be looked at later, in Chapter 3). All this suggests something very important about the nature of the Bible. It suggests that it is not, as a whole, dictated by God, but that God works in a much more indirect way to communicate the truths of revelation through the words of the Bible. Inspiration is not the same as dictation.

The usual Christian view always has been that God 'inspires' the Scriptures, but does not dictate them. But what is inspiration? We might get a clue from the Greek word *pneuma*, from which *pneustos* derives. *Pneuma* is breath, wind or spirit. Wind is what drives along boats under sail. Breath is what enables an organism to live and move. Spirit is the giver of life and new vitality. Genesis 2.7 says that 'The Lord God formed the man from the dust of the ground and breathed into his nostrils the breath of life'. Human beings, the Bible says, are 'God-breathed'. They are brought to life, they are given life, by God. This does not mean that God dictates every human action. On the contrary, it implies that God gives humans freedom to live and choose whether to obey God or to reject God. The breath, or Spirit, of God, gives life and freedom, but it does not dictate.

If this is a good biblical analogy, then we could say that the Scriptures are God-breathed, because God's Spirit hovers over the prophets and the writers of Scripture to give them insights, to enliven them, to raise their minds towards divine reality – but not to dictate to them what they shall say. This is what the mainstream understanding of the inspiration of Scripture has always been. God's Spirit shapes and guides the thoughts of the writers, but does not actually put words into their mouths (as Muslims say God put words into the mouth of Muhammad).

It has seemed to many Christians that if God shapes someone's thoughts, God will prevent errors occurring, so Scripture must be without any errors. But that is not obviously so, and the Bible never explicitly says it is so. Belief in biblical inerrancy is not based on what the Bible explicitly says. It is based on an argument that if God inspires Scripture, then God will prevent any errors occurring in it.

But that argument seems to be undermined by Scripture itself. There are many small mistakes in the Bible. For instance, Matthew's Gospel says that Mary Magdalene, coming to Jesus' tomb with 'the other Mary', saw an angel roll away the stone from the tomb (Matthew 28.1–2), whereas John's Gospel records that Mary Magdalene, coming alone to the tomb, found the stone had already been taken away when she got there (John 20.1). To take another example, Mark reports that Jesus defended his disciples plucking grain on the Sabbath by referring to what David did when Abiathar was High Priest (Mark 2.26). But a quick reference to the Old Testament (1 Samuel 21.1–6, for example) shows that Ahimelech, son of Abiathar, was High Priest at the time. These are very small points, but they are discrepancies. One of each pair of accounts must be mistaken. What they show is that small errors, at least, do occur in Scripture.

Accordingly, those who do accept that Scripture is inerrant usually say something rather more sophisticated. The Second Vatican Council of the Roman Catholic Church put it very well: 'the books of Scripture, firmly, faithfully and without error, teach that truth which God, for the sake of our salvation, wished to see confided to the sacred Scriptures'. (This is quoted from the Council's *Dogmatic Constitution on Divine Revelation*, ch. 3, para. 11.) This phrasing is very careful. There may be discrepancies and errors in the sacred writings, but those truths that God wished to see included in Scripture, and which are important to our salvation, are placed there without error. In other words, God makes sure that the essential truths of salvation are faithfully recorded in Scripture. But God does not remove all errors of memory and give absolutely perfect recall of the precise words Jesus used many years earlier, as if by magic. This Catholic statement is one that I find wholly reasonable, and compatible with what is actually in the Bible. The Bible is not inerrant in detail, but God has ensured that no substantial errors, which mislead us about the nature of salvation, are to be found in Scripture.

When the second letter to Timothy says that all Scripture is useful for teaching, he is not saying that it is just a collection of true beliefs that we have to learn by heart. He is saying that prayerful reflection on Scripture, continual exploration of its difficulties and mysteries, and a search for its often hidden meanings, will be of great spiritual profit, and is an excellent training in prayer. Biblical texts convey insight by evoking discussion, calling forth different responses from different readers, leading people to explore the riches of God's truth in their own way, while listening carefully to the insights of others. Fundamentalists point out, quite rightly, that Jesus accepted the Old Testament, the Hebrew Bible, as inspired by God. But it begs the question to assume that means that he accepted it as dictated by God. It has authority, but that authority is not unchangeable, final or complete. This is made quite clear in Matthew's Sermon on the Mount (Matthew 5—7), where Jesus does not hesitate to declare some of the Old Testament laws obsolete ('You have heard that it was said, "Eye for eye, and tooth for tooth." But I tell you, Do not resist an evil person,' Matthew 5.38–39). That does not imply that we are all free to declare biblical teachings obsolete if we feel like it – we are not, after all, divine. But it does entail that written texts in the Bible cannot always be taken to apply literally to us. We must think very carefully about how to interpret biblical texts. It is never enough to say, 'God dictated this, so it must be true, and it must apply to us.' The words of Jesus make it quite clear that some teachings in the Bible need to be amended or completed or inter-preted in new ways in new situations. The hard question for us is not whether to do that, but how we can do it in a way that is most faithful to the life and teachings of Jesus.

To sum up, I think the natural way to take the text from 2 Timothy is to say that God has 'breathed over', inspired, the minds of the many writers of Scripture so that, with all their varying viewpoints and dif-ferences of approach, the Scriptures build up an authentic and trust-worthy testimony to the loving-kindness of God, and to the divine plan to reconcile the world to the divine life. The Scriptures must be read prayerfully, with an eye to their inner spiritual meaning. It really is a misunderstanding and a trivializing of Scripture to think that it is a record of guaranteed facts that we just have to assent to, without searching, often tentatively and provisionally, for what it discloses of the ultimate mystery of God.

What biblical revelation is

The most misleading thing about fundamentalist use of the Bible is that it misunderstands, not just some specific texts, but the whole nature of the Bible itself. It imposes upon the Bible a view of revelation that is alien to the Bible, and that the Bible refutes by its form and character as well as by its content. That alien view is that revelation consists of a set of clear doctrines uttered by God and put directly, without any human interpretation, onto the pages of Scripture. When fundamental-ists appeal to the Bible, they select some passages of it as providing such doctrines, straight from the mouth of God. They have to ignore huge amounts of biblical writing, but they get away with it because most people do not know the Bible well enough to refute them. The refuta-tion does not consist in denying the texts they cite. It basically consists in simply pointing out what the nature of biblical revelation is. It is not a set of doctrines, and it does not record the direct thoughts of God without any human interpretation. We need to read it carefully to see just what it is. But once we have seen that, we can never be tempted by fundamentalism again.

Ironically, perhaps, the view of biblical revelation adopted by funda-mentalists is more like that of Islam than it is of Christianity. The Holy Qur'an of Islam is believed by Muslims to be the very words of God, in the Arabic language. The Prophet recites the words he hears, but the author of the Qur'an is God, and human minds add nothing to the text. For that reason, the Qur'an must always be recited in the original

Arabic in worship, and translations are viewed with suspicion by Muslim theologians.

Christians have sometimes spoken as though the Bible is like this, but it is very plainly not like this at all. The Bible was written by many different people, at very different times, and in different languages, mainly Hebrew and Greek. Christians do not in fact worry very much if they read the Bible in English, or in some other language – which shows that they do not really think the exact words, in the original language, are sacred and given by God. Moreover the Bible expresses many different points of view. Some books seem to be almost totally pessimistic, like the book of Ecclesiastes: '"Meaningless! Meaningless!" says the Teacher. "Everything is meaningless!"' (Ecclesiastes 12.8). Other books are filled with hope, like the latter parts of Isaiah: 'I will create Jerusalem to be a delight and its people a joy' (Isaiah 65.18). There are hymns, poems, proverbs, predictions of disaster and promises of hope, novels, histories, laws and letters. The 66 books of the Bible differ from one another in style and in perspective. They are not, in any straightforward sense, written by one author or given all at once to one reciter. They express the responses of many human writers to the inspiring presence and action of God in their experience and the experience of the children of Abraham and Isaac.

These facts have always been obvious, but it is amazing how radical and worrying they were thought to be when they were stated explicitly in the nineteenth century. It is as though Christians always wished they had a sacred text that told one continuous story, from one (God's) point of view, without any diversity of perspective or human reaction. There seems to be a hankering for a clear set of facts, set out without error or ambiguity, guaranteed by God, leaving virtually no room for interpretation or argument. That expresses a particular ideal of what revelation is – the communication without mistake or interpretation, of a set of truths direct from the mind of God, to be simply accepted without discussion, argument or personal interpretation.

If that is the ideal of revelation we have, then the Qur'an is its nearest historical expression (though I doubt if even the Qur'an manages to dispense with ambiguity and the need for interpretation). In the light of that ideal, the Bible makes a rather poor showing. This obviously worried people who first came up against the scholarly study of the diverse origins and contexts of the biblical writings in the nineteenth century. But what it really suggests is that this ideal of revelation is misleading. The Bible does not support it. The Bible supports a rather different view of what revelation is.

The primary sense of 'revelation' in the New Testament is that of disclosure of something that had been hidden or unperceived. Paul says, '[God] was pleased to reveal his Son in me' (Galatians 1.15–16), and the reference is to his personal vision of the risen Christ on the road to Damascus. The 'revelation' is the experience of Paul, when 'a light from heaven flashed around him', and he heard Christ address him by name (Acts 9.3–9). This experience made apparent to Paul what had been hidden from him, that Jesus was risen and alive.

The first letter of Peter refers to 'the glory to be revealed' (1 Peter 5.1). Again, the thought is of the making apparent of the beauty and power of God, which is usually ambiguous or concealed.

In Luke's Gospel, Jesus says, 'No-one knows . . . who the Father is except the Son and those to whom the Son chooses to reveal him' (Luke 10.22). The knowledge in question is personal acquaintance, and what Jesus is claiming is that only he has direct personal acquaintance with the true nature of the Father, but that he can make such acquaintance possible for others.

So revelation is primarily an unveiling and knowledge of the reality of God, especially in the person of Jesus. It is not primarily a communication of true propositions.

Of course there are truths that are communicated in revelation. Jesus says to Paul, 'I am Jesus, whom you are persecuting' (Acts 9.5). That is meant to be a true statement. The writer of 1 Peter accepts as true that God will be clearly known in future. And personal acquaintance with God entails that we know some truths about God – that God is loving and compassionate, for example. There are truths of revelation. But the primary and most important thing is the apprehension of God, and our words may not be able to communicate that apprehension very well.

The importance of personal experience is clear in the records we have in the New Testament of the early Church. 'Revelations' were, along with 'knowledge or prophecy or word of instruction', speaking in tongues and interpretation, given to members of early Christian congregations (1 Corinthians 14.6). These were 'spiritual gifts' (1 Corinthians 14.12), and Paul says they are eagerly to be desired (1 Corinthians 14.39). Personal experience is important, for it is in the church community, gathered in worship, and in a heightened awareness of the presence of the Spirit, that revelations occur. In fact most Spirit-inspired utterances, to this day, consist in praising and thanking God for the divine goodness, not in providing new information. Nevertheless beliefs are obviously involved, and it is hard to imagine any personal experience that does not involve some knowledge.

So we might say that revelations occur when we are taken up into the Spirit, and the Spirit manifests in and through us. This involves an experience of disclosure and union, but the words we hear or speak in such a state can also be called 'revelations'.

The key question is whether we continue, in such a state, to speak out of our own characters and personal histories, and in ways that usually express a partial, limited or incomplete grasp of the reality we truly apprehend. The Bible does not explicitly answer this question. But the natural meaning of the word 'inspiration', both in ancient classical sources – where writers sought inspiration from the gods or muses – and in modern English – where writers sometimes feel themselves to be taken over by a force beyond their conscious selves – does not remove individuality. It increases stylistic diversity and also the distinctiveness of individual insights and perspectives, and it certainly does not give infallibility to writers. Of course it may be different in the case of the Bible. But this is not something the Bible explicitly claims.

Why are there four Gospels?

More important than what is explicitly claimed, however, is the immense diversity of content within the Bible. It must, for example, be an immense puzzle for anyone who thinks God just uses the Bible to communicate factual information that there are four Gospels. Why did God not just send down a full and accurate record of the life of Jesus, as it really happened? The four Gospels present the life of Jesus from very different perspectives. They often have different content, and often they present the content in very different ways.

In the first three Gospels Jesus teaches that no miraculous sign 'will be given to [this generation] except the sign of the prophet Jonah' (Matthew 12.39; Luke 11.29, Mark 8.12). But John's Gospel is a Gospel in which Jesus gives many great and public signs of his divinity, so that people 'followed him because they saw the miraculous signs he had performed' (John 6.2). In John's Gospel, Jesus apparently performed miracles so that people would believe he was the son of God – 'This, the first of his miraculous signs, Jesus performed in Cana in Galilee. He thus revealed his glory, and his disciples put their faith in him' (John 2.11). Did Jesus use his miracles as signs of his special status, or did he refuse to do so? The Gospels seem to differ about this. They all agree that Jesus performed miracles, but the first three Gospels, and especially Mark, do not see the miracles as 'proofs of divine approval'. Mark even has Jesus warn the disciples not to tell people that he is the Messiah (Mark 8.30). But in John's Gospel Jesus goes about openly telling people that he is 'the light of the world' (John 8.12), and he does not conceal his divine status at all.

These differences of emphasis have puzzled biblical scholars for many years. All are agreed that there is a problem, but no solution is universally accepted. The basic facts about Jesus are agreed (though there is disagreement about how many times he went to Jerusalem, and about the order in which the events of his life occurred). But there are some broad differences of emphasis between the four Gospels. Matthew seems concerned to stress that Jesus was a defender of Jewish orthodoxy, if in a very humanitarian sense. Mark stresses the hiddenness of Jesus' Messianic claims, and hardly refers to Jesus' teaching at all. Luke has a distinctive stress on the parables of God's compassionate love. All these Gospels represent Jesus as speaking in short cryptic sentences, and using vivid parables and metaphors. But John places a series of long discourses in the mouth of Jesus, in which the Saviour elaborates in some detail his mission and purpose, with hardly any recourse to parable.

It is virtually impossible to maintain that all of these views represent in literal detail what Jesus actually did and said. We have to say that they are interpretations of the life and teaching of Jesus, four portraits from different points of view. As is often said, these are not biographies at all. They are documents meant to present Jesus as the Christ, the Messiah, the Lord of the Church, the one who was raised from death by God, and to present various remembered accounts of his life in that light.

If we assume that God meant there to be four Gospels, then we have to say that in the New Testament, interpretation enters into revelation in an inseparable way. That is, in the documents that reveal Jesus as Lord, diverse interpretations of that basic fact are already present within the texts. These accounts of Jesus include human responses to his reality as the act and image of God. Those responses cannot be eliminated, leaving a wholly literal account of 'the historical Jesus'. More importantly, they ought not to be eliminated. They are part of God's revelation.

Fundamentalists often basically misunderstand biblical revelation. They want the Bible to contain one completely accurate and agreed account of the life of Jesus, so that all the Gospels are in total harmony, and all we have to do is say, 'Amen'. But the Bible is not like that. The Gospels manifest genuinely different interpretations of the life of Jesus, and those differences force us, the readers, to make up our own minds about our personal relationship to Jesus. We are not, after all, historians who want to know 'what really, literally, happened'. We are devotees, disciples of the risen Christ who is known as a personal presence in the Church. What the Gospels give us is a diversity of personal responses to the risen Christ, which reflects and validates something of the diversity of spiritual perspectives present within the Church.

If we look at it in this way, we can see John as putting those long speeches into the mouth of Jesus in order to give an account of the nature and mission of Jesus from a post-resurrection point of view. Jesus is known in the Church as the light of the world, the good shepherd, the bread of life, and the Son of God. John uses the historical material he had to hand, but his purpose is to present the risen Christ in the full glory of his manifestation as the eternal Word.

The other gospel writers present Jesus in rather different ways, and it is not surprising that each Gospel tends to appeal to different sorts of people. Matthew (that is, the unknown person who collected together all the materials that make up this Gospel) seems to be rather a judgemental, authoritarian and legalistic sort of person. He is the one who has Jesus say that not a point of the Torah will be abolished (Matthew 5.18), who frequently repeats that there will be 'weeping and gnashing of teeth' (Matthew 13.42) on the part of those excluding themselves from the Kingdom, and who recommends the excommunication of sinners from the Church (Matthew 18.17).

Mark, on the other hand, suggests that Jesus repealed the Torah by declaring 'all foods "clean"' (Mark 7.19), and says nothing about the Church or the 'power of the keys'. Luke has a sermon on the plain (Luke 6.17–49) instead of on a mountain, as in Matthew, and has a number of sections on Jesus' last journey to Jerusalem, which no other Gospel contains.

Any careful reading of the Gospels, preferably using a Synopsis which places biblical passages alongside one another, and which contains the Greek text, reveals huge numbers of differences in presentation of the material, along with an agreement on a number of basic facts. What the Bible seems to be teaching is that there is no unbiased, interpretation-free record of divine revelation. We always need to take account of the predispositions and interests of the writers. Putting the four Gospels alongside one another enables us to do this, by showing the different attitudes they have to the same material, and by seeing what items they select for inclusion and what they exclude.

When we read the Gospels, we are challenged to interpret the interpreters of the disclosure of God in the person of Jesus. We cannot be content with repetition. Seeing the diversity, we see that we do not have the direct words of God – it is no accident, after all, that Jesus did not write anything down, and his actual Aramaic words are not even recorded. What we have are reflections on memories held in the early Christian Church of a disclosure of God in Jesus, and especially in his resurrection. As we read them, we must bring to them our own experiences of God and the reflections of many Christian centuries. The work of interpretation must continue, and it is licensed by the nature of biblical revelation itself. The fourfold Gospel of God compels us to compare, recognize diversity, learn from it and respond in a personal way to the living Christ.

The Bible and the Church

What, then, do we mean by saying that the Bible is 'inspired'? Some fundamentalists speak as though the books of the Bible somehow selected themselves, with humans looking on in amazement. There is a legend that there were 70 translators of the Old Testament into Greek (the Septuagint) who worked independently, and all came up with exactly the same translation – proving that God had chosen the words. But it is a legend, and we know that the canon of Scripture was decided upon by committees, after much discussion and argument. Even today, different parts of the Church disagree about what exactly is to be included in the Bible, but there was broad agreement on most of it from early times. Gospels that were too fantastic were excluded, as were 'Revelations' which were thought to be too far outside the tradition. The Song of Songs, a collection of erotic poems, just made it, and Luther at least wished that the letter of James had never been accepted (it seems to place too much emphasis on works for Luther).

The Bible is quite clear that the majority of people who call themselves prophets are not truly inspired by God. Jeremiah 28 records a dispute between two prophets, Hananiah and Jeremiah, both claiming to speak in the name of God. Hananiah said, 'This is what the Lord says: "In the same way will I break the yoke of Nebuchadnezzar"' (Jeremiah 28.11). But Jeremiah replied by saying, 'This is what the Lord says: "I am about to remove you from the face of the earth"' (Jeremiah 28.16). Jeremiah was validated as a true prophet because Hananiah died, and peace did not come to Jerusalem as Hananiah had predicted. A true prophet is known by his fruits – his words come true. Unfortunately, we cannot really know until after the event.

Things can get very complicated, however, and on at least one occasion the Bible says that 'the Lord has put a lying spirit in the mouths of these prophets of yours' (2 Chronicles 18.22). Telling a true from a spurious prophet is no easy matter, and what the Bible teaches is that there are many who claim to be prophets who are not from God, and that the decision about truth can only really be made when time has shown who was right. Those who have experience of 'prophecies' in the Church today know that the same is true. Many claim to prophesy who turn out not to have spoken truly. That does not mean there are not true prophets. It means that we should be rather careful about saying who the true prophets are; we must test the spirits – 'do not believe every spirit, but test the spirits to see whether they are from God, because many false prophets have gone out into the world' (1 John 4.1). This testing or discerning of spirits is itself a gift of God (1 Corinthians 12.10).

The New Testament seems to offer a fairly simple test for authenticity. 'Every spirit that acknowledges that Jesus Christ has come in the flesh is from God' (1 John 4.2). But this fails to allow for hypocrisy and deceit, as well as honest delusion. The reference to Jesus as God incarnate is important, however. The spirit of Jesus is the spirit of the figure depicted in the Gospels as loving, reconciling, suffering and forgiving, as keeping company with the socially unacceptable, and as opposed to the hypocrisy of the religious. 'But the fruit of the Spirit is love, joy, peace, patience, kindness, goodness, faithfulness, gentleness and self-control' (Galatians 5.22). The depiction of the life of Jesus in the Gospels is the test of whether a Spirit is the Spirit of God. Only the disciples recognized these things in Jesus – others saw him as a threat, a blasphemer or a dangerous radical. There is no escape from this circle – only those moved by the Spirit can recognize the Spirit for what it is.

This is not a vicious circle, but an inevitable one. Only a good musician can recognize a great musician. Only a good mathematician can recognize a mathematical genius. So only a person who is moved by the presence and love of God can recognize a person, Jesus, who embodies the Spirit in a uniquely full way. And how do we know who is a good musician, mathematician or disciple of God? By the common judgement of the community of relevant experience and expertise. The discernment of the Spirit takes place, not in some isolated private experience, but within the community of the Church.

It is the cumulative tradition of the Church that judges the authenticity of prophecy and inspiration. It is the Church that defines the canon of Scripture. At the first Council of the Church in Jerusalem, the apostles and elders and the whole church sent a letter to Antioch, saying, 'It seemed good to the Holy Spirit and to us . . .' (Acts 15.28). The whole Church, meeting together, heard a dispute about how much of Torah should be kept, and came to a decision. They formulated that as the decision of the Holy Spirit. So the Bible teaches that a meeting of the whole Church (what later came to be called an ecumenical Council) could claim to speak in the name of the Holy Spirit. It would be absurd to hold that such claims ceased after just one Council. Christians are brought up within and taught by the Church. While individuals can add their own insights to tradition, reception by the church community is important to any claims to divine inspiration. This is surely part of what is meant by 'the power of the keys' – 'whatever you bind on earth will be bound in heaven' (Matthew 16.19, repeated at Matthew 18.18). Jesus says this first to Peter, and then to all the disciples, so giving to the Church a power of deciding what is essential to faith.

The history of Christianity is unfortunately filled with disputes as to what the 'true Church' is, but there can be no doubt that the Bible gives to the Church, however it is defined, a power of decision-making which is inspired by the Spirit. It is the Church that decided that just these writings were to be officially confirmed as inspired by the Spirit, and so included in the canon of Scripture. And in choosing to include a diversity of interpretations in the canon, the Church committed itself to the acceptability, or even the necessity, of a diversity of interpretations of the truth revealed in Jesus. The Church did not deny that other writings or utterances were inspired by the Spirit. It is highly unlikely that only Paul's letters were inspired, while all the others, now lost, were totally uninspired! Neither did the Church affirm that everything in these writings was true or to be accepted just as it stands. When it included Jesus' sayings, 'Do not call anyone on earth "father"' (Matthew 23.9), and 'Do not swear at all [on oath]' (Matthew 5.34), it did not mean to forbid calling priests 'Father' or to forbid priests to swear on oath that they would obey their bishops.

What the Church was doing in framing a canon of Scripture was to declare that these writings were truly inspired by the Spirit, and were suitable, taken together, to frame a normative rule for Christian believing. But it was taken for granted that the Scriptures were hard to interpret, requiring discernment and judgement, and that they expressed human responses to disclosures of the divine in and through Jesus, responses which could continue to be built on and extended and complemented by subsequent human experience.

When Jesus said, 'when he, the spirit of truth, comes, he will guide you into all truth' (John 16.13), he did not add, 'But only for a short time'. Jesus said, 'I have much more to say to you, more than you can now bear' (John 16.12). The implication is that Jesus did not give even his closest disciples a full and final revelation of the truth. There is more to be learned, and the Spirit has more to teach. Every generation of Christians adds to revelation, as it learns more of what God wants for human creatures and for this world.

In this process, the Bible has a unique role. It bears a direct witness to the historical Jesus, in a way no longer possible. It describes the earliest foundation of the Christian Church. It expresses a norm of faith in the personal disclosure of God in Jesus that must remain central for all subsequent history. But it is very important to remember two things: the Bible is essentially, and by God's decree, diverse, presenting different perspectives of faith, not one harmonious narrative or set of doctrines. And the Bible, while having a uniquely definitive status, points on to future disclosures of God in the community of the Church, in so far as that community is guided by the Spirit.

It follows that discussion, debate, reflection and exploration should be an essential part of church life, always looking for new disclosures of the unfailing love of God in new contexts, and looking to the Bible as a model and inspiration for such creative exploration, rather than as an unchangeable barrier to any new thought. The Bible is a signpost to new exploration of the mind of God, not a barrier to all original thought. That is what the Bible teaches about itself, by its form and structure and by the nature of the revelation, the disclosure of God as personal presence in Jesus and in the Spirit, towards which the Bible points. The Bible, we might say, is not itself the revelation of God. It is the Church's witness to the revelation of God in Jesus, and an expression of the diversity of human responses to that revelation from the first moments of its life. As such it has an irreplaceable and central place in Christian life. But it loses its main spiritual function and importance if we fail to see that it is not the incarnation of God's word. That took place in the living person of Jesus, and the Bible remains important only because and in so far as it bears witness to the revelation of God in Christ.

♦ 2 ♦

Interpreting the Bible

This is an adversarial book. It attacks Christian fundamentalism, and that may seem a very uncharitable thing for a Christian writer to do. However this is an important issue of truth, the truth of how to interpret the Bible and of what it teaches. The fact that I think my fundamentalist friends are wrong does not at all mean a break in fellowship with them. I am happy to live with differences in the Christian Church, and indeed I think that if people of very different views did not exist in the Church, the Church would not be doing its job of offering the life of Christ to all.

Some may say, 'There must be a limit to who can really be a member of the Church.' But why should the limit not simply be the love of God as revealed in the person of Jesus Christ? If anyone sincerely accepts that, or wants to explore that, they are in the Church. This includes fundamentalists and people like me, and people much more radical than I am. So I do not want to break fellowship with fundamentalists, throw them out of the Church, or think of them as inferior Christians.

Why am I so adversarial, then? Simply because I think fundamentalists are wrong, and I think that needs to be clearly said. They are wrong about the Bible, wrong about the nature of Christian revelation, and wrong about the nature of the Church. They think the Bible is a set of clear doctrines delivered personally by God. They think Christian revelation is a book, miraculously free from any errors. They think the Church is only for those who agree with them on many difficult points of doctrine.

They are wrong about all these things. Nevertheless, somehow they have managed to persuade a great many people that theirs is the authentic voice of Christianity. I often meet people who say, 'I am not a Christian. But if I were, I would believe the Bible literally. If you are going to get into religion, you may as well go all the way. Let's have none of this wishy-washy liberal stuff, which picks and chooses what it wants out of the Bible, and replaces the revelation of God with the theories of human beings. Of course, I repeat, I do not believe all that stuff. But I think Christians ought to.'

This is all a terrible mistake. Worse, it is anti-biblical. For the Bible does not take itself literally. It is the fundamentalists who pick and choose, omitting or reinterpreting huge chunks of Scripture so that it will fit into a neat theological scheme, which was not invented until the sixteenth century. If we are going to be Bible-believing Christians, we have to be very careful how we interpret the immensely complex, diverse and often cryptic set of writings that go to make up the Bible.

Six principles of biblical interpretation

1. The principle of contextualization

So how do we know what the Bible really teaches? I suggest that there are six major principles of interpretation that should govern our reading of Scripture. All Bible-believing Christians should use these principles, and only when we do can we see what the teaching of the Bible really is.

First of all, when we read a specific biblical passage, we should try to discover what sort of text we are reading. The Bible is full of all sorts of different writings. There are histories, laws, proverbs, hymns, stories, dreams, visions, prophecies, letters and allegories. These were written at many different times in history, and for very different groups of people. We cannot read a biblical passage as though it had just fallen out of the sky and was addressed to us personally. We have to try to see who wrote it, when, why and for whom. What were their problems? If we do not have those problems now, how can the passage speak to us?

What is needed here is a good commentary on the Bible. A good scholarly commentary is the *Oxford Bible Commentary*, published in 2001 and edited by John Barton and John Muddiman. This is a commentary that contains the results of the best reliable investigations into the context and the meaning of the biblical texts.

Fundamentalists tend to use only commentaries that are written by 'sound' scholars, people who agree with their own beliefs. In one way that is understandable. After all, biblical scholars differ quite a lot in their approach to the Bible. Some take it to be literally the word of God. Others do not believe in God at all, and think it is a set of purely human documents. Most lie somewhere in between those extremes.

However there is good and bad scholarship. In physics, most decent physicists know who the really first-rate physicists are. The same is true in Bible studies. We know a good biblical scholar because they have mastered Hebrew and Greek, because they have read the original documents, because they know just what other scholars in the field have said, and because they have published research work in peer-reviewed journals. All good biblical scholars know who the first-rate scholars are, because those leaders in the field have published weighty books which have set the agenda for discussion and new research.

The best scholars may not believe the same things that we believe. They may have a very different sort of Christian faith, if they have one at all. But any responsible reader of the Bible should be aware of who they are, and what they have said.

This may seem like bad news for most average readers of the Bible. Do we have to do a degree in theology before we can read the Bible? No, of course not. But all readers of the Bible depend on the work of scholars. Most of us depend on having a good translation. We need to refer to a good commentary to help us to see what that translation means. It is just silly to think that we can work out the meaning of a biblical passage for ourselves, when we may not even know the original language it was written in, and we know nothing about how or why it was written.

This means that when we read the Bible we will be relying on authority – not the authority of God, but the authority of translators, historians and theologians who give us our Bible translations and commentaries to help us understand them. Now the present situation in biblical studies is this: there has been an immense amount of work in the past 150 years which has told us a great deal about the writing and collection of the biblical 'books', and there is general agreement among competent scholars on the main results of this work. However, there are still many disputes about some important topics – like whether there was a document, Q, lying behind the Synoptic Gospels, or about how many different traditions, writers, and editors lie behind the final version of the Pentateuch (the first five books of the Bible).

The Bible can be read for many reasons – for spiritual comfort, for prayer and meditation, or out of interest in the origins of Christian doctrines. Some of these reasons do not require any great biblical scholarship. But if someone is setting out to say what the Bible actually teaches then scholarship becomes vitally important. It is a precondition of scholarship that we know what the best scholars in the field have said, and that we know where the main disputes lie and what the reasons behind them are. Anyone who is honest will then say that there is a scholarly consensus on some things, while many points are uncertain or disputed. It will become impossible to say, 'The Bible teaches exactly this, and it is clear to all true believing Christians.' What the Bible really teaches is usually not very clear, and is often widely misunderstood. In other words, what the Bible really teaches is not just one thing, clearly stated, which it is faithless to doubt or deny.

A good example of what I mean is the dispute in the fundamentalist world about the interpretation of the first two chapters of Genesis. Do these chapters teach that the world was created in six days, so that the whole evolutionary story of the cosmos is incorrect? Or are those passages a different sort of writing, a 'myth of origins', so familiar to students of primal religions, not to be taken literally, but conveying spiritual meaning? Well, this is where a good Bible commentary will help. But it would not help if the commentary just reinforced a literalist interpretation of the text, and said that all true believers will take it literally. Such a commentary would actually be very misleading, as it would not refer to the scholarly work that has been done on the texts, or to other excellent commentaries that do refer to that work. It would thus give a misleading account of what most Christians think the text means.

What scholars have done is to look at other Middle Eastern creation texts from around the same date, to look at the way symbolic language is used in non-literal ways throughout the Bible, to look at Rabbinic commentaries which have explored what the text means for religious life, and to explore the whole question of the relation of religious texts to scientific investigation. Any responsible account of what the Bible teaches about creation would need to mention all these facts, and to set out the range of scholarly opinions on these issues.

After all that, it might still be possible to recommend a literal reading of Genesis. But that would have to be done in full acknowledgement that it is a minority opinion among Christians (the Roman Catholic Church, to take just one case, rejects it), that there are many scholarly reasons to reject it, and it is therefore not the only possible, or even the obvious, reading of the text. What often goes wrong with fundamentalism at this point is that it ignores all scholarly work with which it disagrees, and suggests that disagreement is lack of true faith. That is not conducive either to the search for truth or to respect for the freedom of conscience of which Protestants are rightly so proud.

So the first principle in finding out what the Bible teaches is to get a good knowledge of the background of the passage we are reading, to see the range of interpretations that have been given of it by responsible scholars, and to see what sort of text it is – whether it is an allegory, a history or a piece of occasional advice in a specific context.

2. The principle of consistency

The second principle sounds much simpler, but it is much harder to apply than we might think. It is the principle of consistency. We must treat like cases alike. So, for instance, we should not take some sentences of the Sermon on the Mount literally (like 'do not swear [on oath] at all', Matthew 5.34), when we take other sentences from the same Sermon metaphorically, or as exaggerated statements to make a memorable point, but which are not to be applied literally (like 'give to the one who asks you', Matthew 5.42). Statements from the same sort of text should be treated in similar ways. We could take them all literally, or we could take them all metaphorically. But we should not pick and choose so that we take some literally and some metaphorically, just because we feel that way. The statements of the Bible must be read in a consistent way.

Another example would be the notorious statement from the book of Deuteronomy, 'in the cities of the nations the Lord your God is giving you as an inheritance, do not leave alive anything that breathes' (Deuteronomy 20.16). This is part of the Torah, the Law, said to have been given by God to Moses. It is a test-case of how we are going to use biblical authority, because it so obviously flaunts every moral intuition of most civilized societies. More to the point, it flaunts the biblical principle that you should 'Love your enemies, do good to those who hate you, bless those who curse you, pray for those who ill-treat you' (Luke 6.27). Most Christians would probably agree that the Law has been superseded by the teaching of Jesus and that, whatever used to be the case, genocide is ruled out for Christians. But that clearly entails that statements of the Law cannot be just accepted as they stand. The rule of consistency requires that we look at every statement of the Law (that is, every moral rule from Genesis to Deuteronomy) in a similar way. Any and every Law might be superseded, and we have to look carefully to see whether it is. That will stop us from saying, 'You must do this, just because it is in the Bible.' Reading the Bible consistently means that we must think very carefully before coming to conclusions about what the Bible is telling us to do.

3. The principle of comprehensiveness

The necessity of comparing different passages from the Bible, and weighing different texts against one another, points to the third principle of Bible interpretation, the principle of comprehensiveness. In reading any passage of the Bible, we must consider all relevant biblical material, and not take passages in isolation and out of context. So when reading passages about the 'second coming' of Christ, like Mark chapter 13, we should read them in the light of the Old Testament passages on which they are based (they can be found in any good reference Bible). When you do that, you will find a well-established tradition of the use of symbolic speech by the prophets. When you see what the symbols mean in their Old Testament context, that will give you a good clue about how to interpret what they mean in the Gospels. What might at first seem like literal predictions about the end of the world turn out to be to a very great extent comments about the political and religious situation of Israel in a hostile environment. This is a topic I will treat in detail in the next chapter. The point for now is that you need to get a sense of the whole biblical picture before we see how particular parts of the Bible fit into that picture in a coherent way. It is the Bible as a whole that gives meaning to its parts. The difficulty with fundamentalism is that it lets some parts, taken largely out of context, determine the meaning of the whole. This is an upside-down way of reading the Bible.

Similarly, on another topic I will discuss in more detail in Chapter 10, when we read New Testament passages about the subordination of women, we should also read all the Old Testament passages about polygamy, concubines, and the compulsory divorce of 'foreign wives', before we decide whether any of these passages are binding on Christians today. It may again become apparent that many rules clearly stated in the Bible have been amended by later teachings. That may – and I think it should – lead us to ask whether this process of amendment came to an abrupt stop with the writing of the latest document in the Bible. It will then lead us to try to discover, within the Bible itself, the principle which underlies this process of amendment, and to see how and in what way it might have to be continued beyond the biblical text. For instance, monogamous marriage is nowhere explicitly commanded in the Bible. The idea developed outside the biblical text, as a way of further developing moral principles that were already implicit within the Bible. But to discover those principles, we have to gain a general sense of the whole range of biblical writings, and the way in which they include developments of insight. The principle of comprehensiveness requires us to get a general sense of what the Bible is teaching, and then interpret particular passages in the light of that whole.

4. The principle of sublation

I have talked about some teachings superseding others, and about developments in biblical teaching. This is so important that it ought to be included as a fourth principle of Bible reading, the principle of sublation. This is not a very common word, but it is a very useful one. To 'sublate' means to negate and yet to fulfil at the same time. The best example of it is in Matthew's Gospel, chapter 5. There Jesus says, 'Do not think that I have come to abolish the Law or the Prophets; I have not come to abolish them but to fulfil them' (Matthew 5.17). Jesus is not simply throwing the Old Testament laws out, as if they are useless. He is 'fulfilling' them. But when we go on to read the Sermon on the Mount, we will see that he actually does negate them in their literal and obvious sense. Thus 'You have heard that it was said, "Eye for eye, and tooth for tooth". But I tell you, Do not resist an evil person' (Matthew 5.38–39). In other words, you should not require strict retribution, even though the Law says you should. The Law has been negated in its obvious sense, but only because its inner meaning has been fulfilled by a 'higher law'. That is what sublation is, cancelling an obvious or literal meaning by discovering a deeper spiritual meaning that can be seen to be the fulfilment to which the literal meaning points.

Many biblical passages are sublated by later teachings, so that they no longer apply literally, but can be seen to point towards a deeper spiritual meaning. For instance, a passage from Psalm 139.21–22 reads, 'Do I not hate those who hate you, O Lord? . . . I have nothing but hatred for them'. But Jesus says, 'Love your enemies' (Matthew 5.43). Jesus' teaching sublates that sentiment from the Psalms. Hatred must be reinterpreted so that we hate the sins but not the sinners. The Bible is filled with sublations, which means that many biblical passages, taken in their straightforward sense, must now be accounted false. It is a vital principle of biblical interpretation that we gradually learn to discern when and in what way specific biblical texts are to be sublated by others. This means that interpreting the Bible is never easy and straightforward. It requires spiritual insight, sensitivity and judgement. We must be very cautious when we claim, 'The Bible says . . .'.

5. The principle of spiritual interpretation

Sublating a text often means finding a deeper spiritual meaning that underlies its literal form, and that may even negate the literal form in new and different circumstances. This is the fifth principle of Bible reading. It might be called the principle of spiritual interpretation. In medieval times, it was widely accepted that there were four different sorts of meaning that biblical passages had, and the wise interpreter would look for all of them. First was the literal meaning. But the other three were the moral – what a text implies that we should do – the ana-gogical – how a text might point to some future fulfilment, and so be a basis for Christian hope – and the allegorical or spiritual interpretation.

To take one well-known example, the account of the escape of the Israelites from the Egyptians (Exodus 14) can be read as literal history. But it also has a moral message. It calls for the liberation of enslaved peoples and thanksgiving for God's liberating acts. For Christians it points forward to the liberating death of Jesus on the cross (which Luke describes as his 'exodus', Luke 9.31 – *exodon* in Greek, translated as 'departure' in the New International Version). That is at least one aspect of its future fulfilment, what the medievals called its anagogical meaning. And of course the exodus has a spiritual meaning. It counsels us to leave the world of greed and enslavement to sin, in order to fol-low the call of God, even when that means adventuring into the unknown.

Today we might simply speak of the spiritual meaning of biblical texts, and we could include in that all the three non-literal aspects just described. Sensitively read, biblical passages will point to truths about God and about the path to knowing God – this is the inner or personal aspect. They will foreshadow the objective working-out of God's pur-poses in history. And they will have implications about what we should do to obey God's will.

It is clear that we must never be content with just the literal sense of a biblical passage (though of course some reports in the Bible are liter-ally true). We must seek the spiritual sense, and sometimes the literal sense will be irrelevant to this, or it might become obvious that the text need not, or should not, be read literally at all. For instance, in 1 Corinthians 10.4, Paul makes a mysterious comment about 'the spiri-tual rock that accompanied them [the Israelites in the wilderness]', and that rock, he says, 'was Christ'. The Old Testament never says that there was a rock that went about with the Israelites, from which they drank. They did, however, drink from a rock. What Paul seems to be doing is elaborating the Old Testament account, perhaps in accordance with an old Jewish tradition, so that a moving rock which gives water becomes a symbol of the Messiah, the spiritual water which cleanses and refreshes the people of a renewed Israel. The symbols of rock and water are profound, and form the heart of Paul's comment at that point. It does not really matter whether a rock moved around the desert or not. The literal meaning can easily be rejected, without loss of the spiritual meaning.

So it may be that many parts of biblical history were actually written to convey a spiritual meaning, and it does not matter much whether they actually happened as described. The story of Jonah and the whale, or big fish which swallowed him alive (Jonah 1—2), is probably a fictional account, the spiritual meaning of which is about keeping faith in desperate circumstances.

Sometimes, indeed, it would be a mistake to take biblical teachings literally at all. Their true importance was always spiritual. When the Bible speaks of God coming down from his temple and walking on the earth, so that 'the mountains melt beneath him' (Micah 1.4), it would be blasphemous to take this literally, as though God was a giant. This is symbolic speech. These are images and metaphors, and they have to be rejected in their literal sense precisely because it would demean God to apply them literally.

An even clearer case is the prophetic writing that says of God, 'Sun and moon stood still in the heavens at the glint of your flying arrows, at the lightning of your flashing spear . . . you trampled the sea with your horses, churning the great waters' (Habakkuk 3.11, 15). God does not literally ride a horse, shoot arrows or shake a spear. It is clear to all that this is inspired poetry, not literal description.

It is not easy, however, to know just when the Bible needs to be taken literally, and when its spiritual sense is better expressed in symbol and metaphor. Is talk of Jesus ascending into heaven symbolic? Since heaven is not up above the clouds, I would think this should not be taken literally. But as C. S. Lewis once said, if ascending would make a point to the apostles, who are we to say that Jesus did not ascend into the sky before disappearing from this universe altogether? Probably in this case it does not matter much. We can afford to be agnostic, once we have given up the superstition that the only important meaning is the literal one, and we see that the spiritual meaning does not necessarily require it.

Is talk of the creation and end of the world symbolic? Perhaps again the literal pictures are just the most effective way of expressing a mysterious spiritual truth, at a particular point in history. If we can recover and state this spiritual truth, or at least see the accounts as expressing a truth that perhaps we can never state with complete clarity, we need not be concerned about whether non-scientific writers could have had miraculous insights into the origin and end of the universe. God did not

reveal the laws of physics to the prophets. But God could reveal important spiritual truths about the nature of human relationship to the
Creator, in the memorable symbols of the 'days' of creation.

Is Jesus' talk of camels going through the eyes of needles (Matthew
19.24) symbolic? It clearly refers to a literal impossibility. When we find
that the use of exaggeration to make a point memorably was a common
device of Jewish teachers at the time of Jesus, we need not hesitate to
say that this is symbolic or figurative language. Its point is not to show
that God could shrink camels if he wanted to, but to show that it is
impossible to know or achieve true relationship to God by our own
efforts. Symbolic speech is the best and most memorable way to make
this spiritual point.

Poetic figures of speech might convey spiritual meaning more effectively than pedestrian literalism ever could. The Bible is a deeply poetic
and spiritual work, and to understand that poetry and symbolism takes
all our resources of imagination and discernment. We need always to
bear in mind that the Bible is primarily a spiritual text. That means it
deals with the relationship between time and eternity, finite and infinite,
and with how humans bound by time can achieve a healing and fulfilling relationship to that which is eternal and infinite, to God.

To discern a spiritual meaning is to see how statements evoke an
awareness of God which turns the heart to God for healing, which
reveals our own spiritual condition of estrangement and self-deception,
and which brings wholeness and fulfilment of life by union with the
divine. A key question for any proposed biblical interpretation is: Does
this interpretation increase my self-awareness, disclose the nature of
God as it is seen in the great key-events of revelation, and increase in
me the spiritual fruits of compassion, love, kindness, and sensitivity to
others? Does it deliver me from attachment to selfish desire, and relate
me in love to a God of supreme loving-kindness?

To read biblical accounts as symbolic representations of the unity of
divine and human, of time and eternity, is to read them as profound
symbols of unpicturable spiritual realities, and not as just literal
accounts of amazing physical occurrences. Of course, the Bible is not
merely a set of symbolic accounts. It is important, for instance, that
Jesus literally lived in Judea and died on the cross. Otherwise it would
not be true that Jesus truly manifests what the eternal is under the
forms of time. It is not very important, however, how many times he
visited Jerusalem, or whether he entered Jerusalem on one donkey or
on two (cf. Matthew 21.2, where Jesus rides on a donkey and her colt,
compared with Mark 11.4 and Luke 19.33, where Jesus rides a colt).

Readers need to cultivate a feeling for the spiritual sense of Scripture, and this requires personal discernment and maturity. Much of the Bible's importance lies in its symbolism, and to have a feeling for that symbolism is essential if the Bible is to be adequately read.

6. The principle of Christ-centredness

One of the problems with spiritual readings of the Bible is that they can sometimes become fantastic, reading very strained allegories into every text, or finding all sorts of mystical meanings hidden in such apparently trivial matters as the numbers of soldiers in the Israelite army. For this reason, it is important that our readings of Scripture are controlled by a sixth principle of interpretation, the principle of Christ-centredness.

For a Christian, every part of the Bible must in some way point to Christ, to the living person of Jesus who is the Christ, and to the un-limited, liberating love of God which is revealed in Christ. To put it bluntly, it is not the words of the Bible that are 'the way, the truth and the life'. It is the person of Christ, to whom the Bible witnesses. This means that any interpretation of a biblical text that fails to see it in the light of God's will to redeem all humanity, to go to any lengths to do so, and finally to accomplish what God intends, fails to get the meas-ure of the Bible. It is because of this that any interpretation which depicts God as vengeful, vindictive, exclusive to just a few chosen people, or purely retributive, falls short of the Christian insight that 'God is love' (1 John 4.16), and that God's love knows no limits ('neither height nor depth, nor anything else in all creation, will be able to separate us from the love of God that is in Christ Jesus our Lord', Romans 8.39). The Bible gives us its own main principle of interpreta-tion when it tells us that the love of God in Jesus is the culminating point of its teaching. Only when we keep that firmly in mind can we be sure of being true to what the Bible really teaches.

In what follows I shall try to use these six principles of interpretation to look at some key issues on which I think fundamentalists contradict or misinterpret the Bible. I have already suggested that they misunder-stand the nature of biblical revelation itself. They tend to read the Bible as a set of facts and direct commands inerrantly dictated by God, instead of as an inspired record of God's progressive self-disclosure to the people of Israel, and of that people's varied responses to God's rev-elation. In the next chapter I will attempt to show how the profound doctrine of Christ's final appearing in glory is literalized and trivialized by a fundamentalist interpretation that contradicts the plain sense of the texts. Then in Chapters 4–6 I will show how the very restrictive fundamentalist understanding of salvation as something limited to a few like-minded people perverts the New Testament teaching of God's freely given salvation for all. In Chapter 7 I will show how the fundamentalist's favoured interpretation of Jesus' sacrifice on the cross – called the substitutionary theory of atonement – misunderstands biblical teaching on sacrifice, and falls victim to accusations of injustice on the part of God. Chapter 8 shows how fundamentalists literalize biblical teaching on resurrection, and so miss the point of Paul's teaching about the renewal of the whole universe in Christ. The ninth chapter shows how vindictive fundamentalist doctrines about eternal hell and their rejection of an intermediate state, whether called purgatory or not, either misinterpret biblical imagery or simply deny some fairly clear biblical statements on these matters. And in the final chapter I show how fundamentalists ignore clear New Testament teaching on the triumph of grace over law, arbitrarily choose to obey some moral rules in the Bible while blatantly ignoring others, and disobey the teachings of Jesus, apparently without realizing it.

I am not claiming to have the one true interpretation of Bible teaching. Indeed, that is one of the things I am accusing fundamentalists of doing – saying that there is just one correct interpretation, which is obvious just by reading the Bible. What I am claiming is that fundamentalists are not right in saying that theirs is the true interpretation of the Bible. There are many parts of the Bible that they seem to ignore, others to which they give a rather odd interpretation, and some which they erect into a dogmatic system that is based more on Calvin or some other theologian than on the Bible itself. So fundamentalism is not entitled to call itself more Bible-based than other Christian interpretations. It is in this sense that I think the Bible contains some shocking facts for fundamentalists. Realizing that will turn them into more open evangelicals.

♦ 3 ♦

Interpreting Biblical Teaching about the Coming of Christ in Glory

There are many Churches which call themselves 'Bible-based', and which pride themselves on having 'sound' doctrines, derived solely from biblical teachings. Very often, however, they are wrong, and this can be shown by an attentive reading of the Bible itself. The views of such Churches are usually based on the teaching of various theologians of the sixteenth century or later – theologians like Calvin or Luther, or sometimes even later writers like Carl Henry. These may be very good theologians, and certainly their views must be taken seriously. I am happy to have fellowship with any Christian who accepts views like theirs. But what is certainly wrong is to claim that their views are the obvious or most natural readings of the Bible, or that they are unequivocally backed by the Bible itself. As interpreters of the Bible they are in a minority in the Christian world as a whole, and their interpretations of the Bible are very selective, and biased quite strongly in many ways. They pick and choose what to believe, taking some passages fairly literally, and ignoring or even denying others without a blink. It is extremely ironic that such Churches accuse others of 'picking and choosing' when that is exactly what they do. They also often claim that 'the Bible is its own best interpreter'. I shall try to follow that rule, seeking only interpretations that can be seen to arise from the Bible itself. My argument is that the Bible's own principles of interpretation are often quite different from the principles used by fundamentalist Christians. They lead to very different conclusions, and on some matters fundamentalists seem to have simply got the Bible wrong. They are anti-biblical at crucial points, and they are importing an alien man-made philosophy (usually some altered and over-simple version of Calvin) into their reading of the Bible. Calvin was undoubtedly a major theological writer. But he himself taught that you should never accept the authority of any theologian, and he might have been quite surprised at the way some of his opinions have got

hardened into unchallengeable dogmas in the more extreme parts of
the evangelical world.

This perhaps sounds so surprising that it will seem hard to believe.
But that is only because fundamentalist teaching continually repeats
certain verses that are undoubtedly in the Bible, so they seem to be able
to quote biblical texts to support what they say. However, their sins are
sins of omission. It is the many biblical passages they never quote, or
manifestly distort, that undermine their case. We need to learn to read
the Bible in the way the Bible itself truly requires. We need to attend to
the passages fundamentalists never quote. We need to ask what has
driven fundamentalists to interpret the Bible so selectively, and impose
a particular fairly modern theological system, devised by human minds
(the minds of Calvin, Luther or Carl Henry) on the Word of God.

The expectation of Christ's return

I shall begin by considering a set of passages that are very well known.
They even form the central core of much fundamentalist teaching. Yet
fundamentalists interpret them to mean the opposite of what they actually, and quite clearly, say. As I say, the teaching is very clear. It is not
at all ambiguous. But it immediately leads to a conclusion that completely undermines the fundamentalist approach to the Bible. Therefore
fundamentalists have to say that it does not mean what it says at all. At
this point, so important to many of them, they do *not* think the Bible
means what it says. The teaching is found many times in the New
Testament, but here is an especially clear instance of it, in the words of
Jesus: 'I tell you the truth, this generation will certainly not pass away
until all these things have happened' (Matthew 24.34; Mark 13.30;
Luke 21.32).

All these passages in the Gospels depict Jesus talking about the judgement of God on the nations, and the coming of the Son of Man on the
clouds with glory. They all end with the remark that these things will
happen before the generation (*genea*) to which Jesus speaks has died.
The New International Version has a footnote saying that *genea* could
mean 'race', presumably the Jewish race. That is true, and it occasion-
ally does (once in the Bible). But in this context it is a very forced reading, which would only mean that some Jews, or perhaps even some
human beings, would still be alive when the Son of Man comes – and
that gives no sense of urgency to Jesus' teaching at all. The literal,
straightforward sense is plain: before everybody Jesus spoke to died,
the Son of Man will have returned in glory. The term *genea* is used quite

clearly to mean 'generation' in Matthew 1.17: 'there were fourteen generations in all from Abraham to David'. There is little reason to think it has a different meaning in chapter 24, and the fact is that many of the earliest Christians thought the Son of Man might come soon, and not at some unspecified time in the far future.

The whole New Testament resonates with an early expectation of the coming of the Son of Man in glory. 'Dear children, this is the last hour', we read in 1 John 2.18. The feeling that believers in Jesus as the Christ are living at the end of time is strong: 'remember what the apostles of our Lord Jesus Christ foretold', says the letter of Jude (17–19). 'They said to you, "In the last times there will be scoffers" . . . These are the men who divide you.' The universe had, in their belief, come into existence only about two thousand years ago, and it had now reached its culmination. So the first Christians prayed fervently for the coming of Christ. The great revelation of John the Divine ends with the ringing phrase, 'He who testifies to these things says, "Yes, I am coming soon"' (Revelation 22.20). And the writer says, 'Amen. Come, Lord Jesus.' There can be little doubt that many Christians thought they were living at the end of time, in the very last hour, when God's promises were at last about to be fulfilled.

Not only is this teaching about the imminent coming of the Son of Man found in the Gospels, it is even clearer in the very first piece of writing we have from the early Christian Church. Most New Testament scholars agree that the first letter from Paul to Christians in Thessalonica is the first document now in the New Testament to have been written, possibly within 20 years of the death of Jesus. While it hardly gives a full account of early Christian beliefs, it does vividly depict some central beliefs that were clearly important to at least some early Christians. There can be little doubt that the beliefs of this group, and of Paul at this time, were millennialist.

A millennialist is someone who thinks that the end of the world is at hand, that it will come with terror and destruction, and that a small group of the 'elect' will be saved from it by being taken directly into heaven. Millennialists typically speak of the destruction of their oppressive and cruel enemies, of salvation from this coming destruction by the miraculous return of a seemingly dead saviour figure, and they usually believe that this will happen very soon, within the lifetimes of some believers. In the history of religions, there have been many forms of millennialism. They are found in Judaism, in Islam and in many tribal religions throughout the world. It is a fairly common form of religious belief. But all the forms of it share one thing in common – they have all been mistaken. The end of the world and the transformation for which they looked has never happened. That is true of Christian millennialists too, and careful readers of the Bible have to ask why millennialism existed in the early Church, and what we are supposed to do about it now. When those questions have been squarely faced and answered, profound truths about the Christian gospel are uncovered. The trouble is that fundamentalists do not face up to those questions. They pretend there is no problem, and that we should just go on believing the whole universe might end tomorrow, when any physicist can assure us that even if the whole solar system ceased to exist, the rest of the universe is likely to endure for billions of years.

It is possible that life on earth may cease at any moment – perhaps by a nuclear disaster, perhaps by collision with an object from space. But that will not be the sudden divine intervention for which millennialists look. It will be a disaster, and the ending of God's purpose for future humanity – a purpose that is much more clearly evident in the pages of the New Testament than texts about a sudden end of the world. Presumably God has a way of coping with such a disaster, should it occur. But it is very different from a direct divine decision to end history and create a new heaven and earth, which some parts of the New Testament imagine. So there is a problem about the occurrence of millennialist beliefs in the New Testament. The Bible itself contains the resources for coping with this problem. But if it is to do so the Bible must be read sensitively and carefully. The trouble with fundamentalism about this topic of the end of the world is that it claims to take the Bible literally, and yet it has to change the plain meaning of the biblical texts to make them conform to a sort of 'extended millennialism'.

This failure to see a problem is a failure to read the Bible properly, and to admit that some of the things it says were not literally so. Many early Christians, and indeed some of the very first ones we know about in the New Testament, were millennialists. Millennialism was false then, and it is false now. What are we going to do about it? We need to read the Bible patiently and wisely to find out.

The first letter to the Thessalonians speaks of Christians as people who 'wait for his [God's] Son from heaven . . . who rescues us from the coming wrath' (1 Thessalonians 1.10). Later, Paul adds that 'we who are still alive, who are left till the coming of the Lord, will certainly not precede those who have fallen asleep' (1 Thessalonians 4.15). We will be gathered up in the clouds to meet the Lord in the air. He does not say, 'those who are alive' (which could refer to some far future and as yet unknown group), but 'we who are alive', showing his expectation that the Lord will come before Paul's death. Paul even thinks that this is 'the Lord's own word' (1 Thessalonians 4.15).

Whether or not Jesus himself was a millennialist, Paul certainly was when he wrote this letter (though he changed his mind later, as we shall see), as were the Christians to whom he wrote it. Most New Testament scholars are agreed on these basic facts, for they simply give the plain sense of the letter.

The fact is that the end of the world simply did not come before Paul's hearers had all died. If belief in the end of the world and in Christ's return is to be retained at all (and it is retained in some sense by the great majority of Christians), it must be given some other non-literal sense. This is an absolutely vital point, because it means that the Bible cannot simply be read literally. Some of its earliest and most important teachings must be taken in a non-literal way. We have yet to discover what that way is. But it is wrong to say that the correct way to interpret the Bible is to take it literally. This quite unambiguous teaching about the return of Christ before his hearers have died demonstrates that conclusively.

Literal and symbolic interpretations

The millennialist belief that is so apparent in parts of the New Testament provides a crucial test-case for discovering a consistent and comprehensive principle of interpreting biblical texts. For it shows that there are important beliefs in the New Testament which, taken literally, are false. These beliefs must therefore be interpreted in a non-literal sense. We need to discover just what that sense is, but at least it is established that the presence of a literal statement of belief in the New Testament is not binding on believers in its literal sense. We must, if we are to accept it at all – and most Christians will feel they should accept it in some sense – find lying behind it some non-literal sense which was appropriately expressed for that time in that way. Here then is one vital principle of interpretation: some statements of belief which are found in the Bible are false in their literal sense, and a non-literal, or symbolic, interpretation of them needs to be found.

It is important to note that it follows from this that it cannot be a requirement of contemporary Christian belief that we should believe just what the first generation of Christians, or the apostle Paul, believed. For they believed Christ would come before Paul died, and it is not possible for us to believe that. We have to say that some of their beliefs were false. There is a natural reluctance on the part of Christians to say that an apostle, or the Bible, ever expresses false beliefs. If we think that these beliefs have a symbolic interpretation, then we can share that belief with the apostles. But even if we think the symbolic interpretation is the important one, we must admit that Paul also seemed to take these beliefs literally. And in that we must disagree with the apostle. So we must add a corollary of our principle of interpretation: some of the apostles had beliefs that we cannot share, and must indeed reject in the sense in which they accepted them. We do not know in advance which these beliefs are, but it is fairly clear that belief in an imminent return of Christ was falsified by historical facts. We may well wish to emphasize that these beliefs always had a real symbolic meaning that was present then, and remains still. Nevertheless, the principle of interpretation and its corollary presented here will turn out to be vital general principles of biblical interpretation, and they need to be constantly kept in mind.

A non-literal interpretation is not just an option, not some aberration of the liberal mind that has given up the plain sense of Scripture. It is forced on Christians by the plain facts. Jesus did not return before the first generation of believers had all died. His return was not 'soon'; it has at best been indefinitely delayed. And if it is literally false that the Lord was to return soon, then it might well also be literally false that he will come in the clouds, with the sound of a trumpet, and draw living people up into the sky to meet him. I shall show in a moment that these statements too are almost certainly false, in a literal sense.

There are some groups of Christians today who still look for a literal return of Christ in glory in the near future. It should be recognized that these Christians are changing the plain sense of Scripture. They are drastically reinterpreting it so that a return of Christ soon, or even 'within one generation', becomes a return at some future time in history. Whereas in the Gospels Jesus says that no one knows the 'day or hour' of this event, revisionists have to say that no one knows the year or century either. There is a huge difference of meaning here. Just think what we would say if the train timetable said 'The train will come in the next hour', and three weeks later it had still not arrived. We would have to say the timetable was wrong! So fundamentalists have to say that the literal sense of the biblical text is false. But, they can say, it was not really a timetable at all. It was a promise of a return at some unspecified future time. The timing cannot be taken literally. That is absolutely true. My reason for labouring this point is that fundamentalist Christians sometimes claim to take the biblical texts in their literal sense, and insist that this is the true sense. Whereas it seems beyond dispute that they reject the literal sense of Matthew 24.34, and interpret it to refer to a future return, but not at the time specified (which is within the generation contemporary with Paul).

It is in this sense that there are not, and cannot be, any Christians who truly take the Bible in its literal, plain sense. Biblical literalism is thus deeply anti-biblical. Assertions that we must take biblical assertions in their literal sense, that it is clear what their true sense is, and that we must today believe whatever is asserted in the Bible, are false. Their falsity is shown by a careful reading of the Bible, which therefore frees us from all forms of biblical literalism. Such literalism is shown to be a perverse reading of the Bible, it is always inconsistent in its application, and it is often unaware of its own arbitrariness and prejudice. That gives rise to a fundamental principle of Christian theology. The theological problem is: what sort of reinterpretation is acceptable? Groups that think they are conservative say, 'The Return will not happen *when* it says; but it will happen.' But using exactly the same principle of interpretation, we could equally well say, 'The return will not happen *in the way* it says; but it will happen.' That is, there will be no literal trumpet, no coming in the clouds, no ascent of the elect into the sky. Just as the Bible does not give a timetable for the Return, so it does not give a literal description of what it will be like. These are non-literal, symbolic, ways of depicting the return of Christ in glory at the end of time. Exactly how we should interpret that is not set out in the Bible or anywhere else. The theological task is to give some non-vacuous meaning to talk of the return of Christ, to provide some explanation for the forms of symbolism used to depict Christ's coming in glory in the Bible, and perhaps to suggest other forms of symbolism which might perform a similar task in today's very different context.

The Old Testament sources for beliefs about 'the end'

This is I think the consensus of Christian opinion on the matter. Most Christians today would probably find a literal interpretation of the return of Christ both vastly improbable and religiously shallow. How can Jesus appear in the sky to everyone at the same time on a spherical planet? And what are we going to do when we get into the sky anyway? Fortunately there is not much difficulty in finding non-literal interpretations within the Bible itself. All we have to do is trace the Old Testament sources of the millennialist texts, and we will at once find symbolic interpretations ready to hand.

The key millennialist passages in the Gospels are found in Matthew

24.4–36, Mark 13.5–37 and Luke 21.8–36. They have a common structure, and speak of a time of great tribulation, followed by the darkening of the sun and moon, the fall of the stars from heaven, and the coming of the 'Son of Man' on the clouds with power, a trumpet call and the gathering of the elect from the four winds.

All these elements refer back directly to Old Testament passages, which pretty clearly reveal their symbolic meaning. The darkening of the sun, for example, is found in Isaiah 13.9–10, where it is connected with the fall of Babylon, the great oppressor of Israel. The fall of the stars from the sky refers back to Isaiah 34.4, where the topic is the defeat of Israel's enemies and the return of the Israelites in triumph to Jerusalem. Events in the cosmos are used as symbols of historical events like the fall of Babylon and the return from exile to Jerusalem. The cosmic events, the darkening of the sun and fall of the stars, are not literal events. They are symbols for historical events, poetic images that describe the destruction of Babylon in literally exaggerated forms. The literal, historical reference is not to the end of the world. It is to specific events in the political realm, and the 'day of the Lord' is the time of the overthrow of the armies of Babylon by the Persians. History will continue beyond that day, but in a 'new age', a new political order. So the first principle given by the Bible for interpreting the symbols of the Apocalypse is to look for a historical situation that they describe in veiled, metaphorical terms. There is a historical reference, but it is not to a miraculous intervention bringing history to an end, whether sooner or later. It is to a specific historical situation, which the prophet interprets in terms of divine judgement and redemption. Using this clue to interpretation, we can see that the New Testament apocalypse is talking about a series of historical events that occurred and was completed in the generation of Jesus and Paul.

But the Old Testament oracles are not just political predictions, foretelling that an oppressive military power will be overthrown, and that Israelites will return from exile to Jerusalem. They are oracles of a prophet, and the prophet sees those events in the light of God's judgement and redemption. There is accordingly a further level of interpretation to the accounts. They are addressed directly to the hearer, and intended to relate the believer to God in an appropriate way. 'For the Lord Almighty has purposed, and who can thwart him?' asks the prophet (Isaiah 14.27). He calls his hearers, the people of Israel, to renew their faith in God, whose purpose is for good, and whose power is invincible. They are to know and acknowledge God as the One in whose hands all history ultimately lies, and they are to accept God's power to save them from the destruction that is the reward of injustice and oppression. This is the spiritual dimension of the utterances.

Because it is a spiritual dimension, its interpretation will depend in part upon the spiritual condition of those who hear it. When Jesus explained why he taught in parables, he refers to Isaiah 6.9 – 'For this people's heart has become calloused; they hardly hear with their ears, and they have closed their eyes. Otherwise they might see with their eyes, hear with their ears, understand with their hearts and turn, and I would heal them' (Matthew 13.15–16). So it is possible to hear the teaching of divine judgement and redemption, and yet to be filled with secret hatred, pride and resentment. This happens if we take the divine judgement to be a vindictive destruction of other people, who deserve all that is coming to them, and whose torments will fill us with the glee of vengeance satisfied. The fact that we think this is a concern for justice, and that our real desire for vengeance remains unrecognized, only intensifies the fact that the teaching of divine judgement has not been 'understood with the heart'. We have not yet seen the universality and inescapability of divine judgement. It is not just for others. It is for us.

What is spiritually wrong with such an interpretation is that it does not lead to a turning to God for healing. It fails to perceive the injustice and egoism in our own lives, which falls under divine judgement as surely as does the more obvious evil done by others. As Jesus asked, 'Why do you look at the speck of sawdust in your brother's eye and pay no attention to the plank in your own eye?' (Matthew 7.3). The first lesson of the prophetic oracle is that divine judgement does not just apply to the Babylonians or the Romans. It applies to Israel, to the Church, and to us. 'For all have sinned, and fall short of the glory of God' (Romans 3.23). The prophetic oracle is meant to call forth this perception, not to celebrate the vengeance of God on our enemies.

A similar misinterpretation occurs if you take redemption to be the rescuing of you and your friends from harm, leaving the rest of the world to a horrible fate. Such a view is wholly lacking in compassion for the sufferings of others, and wholly obtuse to what it means for God to be a God of loving-kindness and compassion, who cannot be content to let any soul be lost without going to the utmost lengths to redeem it. Jesus said, 'your Father in heaven is not willing that any of these little ones should be lost' (Matthew 18.14). And if you are tempted to say that 'these little ones' are only Jews, or Christians, you still have not seen that perfect love requires the breaking down of all limitations and barriers – 'There is neither Jew nor Greek, slave nor free' (Galatians 3.28). God may have a special vocation for Jews or for

Christians. But that vocation must be concerned with the salvation of
the whole world from the domination of evil, not with the salvation of
a privileged few.

In fact a major reason for thinking that the return of Christ would
not, after all, come soon, was that if it did it would leave countless millions apparently without the hope of salvation. There must be sufficient
time for the gospel to be preached to all nations, and that will take
much longer than one generation. The perception of the requirements
of unlimited divine love led to a growing belief that the Church would
exist for many generations, and that Christ would not come in glory
within a generation. The spiritual principle at work here is that Christ
does not come to save a fortunate few who happen to have heard the
gospel. He comes especially to save the lost and the unfortunate, and
any interpretation of Christ's coming in glory must be consistent with
that insight. Jesus said, 'whoever wants to save his life will lose it, but
whoever loses his life for me will find it' (Matthew 16.25). To think that
we belong to the 'chosen few', who will be saved while others live in
anguish is to care about our own life more than we care about others.
And that is not an acceptable spiritual principle.

Applying the principle of sublation

Here then is another important principle of biblical interpretation –
some beliefs, like that in Christ's imminent return, were false. But they
were not just mistakes. Further reflection on central principles of the
gospel – in this case, on the unlimited love of God, shown in the life and
teachings of Jesus – led to changes in belief. We can see such changes
within the New Testament. We might say that the earlier belief is sublated by deeper reflection on the gospel.

So belief in Christ's imminent return is sublated within the New
Testament itself. It is denied in its literal sense, but only on condition
that the underlying principle – of Christ's will to save the whole world,
and unite it to him in glory – is accepted. But exactly what that underlying principle is, and how it will be actualized, is a matter for sensitivity, judgement and creative skill, in short for spiritual insight. There is
no one absolutely correct view of such matters, though the sort of view
that will be acceptable is clear in its broad outlines.

The underlying spiritual principle of talk about an 'end of the world'
is clearer when we remember that the Old Testament naturally has a
major interest in the vocation and destiny of the Jewish people, the
people of the covenant, and so the prophetic oracles of the Hebrew

Bible are concerned with the liberation and destiny of the Jews. It is in the context of God's providential dealings with the Jews that the biblical spiritual teachings concerning repentance and faith are developed. The prophetic symbols of the Old Testament interpret historical events as occasions of divine disclosure that, over many generations, establish and develop a normative understanding of the appropriate spiritual relation to God. That is what the Bible primarily is – an inspired record of God's progressive disclosure to one historical people, who became the people of Israel.

Christians believe that Jesus of Nazareth develops this understanding in a decisively new way. He is believed to be the Messiah, the appointed liberator and King of Israel. But the Christian idea of Messiah requires a sublation of its Jewish original. Within Judaism, there is a very wide range of interpretations of who or what the Messiah is. Some have seen the Messiah as a political figure, establishing the state of Israel. Others see him as a supernatural figure who will miraculously intervene in history. And some see the Messiah as a symbol for the creation of a truly human, just and compassionate society under God (an excellent survey of Jewish views of Messiah is to be found in *Judaism and World Religion*, by Rabbi Norman Solomon, Macmillan, 1991).

The underlying reality is the defeat of evil and the triumph of God's purposes. The symbols used to depict this are not meant to be taken literally, and they are open to a range of specific interpretations, none of which is definitive, though some may seem more plausible than others. But the interpretations refer both to some historical events that at least partially exemplify divine judgement and divine favour, and also to the ultimate triumph of good in the cosmos.

In the Gospels such prophetic texts from the Hebrew Bible are used to reinforce the claim that Jesus is the Messiah. Whatever else is uncertain about the New Testament, one thing is certain, and that is that the writers thought Jesus was the Messiah. So the symbolic images of the Hebrew Bible are naturally applied to Jesus. He is the one who appears 'like a Son of Man' on the clouds. This image is taken from Daniel 7.13, where the prophet has a vision of the death of four great beasts, followed by the rule of a supernatural being in human form.

It is absolutely clear that these are symbols, not literal descriptions. The prophet himself is confused and asks for an interpretation. He is told by a heavenly being that the beasts are symbols for kings, whose downfall will be followed by the rule of 'the saints of the Most High' who will then receive the kingdom and possess it for ever (Daniel 7.18). It is unclear who the kings are – they are sometimes identified with

Babylon, Alexander the Great, Greece and Asia Minor, but there are other possibilities. The precise identification of the people involved, and of the times involved, are left in obscurity. The general message is that a succession of great military empires will be followed by the institution of a truly humane society, probably the nation of Israel. In that case the 'Son of Man' would be a symbol of Israel, and the vision would express the downfall of Israel's enemies and the future triumph of Israel.

The symbols used in prophetic writings are fairly natural ones. It is understandable that military empires should be symbolized as beasts, and that a truly humane rule should be symbolized in the form of a human being. Other symbols commonly used in the Bible include the sea, used to depict chaos (in the new Jerusalem, there will be no more sea), the dragon or serpent, representing a force of danger or destruction, light as a symbol of goodness, and the Shekinah, or cloud which represents the presence and glory of God. So when the Son of Man comes on the clouds, the meaning is that he comes in the full presence and glory of God.

The general meaning of the symbols is clear. They depict the ultimate powers of existence, the forces that govern human being in the world. These are forces of destruction and oppression, entering into a great cosmic battle with the power of goodness, and eventually being defeated, so that a just and peaceful society comes into being. Moreover in the biblical context the power of goodness is God, the creator of all things, and the vehicle of liberation from evil is the people of Israel, who have a special vocation to implement God's purpose in the world.

The New Testament applies all this symbolism specifically to Jesus. He becomes the representative of Israel and the fulfilment of Israel's vocation. He is the liberator and King of Israel, who comes in the presence and glory of God ('on the clouds'), who gathers together all the scattered tribes of Israel from the four corners of the earth (at the trumpet-sound, the twelve tribes are gathered from the four winds – Isaiah 27.13), to live with him in the sky (in heaven, the full consciousness of the presence of God).

Jesus becomes the focal point of all the biblical symbolism concerning the battle of good and evil and the triumph of God's purpose through the mediating vocation of Israel. If we are to be true to the biblical use of these symbols, it would be a great mistake to take them as literal descriptions. They are symbols which depict specific historical events (though the specific reference is sometimes unclear to us), and which see those events as prototypes of the ultimate triumph of God's purpose (writing about future states as though they were already present).

The biblical clue to the meaning of 'the coming of the Son of Man'

There is at once a major problem with applying these Messianic symbols to Jesus, one that Jews find insuperable. Jesus did not overthrow the military empire of Rome, did not become King of Israel, and did not inspire the return of the twelve tribes to Jerusalem in triumph. He died accused of being a criminal, deserted even by his followers, and within a hundred years or so Israel as a nation had ceased to exist. If some of his followers thought that he would return soon to restore the nation of Israel as a political entity, they were mistaken.

It seems that some of them did think that. Luke 24.21 writes of two disciples who said, after the crucifixion of Jesus, 'we had hoped that he was the one who was going to redeem Israel'. They had apparently followed Jesus as one who would liberate Israel from Roman domination. Was not that the role of the Messiah? They still needed to be taught that salvation had a different meaning, and that Jesus' Kingship was not of this world (John 18.36).

But if he returned in glory, would he not complete the Messianic vocation of redeeming Israel then? No, in a radical, unanticipated sublation of the Messianic symbolism, the Messiah is no longer seen as the political ruler of the nation of Israel. 'Liberation' or 'salvation' is not from Roman rule, but from the sins that oppress and enslave human lives, binding them to desires that are in the end self-destructive. Kingship is not political headship of a country, but the rule of God within the heart. So there is a 'new Israel', not a political or social entity, but a community, or set of communities, of those who acknowledge the rule of God, and who are 'saved', or at least promised salvation, from sin and egoistic desire. The 'return of the twelve tribes' is not a historical series of events culminating in the rebuilding of Jerusalem. It is the formation of a new Israel, a new covenant with God, a new community with the vocation of reconciling the world to God. It is what came to be known as the Church, under the rule of the twelve apostles, whose hope is for a heavenly city, a new Jerusalem not subject to destruction and decay.

There is still a historical dimension to the Messianic symbolism. Bearing in mind the claim that all these events were to happen within one generation (Matthew 24.34), it is not difficult to see the passages about the 'coming of the Son of Man' as depicting the persecution of the early Church (Mark 13.13), the rise of false Messianic claimants like Simeon Bar-Cochba (Mark 13.5), the profanation of the Temple by

Roman occupying forces (Mark 13.14), the destruction of the Temple in AD 70 (Mark 13.2), and the final destruction of the state of Israel and the exile of all Jews from Jerusalem in AD 135 (Luke 21.23).

At that point the Age of Israel had come to a violent end. The revolutionary change of meaning is that it was not the enemies of Israel who were destroyed, but Israel itself. Similarly, it was not the tribes of Israel who returned to Jerusalem in triumph. Rather, the followers of Jesus believed that a new Israel came into being, its members drawn from all over the world, Jews and Gentiles alike (the 'elect' gathered 'from the four winds', Mark 13.27). In place of the old empires founded on military might, the 'Son of Man', bringing near the presence and glory of God ('coming in clouds', Mark 13.26), was enthroned as the King of a new spiritual kingdom, the Church.

All these things did indeed happen within one generation. The prophecy was fulfilled by the destruction of Israel and the birth of the Church, in which Jesus' Kingship is everlasting, and which outlasted the decline and fall of the Roman Empire in both East and West. This interpretation is, of course, basically that of C. H. Dodd (*The Apostolic Preaching and its Development*, 1936), and is commonly known among biblical scholars as 'realized eschatology'. Its unravelling of the Messianic symbolism is consistent with the claim, made in each Synoptic Gospel, that all these things are to happen within one generation, and parallels the use of symbols in the Old Testament to depict historical events in a figurative and veiled way. It therefore seems to give the true sense of Scripture, whereas more literalist accounts ignore the use of imagery in the Old Testament, and have to interpret the 'one generation' text in a very strained and implausible manner.

The time of the end

However there is little doubt that Paul was still looking for the return of Christ to happen in the near future, when he wrote to the Thessalonians. And in the Gospels the Kingdom is still said to be 'near', even though the Church had been in existence for at least 40 years. The Kingdom, which is still to come, cannot simply be identified with the Church. Realized eschatology is not the whole story.

To take account of these points we have to take note of the 'double focus' of Messianic symbolism. It does not only refer to events of history. It also refers to the final realization of God's purpose in creation. After all, the birth of the Church, a set of institutions filled with the ambiguity and weakness and corruption of all human organizations, can hardly be regarded as the complete fulfilment of the divine purpose. Something new may have happened with the founding of the Church. But the full realization of God's purpose still lies in the future.

It is unlikely, therefore, that these symbols refer solely to events happening in the first generation of Christians. Matthew speaks of the gospel being preached throughout the whole world before the end comes (Matthew 24.14), and Luke says that Jerusalem will be trodden down 'until the times of the Gentiles are fulfilled' (Luke 21.24). So there is an ambiguity about whether the coming of the Son of Man will be within a generation or after an indeterminate time.

The clue to this ambiguity is given by referring back to the Old Testament prophecies, which speak of specific historical events, but describe them in terms of a total cosmic catastrophe and a restoration of all things in perfection forever. When a historical event is referred to by such symbols, it is seen as a prototype of the fulfilment of God's purpose. The fall of Babylon was a real historical event, but it is an anticipation and foreshadowing of the destruction of all evil in the created order. The return of the exiles from Babylon to Jerusalem occurred, but is also seen as a prototype of the rule of God over the people of God, when all suffering and sorrow has been overcome forever. In a similar way the Church comes into being as the community in which the Son of Man frees people from sin and rules as King, in an inward and spiritual way. But it is also a foreshadowing of the final coming of the Kingdom, when sin is no more and the rule of Christ is absolute and unequivocal.

'When will these things happen?' (Mark 13.4). It may now be apparent that a threefold answer is required to this question. In the historical sense, the destruction of the state of Israel and the origin of the Church, in which Christ rules as liberator and King, happens within a generation.

But there is also a post-historical sense, referring to the complete extermination of evil and the consciously known rule of God over all who turn to God for healing. That will happen only when history, the story of human life on this earth, has come to an end. We have no idea how long that will be. 'With the Lord a day is like a thousand years' (2 Peter 3.8). The writer of this letter is clear about the reason for the 'delay'. 'The Lord . . . is patient with you, not wanting anyone to perish, but everyone to come to repentance' (2 Peter 3.9). Not until every human being whom God wishes to enter into eternal life has been born and had a chance to reach repentance will the tragic history of human freedom, egoism and conflict be brought to an end.

Finally, there is the spiritual sense, which speaks to the heart and turns us to God to be healed. In this sense, the *parousia*, the being-present, of Christ is imminent at every moment of time. In Matthew's Gospel, when Jesus is on trial before the High Priest, he says, 'But I say to all of you: In the future you will see the Son of Man sitting at the right hand of the Mighty One and coming on the clouds of heaven' (Matthew 26.64; the force of the Greek 'from now' is slightly obscured by its New International Version translation as 'in the future'). The sense seems to be that from the time of the resurrection Jesus is enthroned on the clouds of heaven, even though the world continues on its way.

He can appear at any moment. 'Be on guard! Be alert!', the Gospel of Mark proclaims, 'you do not know when the owner of the house will come back – whether in the evening, or at midnight, or when the cock crows, or at dawn. If he comes suddenly, do not let him find you sleeping' (Mark 13.33, 35–36). It is unlikely to be coincidence when Mark records that it was evening when Jesus unmasked Judas' treachery (Mark 14.18). It was around midnight when Jesus found the disciples asleep in Gethsemane (Mark 14.37). At cock-crow Peter denied Jesus (Mark 14.72). And at dawn Jesus was led in chains to Pilate (Mark 15.1). The master of the house came, and uncovered the secrets of the human heart, secrets of treachery, inattention, denial and hostility. It is the recognition of this fact that turns our hearts to God for healing. So the Son of Man can come at any moment, 'like a thief in the night', and find us ready or unready for his coming. We do not know when he will come, and so we must keep alert, as children of the day.

The idea of foreshadowing is the central clue to the interpretation of these parables of the coming of the Son of Man. Every moment can be a prototype of eternity, of the final consummation of all things. In his dialogue *Timaeus*, Plato speaks of time as 'the moving image of eternity'. Each moment of time is in its way an image, poised between being and non-being, of a reality that is eternal and unmoving. Each moment exists by its participation in the eternal, and those who have eyes to see can discern beneath the transient beauties of time that unfading Beauty upon which the temporal world is patterned.

The Bible also depicts a relationship between the temporal and the eternal, but now the eternal is a personal and active God. God is active in time to disclose the divine being and nature, and to invite created persons into communion with that being. The coming of Christ is the drawing-near of God in the form of the risen Jesus. It is God's self-disclosure, not so much a passive reflection of a changeless eternity as an active breaking-in of the dynamic divine life. Those who have eyes to see, those who 'are awake', can discern in the challenges and possibilities of the present moment the invitation to share in the personal life of the eternal God.

Such moments then become prototypes of eternity, anticipations in an ever-changing time of that life which is beyond yet including all times, with which God intends us to be united forever. They are not just, as in Plato, faint images of a changeless reality. They are foretastes of a completion of time to which our lives contribute and in which all times are sublated and fulfilled. Plato speaks of the Real as lying-behind this world, as it were just beyond and hidden. The Bible speaks of the Real as lying just ahead-of the present moment, in the imminent future, promising a completion of all our unfulfilled possibilities and a redemption of all our failures and vices. The distinctive message of the gospel is that time can be completed in eternity, as our lives are taken up into the life of Christ and united with it. That is the spiritual meaning of the *parousia* of Christ, the drawing-near to us in time of the eternal life that sublates and completes our temporal lives in eternity.

Of such a raising of time into eternity, a raising which Plato did not envisage, the image of Christ raised from death, coming on clouds of glory, gathering human lives to be with him for ever, is deeply appropriate. It is not surprising that some early Christians thought the Day of the Lord had already come (2 Thessalonians 2.2). For they already felt their liberation from sin, their union with Christ, their share in eternal life. Yet, the writer reminds them, they are not yet in fact fully liberated, united fully to the divine life. They are ambiguous inhabitants of an ambiguous world still, and they have work to be done and sufferings to endure before earthly history is ended. So the historical, the spiritual and the post-historical strands of belief in the coming of Christ must all be held together.

The new reality of the Church, which gives participation in the life of Christ, is established in the first Christian generation. In each continuing moment Christ comes to begin in us the process of drawing the temporal into the eternal, a process that had been already fully realized in the unique case of his own earthly life. But only at the end of history will all things be completely drawn together consciously and joyously in Christ.

What this tells us about interpreting the Bible

The symbols of the glorious coming of Christ remain deeply obscure and hard to interpret, requiring exposition of a divine revelation in forms that challenge all our imaginative and spiritual resources. As Thomas Aquinas put it so well, divine revelation is the revelation of ultimate mystery. It is the disclosure of a reality that transcends and includes time, which destroys sin and unites the finite to itself. The poetry of the *parousia* has a profundity which makes all literalistic interpretations seem shallow and superficial. We have to work hard at biblical interpretation, not giving up when it seems difficult, and not claiming a certainty and clarity that is not there. To embrace the poetic vision of the gospel, of the coming of Christ in glory, is to embrace a vision of eternity entering into time, in order that time should be transfigured into eternity.

The symbolism of the coming of Christ in glory still has a central place in Christian faith, but it needs sensitive interpretation. Passages like 2 Thessalonians 1.5–10 speak of a cataclysmic Day of Judgement, when all evil will be destroyed by the searing breath of God, and the raging fires of desire will consume those who have fanned them unknowingly throughout their lives.

They speak of the sudden appearing of the perfection of humanity, transfigured by the radiance of the divine beauty, drawing to itself all whose hearts are not irredeemably blind to its intrinsic attraction.

They speak of the expectation that this will happen soon, at any day or hour, driving into insignificance all our petty concerns for fame, wealth or power, our petty hatreds and dislikes, our petty arguments and plans, concentrating all thought on the flight from destruction – now! – and the fulfilment of a life free from pain and grief – now! – in the one who draws near to us in undying love – now!

What is it to believe these things? It is not a matter of historical pre-diction – as though we said, 'Next week it will rain, and a visitor will come.' It is rather to open a door into the innermost self, the cave of the heart, where hopes and desires and self-deceits and suppressed longings ebb and flow.

The judgement is upon our own destructive and self-serving desires. It is not later and for someone else. It is now and for us. It is love's rejec-tion of all that is not love; or better, it is our rejection of all that makes for love. We throw ourselves wilfully into the flames, praying, perhaps with real passion, that we may not be burned.

The drawing-near of perfect love – is that something we can bear? For love sees through our pretences and illusions, sees what is truly in our hearts, comes to embrace us even as we turn away. Love makes demands, requires honesty and trust, humility and compassion. We have some of these, indeed, but love demands that we put our pride even in these to one side and simply accept, like a child.

We are not ready. Nor are the millions of the unborn, generations yet to exist who can enter into the divine love. So that final ending of evil and that final realization of perfection, so ardently expected in the first excitement of the vision of a redeemed world, is deferred. The Lord will come in judgement and grace – but not yet. And yet he does come, in the secret places of the heart, caressing with shame, searing with love, the making-present of God within the heart, the making-eternal of each present moment as it is taken into the divine life. That is judgement and redemption. It is now and within us. And as such, it foreshadows the fullness and finality of what will be, when all things have reached their end and consummation, in the fullness of time, when time shall be no more.

Within the Bible, within the New Testament itself, there is discernible a development towards this vision, and a sifting out of interpretations which proved unsatisfactory. When Paul wrote to the Thessalonians he thought the coming of Christ would be soon, during the lifetime of his readers. It is no longer possible for us to believe that. Jesus did not return at that time, coming 'in blazing fire' to 'punish those who do not know God' (2 Thessalonians 1.8). The inadequacy of these under-standings of the role of Jesus and of the redemptive purpose of God is recognized within the New Testament canon. They are sublated by the recognition that it is God's purpose 'to bring all things in heaven and on earth together under one head, even Christ' (Ephesians 1.10). That fullness will not be realized until all peoples throughout many genera-tions have heard the gospel, and Jesus' role is not to inflict vengeance, but to offer redemption to all ('God did not send his Son into the world to condemn the world, but to save the world through him', John 3.17).

Paul himself changed his mind about these matters, and in his letter to the Romans, probably one of the last letters we have from his hand, he writes that 'Israel has experienced a hardening in part until the full number of the Gentiles has come in. And so all Israel will be saved' (Romans 11.25–26). Final salvation would not after all be within one generation. The millennialist expectation of the imminence of Christ's coming was even then being reinterpreted by the development of a sacramental theology for which the eternal Christ is made present in the Eucharist in order to include human lives in his own risen and eternal life. The real coming of Christ in bread and wine to incorporate us into the life of eternity is no less than a sacramental reinterpretation of the coming of the Son of Man on the clouds to take believers to live with him in the heavens. So the spiritual meaning of the coming of Christ becomes sublated into the central Christian sacrament of the Eucharist, in which Christ continually comes to take us into his own divine life, in a prototype of that final deliverance from evil that will be the end of historical time.

It is vitally important to realize that interpretations of Christ and his saving role were changing from the very beginning of Christian faith, and can be seen to change within the New Testament. There is not one unchanging perfect revelation, preserved without amendment throughout all time. From the first, and ratified by the Bible itself, there is a process of change, as early interpretations are sublated by later ones that can plausibly claim to disclose more adequately the saving purposes of God in Christ. This suggests that a crucial principle of biblical interpretation will be to distinguish limited perspectives, which are sometimes found within the Bible itself, from deeper spiritual insights, and to use these deeper insights as clues for interpreting the revelation of the love of God given in Christ, which need to be gradually elicited by patient, thorough and prayerful reflection. This principle of creative development and sublation is forced upon us by the Bible itself, in all its subtlety, mystery and complexity. That is why the task of theology is not endlessly to repeat ancient and unchangeable beliefs. It is to advance to new insights into the purposes of God, as the text is reread in ever-changing contexts, and the Spirit of God moves us to deepen our appreciation of the revelation of the being and will of God which was normatively given in and through the person of Jesus.

♦ 4 ♦

Interpreting Biblical Teaching about Salvation

I have looked at some important biblical texts that seem to be misunderstood by fundamentalists. A misunderstanding which is even more serious claims that the Bible limits salvation to just a few explicit believers in Jesus. This is absolutely false, and the whole tenor of the Christian gospel, and many specific texts, show it to be false. The biblical teaching is that salvation is for all, not for the few, and that it is cosmic in scope, not just concerned with a few people on the planet earth. One of the most telling texts is as follows:

> 'And he made known to us the mystery of his will according to his good pleasure, which he purposed in Christ, to be put into effect when the times will have reached their fulfilment – to bring all things in heaven and on earth together under one head, even Christ'. (Ephesians 1.9–10)

This New International Version translation omits the very significant phrase 'in Christ', *en to Christo*. The Greek actually reads: 'to bring under one head all things in Christ'. This expression, 'in Christ', is of tremendous significance for a truly Christian understanding of salvation, and the failure to take due account of it is responsible for many unduly restricted interpretations of salvation. The phrase occurs many times in the New Testament letters, but on the whole Christians have chosen not to interpret it in any very realistic way. Sometimes it is translated by phrases like 'in union with Christ', or in some other metaphorical sense that makes it mere shorthand for some more complex expression. I can hardly fault this, since one main argument of this book is that much of the biblical language is metaphorical or symbolic. Nevertheless, while 'in Christ' is a metaphor – we are certainly not inside the human Jesus – there is a more realist interpretation of it that makes very good sense of biblical teaching about Christ. I shall advocate a plausible interpretation that may be unfamiliar to some Christians, though many of the early Greek-speaking theologians of the Orthodox Church would have been sympathetic to it.

Sometimes people are troubled by the 'scandal of particularity', by the thought that Jesus is just one person in the history of humanity, and that it seems odd for the salvation of everyone to depend on knowledge of that tiny piece of history. The first chapter of the letter to the Ephesians puts this scandal in its proper context. It is better not to start with a search for the minute details of the historical life of Jesus, which is a subject of endless debate and can never be empirically checked. We should start instead from the disclosure of the divine purpose that was made in Jesus. That purpose is cosmic in its outreach. It is no less than that everything in heaven and earth is destined to be united 'in Christ'.

If we begin with that vision, then we are thinking of the whole cosmos, all the billions of galaxies and whatever forms of life that exist in them, as united in Christ. This is not a scandal of particularity, for we are thinking of Jesus as the one in whom this purpose was disclosed, and any such disclosure has to occur at some particular time and place. Of course there could be many such times and places, but each of them will be particular. It is a matter for investigation whether and to what extent there are many particular disclosures of the same sort, or whether one of them is importantly distinctive and normative. Most Christians have assumed that the disclosure in Jesus is unique in the history of the planet earth, and that there is nothing else quite like it in human history. If that is indeed so, it will simply be a fact that in Jesus there is an importantly unique disclosure of the divine nature and purpose. That is not a scandal, however. If anything, Christianity poses a scandal of universality, that the whole of created reality, vast in extent in both space and time, is to be included in Christ.

What could such a Christ be? Obviously not a human person, for it must be beyond all spaces and times to be able to include them in itself. The only reality that is beyond all spaces and times is God. So this passage forces us to think of the unbounded reality of God as somehow taking form in the human person of Jesus, but ultimately as including all things within itself. The whole cosmos is to be included in that infinite divine reality which took human form in Jesus, but is never confined to that form.

Of course the writer of the letter to the Ephesians had no idea of the vast extent of this physical universe. But the writer probably did believe in virtually endless sorts of spiritual beings, angels and demons, and so in speaking of 'everything in heaven and earth', was thinking of a reality far greater than that of the earth. Now we know that the universe is vast in extent, but we do not know whether there are any other conscious life forms in it or not. So we probably are not thinking of there being more developed conscious beings in existence than that first-century Christian writer imagined. So the point is much the same – whatever finite conscious beings there are, or ever have been or will be, will all be united in the divine reality that took form on earth in Jesus of Nazareth.

It is this perception that gives the proper meaning to a text often quoted by fundamentalists: 'I am the way and the truth and the life. No-one comes to the Father except through me' (John 14.6). Fundamentalists usually interpret this to mean that no one can come to God except by explicitly confessing faith in Jesus as Lord and Saviour. Moreover, people have to make such a confession before they die, since there is no possibility of repentance after death. It follows that only a small minority of the earth's population can ever come to God, since few of them have even heard of Jesus, and even fewer have had a realistic chance of professing faith in him as their saviour. On this interpretation, salvation is for the very few, and God is content to condemn millions to hell for no particular fault of their own.

Common human decency might lead us to doubt such an extraordinary interpretation of John's Gospel. A realization that God is a God of unlimited love – which is what John's Gospel teaches – should definitely lead us to reject that fundamentalist interpretation. But the decisive consideration is that, in John's Gospel, the person who speaks these words is not just the historical figure of Jesus. It is the eternal Word of God, who is 'the true light that gives light to every man' (John 1.9), through whom 'all things were made' (John 1.3), and who 'became flesh and made his dwelling among us' (John 1.14). It is this eternal Word who is the way that every creature must follow to come to God. Every creature that comes to God can only do so by following the Wisdom of God and by being filled with that Wisdom, the uncreated light. The eternal Light did become flesh. He is truly enfleshed in the person of Jesus. But he is not confined to that historical figure. He enlightens every human being, and every creature who does not turn away. So Christians believe that in the end all humans will see that they are brought close to God through the eternal Word. They will see that the Word was truly in the person of Jesus. But they may never have even heard of Jesus during their earthly lives. The Light may have come to them in forms unrecognized or concealed. The advantage Christians have is that they are given the opportunity to recognize the Light. But in recognizing him, and precisely in so far as they do so, they recognize the light who gives light to the whole world (John 1.12).

This text from John's Gospel is not limited or exclusive at all. Jesus is saying, 'All created persons can come to God, and God will make it possible for them to do so. But I show you the way to God clearly, the way that all will take after many journeys and many turnings. To you the way is made plain, for I bring it close to you.' The one who speaks is the eternal Word, the cosmic Christ, truly manifest in but never confined to the person of Jesus.

Christians have the amazing privilege to know that salvation only comes through Jesus Christ, but it would be quite wrong for them to think that salvation only comes to them. 'Salvation is found in no-one else, for there is no other name under heaven given to men by which we must be saved' (Acts 4.12). It is not any God, but the God revealed and present in Jesus of Nazareth, who saves all humanity. And that same God, and that same Christ, saves all creation, all things on earth and in heaven, by uniting them in the Christ through whom all things were created, on whom all things are patterned, and in whom all things will find their true fulfilment.

Creation in Christ

This picture is reinforced by what many scholars take to be one of the earliest extant Christian hymns, in Colossians 1.15–20: 'He is the image of the invisible God, the firstborn over all creation. For by him all things were created' (Colossians 1.15–16). Again, this phrase, 'by him', translates the Greek *en auto*, 'in him', and a proper and exact reading would be that all things were created in Christ. Jesus is described as the 'image of the invisible', which is a phrase it is impossible to take literally, since what is invisible can have no visible image or reflection. It cannot mean that Jesus looks like God, or is a smaller representation of a much larger reality of the same sort. To be an image of the invisible is much like being the touch of the intangible or the sound of silent music. It must never be taken to be a literal representation of God.

There is a remote analogy, perhaps, in the pictures of the galaxies that are constructed by the operators of radio telescopes. What those telescopes receive are radio signals. But they are turned into visual pictures by computer technology, using a code that translates particular sounds into colours. There are no colours like that in fact in the data that the radio telescopes receive, but the pictures give us, with our organs of sensation, an idea that we can grasp of what the galaxies are like.

In this case sounds are being translated into colours, and there can be a one-to-one correspondence between them. In the case of a finite human person and God there can be no such correspondence of one sensory input into another. But perhaps we can say that a human person could give us, with our organs of knowledge, an idea of what God is like which we can grasp.

The likeness could not be physical, but it could be spiritual. According to the Genesis creation story, human beings were all created in the 'image' and 'likeness' of God (Genesis 1.26). This has usually been taken to mean that humans have intellectual consciousness and freedom, which does in however faint a way resemble the consciousness and freedom of the Creator. Hebrew scholars often point out that the Genesis picture also, and perhaps primarily, refers to the capacity for conscious loving relationship which exists between God and created persons, and to human responsibility, under God, for the world.

Jesus is said to be the image of God in a slightly different sense, because he is *the* image, not just *an* image of God. A plausible interpretation is that Jesus is a perfect case of the intellectual consciousness and freedom of humanity, who expresses in an uncorrupted way an unbroken and uniquely intimate conscious relationship with God, and who is the representative of God, the responsible ruler of the created order on earth.

All these things, however, could be true of a created human being. They are proper to human beings as such, though few, if any, human beings actually possess such properties. In this respect Jesus, as the image of God, is the image of what humanity under God should be. But he is also described as 'the firstborn over all creation', which is not possible for any human being. Humans are very late arrivals on the cosmic scene. No human being existed before the stars and galaxies, even before the Big Bang that started the universe, on some contemporary scientific views. It sounds as though Jesus is the first created thing – though later theologians pointed out that this is a rather misleading picture.

Yet again, we see that biblical statements often cannot be taken literally. It is actually a mistake to say that Christ is the first created being. What is needed is to say that Christ proceeds from the Father in a way that is something like creation, but which does not generate a wholly independent entity. Later theologians invented a new terminology, saying that Christ is 'begotten, not created'. In doing so, they were elaborating the biblical statement in a way which literally contradicts it, but which can be taken to be a necessary amplification of its implicit meaning. In a word, they sublated it by the doctrine of the begetting of the Son from the Father, a doctrine for which the New Testament writers simply did not have the terminology.

But however exactly we are going to tackle the mystery of the relation of Christ to God, Christ is clearly not just a human being. In some way Christ stands between God and creation. It sounds at first as though he is the first created being. But the hymn immediately goes on to say that 'by [or in – *an auto*] him all things were created'. That places him before creation, and so as identified with the uncreated, that is to say, with God.

It is natural that if God took human nature, that would be a perfect, uncorrupted human nature. But now we have to say that Christ is not just God. He is the 'image' of God the Father, even in his uncreated nature, and before he becomes the perfect image of God in human nature. Christ can now be seen to be the image of God in the stronger sense that, as an eternal divine reality, he reflects or mirrors the nature of God the Father. Jesus Christ is not only the paradigm of perfected humanity. He is also, even in his human life, the authentic image on earth of the divine nature. Theologians worked this out with reasonable plausibility. But they did not develop the thought that all things were created 'in' Christ.

Suppose we try to develop that thought. 'In' cannot mean physically inside. To be spiritually in a spiritual being is to be part of it, not to be externally related to it, but to be an aspect or mode of its being. If the whole creation is in Christ, then it is part of Christ, an aspect of the being of Christ. It would have to be mentioned in any complete account of what Christ actually is.

Since the idea of containment is a metaphor, there is not one precise meaning that it has. It is even rather difficult to spell out just what is meant by being in Christ, as opposed to being externally related to Christ. If something is in Christ, it is not a completely independent self-existing reality. Nor is it simply identical with Christ, in the sense of possessing all the properties Christ possesses. But in this sense any created reality, which only exists because Christ enables it to do so, is in Christ. More than this seems to be implied by 'in'.

If one thing is in another thing, it is a constitutive part of it. It need not be an essential part, by any means. The thing could well exist without it. Yet its being there makes a difference. So if England is in Europe, it is part of what Europe is. Europe could have existed without

England, or with a very different England. But as it happens, to give a complete description of Europe you would have to include England.

This analogy suggests that creation is a constitutive part of Christ, it makes a difference to what Christ is, and is part of the complete description of Christ. That is what has alarmed many theologians, despite its repeated New Testament provenance. They quite rightly shy away from the thought that Christ is made up of created individuals, as though he was no more than a sum of created parts. But why could Christ not have complete and subsistent reality, which is yet filled out, as a matter of contingent fact, with many created things, which make a difference to Christ, and which do determine many aspects of the way in which Christ is and acts?

Paul even writes, 'I fill up in my flesh what is still lacking in regard to Christ's afflictions, for the sake of his body, which is the church' (Colossians 1.24). This passage is admittedly very difficult to interpret, since it is hard to believe that there is anything 'lacking' in Jesus Christ's afflictions. The *Oxford Bible Commentary* suggests a literal translation from the Greek – 'I complete what is lacking of the afflictions of Christ-in-my-flesh.' Then the natural reading would be that Christ is in some way embodied in the Church, so that 'my afflictions' are at the same time the afflictions of the body of Christ. My afflictions are suffered for the sake of that body, so that it may be strengthened and built up. This gives a very strong sense to the presence of Christ in the Church as his body, which is capable of suffering, and so makes a difference to Christ himself.

The body of Christ

It is very hard to avoid the conclusion that this is precisely how the writer to the Ephesians sees Christ – though theologians have tried many contortions to avoid that conclusion! He speaks of the Spirit as giving spiritual gifts 'to prepare God's people for works of service, so that the body of Christ may be built up' (Ephesians 4.12). The body of Christ is surely part of Christ, even if Christ can exist without a body. And that body is to be built up by the activities of ministers in the Church, the community of believers.

The writer goes on to say that we (members of the Church) 'will in all things grow up into him who is the head, that is, Christ. From him the whole body . . . grows and builds itself up in love' (Ephesians 4.15–16). The image is of bodily growth, forming a body whose head is Christ. Most Christians are familiar with saying that the Church is the body of Christ – 'you are the body of Christ' (1 Corinthians 12.27). But they do not always see the implication that this human community grows and is formed as part of Christ, so that Christ grows, suffers and rejoices, in accordance with what happens to the body. In this case 'the head' is not dependent on the body for its existence. But what happens to the body happens to Christ, and what the body does is in some sense done by Christ.

Looking at the frail and often corrupt nature of the Church, we are reminded that not all that bodies do is intentionally done. Sometimes a body can behave in ways that the self of that body completely disapproves of. It is only when the body is completely under the control of the self that what it does is what the self does. So we must say that, in so far as the Church is completely under the control of the self, it does what Christ does, it becomes the presence of Christ in the world. Unfortunately, the Church is rarely under Christ's complete control. The body of the Church is subject to corruption and decay, just as human bodies are. But, like them, it is meant, and it is destined, to be transformed into the perfect form of the divine activity in the world.

According to Ephesians, the Church is part of Christ as his body, and according to Colossians all creation is part of Christ, since 'in him all things hold together' (Colossians 1.17). It looks as though there is a very close relation between the Church and the whole of creation, since in some sense both are parts of Christ. The relationship is rather different, since it is not true that all creation consciously attempts to subject itself to Christ, as the Church does, and most of creation may not even be aware of Christ. We might see the Church as the frail and stumbling vanguard of the body that will be, when the whole creation shows forth clearly and unambiguously the being and activity of God. Then the creation and the Church will be co-extensive, for all things will glorify God, be the unambiguous objects of God's delight, and enact the will and purpose of God.

Just as the human body is a source of delightful experiences, as the senses convey the beauty of the world to the self, so the transfigured universe will be the source of delightful experiences for God. The great hymn to wisdom in Proverbs chapter 8 speaks of wisdom, *chokmah*, as 'rejoicing in his [God's] whole world and delighting in mankind' (Proverbs 8.31). Perhaps this hymn, which runs from verses 22 to 31, was in the mind of the writer to the Colossians. Certainly, Christ is the wisdom of God, and so we might well see this as suggesting that Christ delights in the joyful experiences of created beings, so that they become, so to speak, the senses that convey such delights to him.

Just as the human body is that by means of which the self changes the world and acts in it, so conscious beings in the transfigured universe will be the means by which Christ changes the world, acts creatively in it, and brings about his purposes. That does not imply that created persons have no purposes of their own. But all those purposes can be woven by Christ into one harmonious whole which also expresses the purpose of the Creator, just as the conductor of an orchestra can direct the players to a specific interpretation of a piece of music, while each of them strives to complete their own part as well as possible.

I stress that these are metaphors and analogies. Nevertheless, they are plausible interpretations, even if rather unusual for many Christians in the West. It should really not be any more odd that the universe, in its redeemed and transfigured state, should be the body of Christ than that a particular human being should be the body and mind of the Son of God. In fact, I think it is a much deeper view of incarnation to say that God wills to be incarnate in the whole universe than to say that God only wills to be incarnate in one tiny part of it.

We must appeal to the idea of foreshadowing yet again when we speak of all things being in Christ, just as when speaking of the coming in glory of Christ. These things are connected, since at the appearing of Christ in glory, all things will at last be consciously and freely united in him – everything in heaven and on earth, in the whole created universe.

Now the mystery and splendour of what is revealed in Christ becomes clear. The whole universe is to be transfigured to be the body of the eternal Wisdom of God, and we are called to be conscious fore-runners and vehicles of that cosmic transfiguration. It begins to happen already in us, as we are filled with the spirit of Christ, who lives within us and forms us in his image. It is completed when we are 'being transformed into his likeness with ever-increasing glory' (2 Corinthians 3.18), and at last 'you may participate in the divine nature and escape the corruption in the world caused by evil desires' (2 Peter 1.4).

To participate in the divine nature is to share in the being of God, which is love, to become instruments of that love and experients of that love, bound together in a community beyond ignorance and desire, suffering and sin, where 'there will be no more death' (Revelation 21.4). That is the ultimate meaning of salvation.

How the universe exists in God

For the New Testament letters, there are thus three senses in which the universe is 'in Christ'.

The thoughts of God

First, 'in him all things hold together' (Colossians 1.17). This reflects the quotation from the poet Epimenides in Acts 17.28 – 'In him (God) we live and move and have our being'. The main thought here is, as Acts makes clear, that God is not far away from us. Every part of space and time is immediately near to the one reality of God, and could not exist for one second without God's sustaining presence.

But there is more to it than that. The universe is created 'by him and for him' (Colossians 1.16). It is created by means of divine Wisdom, formed upon the pattern of all possible created things that exists in the mind of God. We might think of God as forming an idea of a created universe, a thought or, if uttered, a Word. Then the universe is the realization of this divine thought. It comes to be through the divine Word.

The universe exists 'for' the Word, in order to realize it fully and perfectly. The universe exists for the sake of realizing the divine Wisdom, of expressing its nature in a particular way, just as written words, in expressing the thoughts of their authors, also express their natures.

In saying that the universe is created by and for Christ, we are saying that the universe exists on the pattern of divine Wisdom and for the sake of realizing divine Wisdom. So we might think of Wisdom forming and completing its own thoughts in a material universe, just as a writer forms and completes thoughts in a printed book.

We do not, however, say that a printed book is 'in' the author. The book might be printed by someone else, and it has a reality independent of the author. Once it has passed out of the author's hands, it becomes public property, which can be sold or pulped at the will of others. In the case of the universe, it never passes out of the control of the divine Wisdom. We might say that the material universe is the materialized thought of God, not an independent reality. It is in God in the sense that a thought is in a human mind. It exists only as long as the thinker thinks it; it has no independent power of existence; and thinking it in some sense modifies the mind of the thinker, in that it is a mode, however transient and unimportant, in which the thinker exists, as thinking this thought (though it might have thought many other, different things).

The Colossians passage, then, pictures the universe as the thought of God. The formation and completion of the thought is at the same time the holding of the thought in mind – and here we bring together 'through' (formation), 'for' (completion) and 'in' (thinking) in one coherent phrase. To say that the universe is in Christ is to say that it is formed, sustained and completed by the creative thinking of divine

Wisdom, and is incapable of existing without the divine thinking activity by which it has being. That is the first sense of the phrase 'in Christ'. We are thoughts in the mind of God. But we are thoughts that have been given a certain limited but real freedom and autonomy of action.

The Church

The second sense relates specifically to the Christian Church. 'The Word became flesh and made his dwelling among us' (John 1.14). We have seen that the whole universe is an embodiment of the Word, a material realization of divine thought. But there is a more specific form of 'becoming flesh' in the person of Jesus. In him, Christians believe, the Word reveals its true nature and purpose in a uniquely clear and normative way. Jesus' whole life shows the love of God in action. In a novel, there may be many characters and many statements, most of which do not represent the actual beliefs and character of the author, but there may be one who does. So in the history of this planet, many created persons do not represent the mind of the author, even though they are in one sense the thoughts of the author. Jesus is meant to represent the mind of the author, and to be the thought, the Word, which expresses, which is in human form the essential nature of the author.

The Church is a community in which that essential nature continues to be mediated to the world. Within it, the Word continues to live and act, even if in a way which is obscured by the failures of the human members of the Church, the 'body of Christ'. To be 'in Christ', in the second sense, is to be a conscious believing member of the Church, seeking to live by the indwelling Spirit of Christ, and to be bound together in a harmonious community that tries to mediate the presence of Christ to the world.

A new heaven and earth

The third sense of being 'in Christ' refers forward to the consummation of all things, the 'new heaven and new earth' (Revelation 21.1). Then all sin and suffering, corruption and decay will be eliminated, and the conscious members of the created universe will consciously and freely be instruments of the Spirit, having the mind of Christ, bound together in one cosmic community whose existence is a perfected finite image of the beauty, wisdom and bliss of God. Then God will have achieved the ultimate divine purpose, which is 'to reconcile to himself all things, whether things on earth or things in heaven' (Colossians 1.20).

Some fundamentalist versions of Christian faith seem to think that Jesus, in human form, will appear soon to save a few believers on earth from divine judgement. God seems to be only concerned with human beings, and then only really concerned with a few of them, who have a very specific set of religious beliefs. If you look at paintings from early modern Europe that have as their theme the Judgement Day or the vision of Christ in glory, they are decidedly anthropomorphic. Apart from a few angels scattered around, the pictures are filled with human beings. Jesus and Mary, looking distinctly human, are in the place of honour next to God, and even God the Father often has a human form. Perhaps Paul himself regarded earth as virtually the whole of the created universe, the stars being lanterns in the sky, and Jerusalem being the centre of the universe. Nevertheless, the cosmic scope of Paul's thought cannot be missed.

Paul's vision of salvation

Paul's teaching was not formed from personal knowledge of Jesus, but from a vision of the risen Christ as a 'light from heaven' (Acts 9.3). He is strikingly not said to have had a human form, but the vision was of such power that it aroused in Paul an intense belief in the transformation of the whole universe as he knew it into a new creation, freed from the power of death. It is that belief which is expressed so strongly in the letters to the Colossians and Ephesians. We are called to share both in the death and in the resurrection of Jesus. 'For you died, and your life is now hidden with Christ in God' (Colossians 3.3). We are to 'be made new in the attitude of [our] minds; and to put on the new self, created to be like God' (Ephesians 4.23).

That is the core of Paul's teaching – death to the old nature and the assumption of a new self, given to us through participation in the life of Christ. But as he explores the implications of this teaching, he is taken far beyond the confines of the Jewish people, of the Mediterranean world, and of the earth itself. It is the whole universe that is to be renewed, and the Christ who was truly seen and fully present in Jesus is the cosmic, all-embracing Word and Wisdom of God.

Modern science expands our understanding of this vision in an enthralling way. Now we see that all the billions of galaxies are to be renewed and united in Christ. Humans can no longer be the centre of the picture of salvation. Who knows what forms the divine Word may take in other star-systems and created universes? It will not be the human Jesus who is the centre of cosmic salvation. It will be the limitless divine Word. For us humans, Jesus *is* that Word. He is the Word in human form. But the forms of the Word may be many, and unimaginable by us. So the manifestation of Christ in glory may be the full manifestation of the divine Word in countless forms of love, of death and resurrection, of sharing in creaturely suffering and renewal of creaturely existence by enabling it to participate in the divine nature.

The whole universe is patterned on the eternal Christ, is held within the mind of the eternal Christ, and exists in order to realize the mind of the eternal Christ in countless particular forms of wisdom and love. That is the vision that is clearly stated in these New Testament letters, and which modern astronomy enables us to understand in a wider and deeper way. We are only now beginning to see the fuller implications of the Pauline vision.

There is here a twofold sublation of specific beliefs that are stated in the Bible. First, the passages in Proverbs 8 and Colossians 1 which speak of Wisdom or Christ as being 'the firstborn of creation', are sublated by the later theological doctrine that Christ is 'begotten, not created'. This forces us to conclude that Christian teaching is not given complete and fully worked out in the Bible itself. It needs to be developed in ways for which the writers did not have the vocabulary, or of which they could not at that time see the implications. Second, the anthropomorphic imagery which the Bible often (not always) seems to suggest needs to be sublated by a greater knowledge of the extent and diversity of the universe, which only post-sixteenth-century science could give.

In both cases the implications of the biblical teaching required centuries to come to light. An over-literal reading of the text is therefore apt to lead to an inadequate theological interpretation of what is really being said, and to a very restricted view of the saving act of God in Christ. The biblical text retains its importance as the source and inspiration of theological thought. But the exact words of the text cannot constrain that thought, if further reflection on a wider range of texts and on the cumulative tradition of Christian experience, or new knowledge which places the biblical teachings in a different context, suggests that texts must be sublated to reveal their real significance.

So consideration of texts such as John 1.1: 'the Word was God', and the experience of worshipping Christ in prayer suggested a sublation of specific phrases in Proverbs and Colossians. And new discoveries of the size and age of the universe suggest a sublation of anthropomorphic imagery about the Judgement Day and the manifestation of Christ in glory. In neither case are the texts simply abandoned. In fact they might plausibly be said to achieve their full significance only when they are sublated by a deeper understanding of the deity of Christ and the cosmic scope of redemption.

If, in the light of our fuller knowledge of the cosmos, we were to paint a picture of salvation now, what would it be like? It would perhaps be a picture of a trillion trillion suns, of uncountable forms of conscious and creative life, of virtually endless reaches of space and time, universe upon universe, all held together in the mind of Christ, raised from the destruction and decay of the material realm to participate in the deathless and trans-temporal nature of divine Wisdom. On one small planet at the edge of a small galaxy, one young man was taken to share in the divine nature, to disclose its final purpose and mediate its illimitable power to the inhabitants of that small world. And what they see is the ultimate transfiguration of time itself into eternity, the final reconciliation of the whole universe in Christ, what the visionary Pierre Teilhard de Chardin called the Christification of the cosmos. What the Bible really teaches about salvation is no less than that.

♦ 5 ♦

Interpreting Biblical Teaching about Evil and Divine Love

Salvation as liberation from evil

The biblical picture of creation, especially in the letters to the Ephesians and Colossians, is of the whole universe being patterned on the eternal Wisdom who is Christ, existing within the divine Wisdom, and being ordered towards the full realization in matter of that Wisdom.

This is a remarkable cosmic vision. Fundamentalists, however, very often reject it, or perhaps have not even heard of it, though it is clearly biblical. Why should that be?

Perhaps it is because such a vision of the very close connection of the whole universe to the being of God, so that the whole universe is destined to be 'united in Christ', is felt to undermine the freedom of creatures, which involves the freedom to sin. Also there is much suffering and imperfection in the universe, which we might not expect to see in a divine incarnation. Most deeply of all, Christians probably have a profound feeling that they are not God, and not even part of God, because they are far removed from divine perfection.

These are all natural human reactions. But how do they measure up to the teaching of the Gospel? It is, after all, a very basic Christian insight to see suffering as involved in incarnation. Christ suffered on the cross, and so Christians are committed to believing that God shared in human suffering. Sin is a different matter. Jesus was 'tempted in every way, just as we are – yet was without sin' (Hebrews 4.15). It is sin that separates us from God, and makes us feel excluded from the presence of God. So the universe can only incarnate God if it is free from sin.

But is that not exactly what we hope for, as the fulfilment of God's purpose for creation? 'The creation itself will be liberated from its bondage to decay and brought into the glorious freedom of the children of God' (Romans 8.21). Now the creation is subjected to futility, disfigured by sin. In the new creation, we will be truly children of God, even as Jesus is the eternal son of God. At that time, we will not be separated from God, fearfully asking for divine mercy. We will be the brothers and sisters of Jesus, and with Jesus we will become manifestations of the eternal Wisdom. He will be the original and archetype. We will 'receive the full rights of sons' (Galatians 4.5) by grace. We will together be one body, one organic community, with Christ as head, and each one of us playing our proper part in the spirit of freedom and the union of love.

However the universe is not at present much like that. We exist in a world of ignorance and desire, suffering and evil, in which human beings use their freedom to do what is evil. Can these things really be thoughts of divine Wisdom? This is hardly a new problem, and it is a problem for any view of a good creator God, not just this one. But it is a problem nonetheless.

The problem is made much worse by two views which are fairly common in modern Christian thought, but which do not in fact have much basis in the Bible. One is the idea of God as purely and simply a 'loving heavenly Father', who so loves his children that he would never harm them, and will always take good care of them. The other is the interpretation of God's almighty power as the ability to do absolutely anything that can be imagined. According to the first view, God would never want any harm to come to his children. According to the second, God is able to prevent any harm coming to them. So the existence of suffering and evil becomes almost impossible to account for.

These views have become so widespread that many people think they express what the Bible teaches. But they do not, and it is important to examine what the Bible actually does say.

The prophet Isaiah is clear that God, as creator of everything, is the creator of darkness as well as light, of suffering as well as of happiness. 'I form the light and create darkness, I bring prosperity and create disaster; I, the Lord, do all these things' (Isaiah 45.7). How can this be? The prophet is at pains to emphasize how difficult it is to discern the mind of God. '"For my thoughts are not your thoughts, neither are your ways my ways," declares the Lord' (Isaiah 55.8). If the universe is a material realization of the thoughts of God, then it could be that the thoughts of God contain, in some way our minds are too limited to discern, negative possibilities as well as positive possibilities.

In a small way, we can see this in our own minds. If we can think of light, then we can also think of its absence. One thought entails the other. So perhaps even God, as the greatest of all possible beings, could not just have thoughts that were all positive. Even in God, if there is a thought of light, there will also be a thought of darkness.

But, we might be tempted to say, could God not keep the thoughts of darkness under control? We are now thinking of God as a person who thinks, and who can keep some thoughts to himself, while making others public – 'creating' them as objects. Yet what right have we to do that? The prophet says, 'To whom, then, will you compare God? What image will you compare him to?' (Isaiah 40.18). We simply have no idea what God may or may not do, or what is involved in creating a universe.

If the universe expresses the thoughts of God, perhaps it would not express those thoughts in a complete way if many thoughts had to be suppressed. I do not think we would want to say that God has to express all possible divine thoughts. But it could be that some positive – 'good' – thoughts could not be adequately expressed without some negative – 'bad' – thoughts.

When St Augustine wrote about this, he used the analogy of a painting. There has to be shade as well as light for a painting to exist. We might think of something we value a great deal, like love of another person. We can see that such love could not really exist if that other person did not have a will of their own, which could conflict with ours, and lead to the breakdown of a loving relationship. We hope the breakdown will never occur. In a perfect relationship, it may be that it will never occur. But we can still see that it could, and that if it could not, if love took no effort, no resilience, patience, persistence and compassion, we would not be talking about love as we understand it at all.

These are no doubt remote analogies for God. But they can give us some idea of how it could be that good things, like love, might entail the possible existence (which we hope will never be realized) of bad things, like the breakdown of relationships. So, in God, the thoughts of some good universes might entail the possibilities of bad things, though God might not positively intend their actualization.

The Genesis creation story

The story of creation in the book of Genesis implies a view very like this. As God created each class of thing – light, the atmosphere, vegetation on dry land, sun, moon and stars, creatures of sea and sky, and animals – the text says that God saw that they were good (*tob*, pleasing or beautiful). When God finished the work of creation, 'God saw all that he had made, and it was very good' (Genesis 1.31). The biblical view is that the created universe is pleasing to God. It is not to be seen just as a realm of suffering, or as an accidental, unplanned and

wasteful process. It is intrinsically good and beautiful. It is meant to be
a creative expression of divine Wisdom, and as such it is elegant, intel-
ligible and well ordered to its purpose.

The biblical account of creation is thus opposed to any evolutionary
view that sees human life as evolving by accident, and in a wasteful and
morally indifferent way. But it is not opposed to evolution as such.
Indeed, the Genesis account sees God's creative work as carried out in
successive stages ('days'). These days are clearly not periods of 24
hours, since the sun did not exist until the fourth day, and accordingly
theologians have always seen talk of 'days' as symbolic. However you
interpret the symbols, it seems that things were not created all at once,
and in the first Genesis account of chapter 1, God successively created
vegetation, sea creatures and birds, and animals. Humans were the last
things to be created.

In the second creation account (Genesis 2.4 onwards), 'the Lord God
formed the man from the dust of the ground' (Genesis 2.7). The Bible
has no objection to humans being generated out of simpler forms of life
– you cannot get much simpler than dust! So the evolutionary theory,
now accepted by the vast majority of working scientists, that *Homo
sapiens* evolved from simpler forms of life over a long period of time,
is quite compatible with the biblical view. What the Bible insists upon
is that this was an intentional, elegant and good process, not a random,
wasteful or repugnant one.

The fact that we are not to take the creation accounts literally is
established by the presence in the book of Genesis of two differing
accounts. In the first of these humans are created last, after the plants
and animals. In the second, humans are created before plants have
sprung from the ground (Genesis 2.5), watered by a mist that rises from
the earth, and before the animals have been formed 'out of the ground'
(Genesis 2.19).

Trying to make these different accounts of creation compatible is a
desperate manoeuvre, which simply misses the point of having two
accounts in the first place. That point is that these are not meant to be
literal descriptions of what happened at the beginning of the universe.
Like the creation stories which exist in most religious traditions, they
tell stories of 'origins' as a way of disclosing 'essences'. They are imaginative stories that convey spiritual truths about the essential nature of
humanity, and its relation to God. Such truths cannot be conveyed literally with any adequacy, and so poetic symbolism and story is used to
express them in a partly opaque, but evocative and spiritually fruitful
way. Diverse stories often need to be used, since one story cannot con-

vey all the truths that clamour to be expressed, and what we need to see is the differing, complementary truths that the different Genesis accounts convey.

Seen as spiritual reading, the two Genesis creation accounts offer inexhaustible resources for deepening our understanding of the essential nature of humanity in relation to God. Since the meanings are inexhaustible, and since a spiritual reading must be intensely personal, I cannot pretend to give *the* meaning of the accounts. But perhaps I can suggest that the first account is primarily concerned with the ordering of the elements of creation, and human responsibility under God for the flourishing of creation. The second account is more concerned with seeing human nature as both material and relational, as the point at which the material is capable of being raised to the spiritual within a relationship of love. Each story, read in this way, should be taken as a separate sacred poem, each presenting its own perspective on humanity's unity with creation and responsibility before God. Taken together, they are like views of a landscape through different windows, or like paintings of such views, each with its own character and meaning, but neither being like a photograph, which simply literally reproduces what is there.

What is common to both is the emphasis on the goodness of the created universe, and the responsibility of humans to oversee it in the name of God. But already, in this notion of human rule over nature in the first account, and of responsibility to 'work and take care of' the garden in the second account, darker possibilities are already present. For human rule may become a destructive tyranny, and those who are supposed to take care of gardens may allow them to be choked with weeds.

Tyrants and weeds are parts of the universe as well as benevolent rulers and flowers. Moreover, God placed the tree of knowledge in the garden, and forbade humans to eat the fruit on pain of death. Possibilities of disobedience and death were present even in the Garden of Eden – a symbolic way of saying that even an earthly Paradise is not free from possibilities of destruction and decay.

The second verse of Genesis hints at this: 'darkness was over the surface of the deep' (Genesis 1.2). The Spirit of God moved over the waters, forming the heaven and the earth. But the waters, *tohuwabohu*, the Great Deep, can be interpreted as the sea of chaos, the power of negativity, of threatening disharmony and entropy, which is found in other Middle Eastern mythologies. Certainly the Bible does not speak clearly of a 'creation out of nothing', as later theologians were to do. It speaks of the beginning of a formation of heaven and earth, and of God's spirit hovering over the Deep.

Is this some sort of material that God must shape or confine, in order to create a good, wisdom-expressing universe? The text allows and even suggests that interpretation, but both Jewish and Christian theologians were reluctant to allow any power external to God to constrain God's creative power. So they thought of the Deep as also created by God – though the Bible does not say that. That means that God first creates the Deep of chaos, then shapes the ordered universe out of it. There are other hints of this power of chaos in the Hebrew Bible.

On the second and third 'days' of creation, God divided the waters, to make the sky and the dry land. To a literalist, this may seem a straightforward physical act, but taken as poetic symbolism it suggests much more. God's conquest over the Deep is a theme found elsewhere in the Bible, where the Deep is associated with the great serpent or dragon who also symbolizes the dangerous power of chaos. 'It was you who split open the sea by your power; you broke the heads of the monster in the waters' (Psalm 74.13). Dividing the sea is a symbol for the conquest of chaos, and that is also the defeat of the dragon, whose name is Leviathan or Rahab. 'In that day, the Lord will punish with his sword, his fierce, great and powerful sword, Leviathan the gliding serpent; Leviathan the coiling serpent; he will slay the monster of the sea' (Isaiah 27.1).

The power of chaos and destruction is obviously not yet wholly defeated, though at creation it suffered grievous injury: 'Was it not you who cut Rahab to pieces, who pierced that monster through?' (Isaiah 51.9). There is an unmistakeable echo here of the Babylonian story of the battle of Marduk, god of Babylon, of city and culture, with Tiamat, dragon of the salt water sea, the defeat of Tiamat and the formation of the human race out of the blood of the leader of her armies, Kingu.

The Bible uses the same mythological material as the Babylonian story, but places it in the context of a firmly monotheistic and ethical faith. The sea, the serpent, and the dragon in the sea are common early Middle Eastern symbols of the formless abyss that always threatens human culture, and needs to be kept at bay, divided and contained. Water is life-giving, and from the Throne of God 'the river of the water of life' (Revelation 22.1) flows out to nourish the tree of life, whose leaves are for 'the healing of the nations'. Yet water is also destructive, and in John's vision of the new Jerusalem, when suffering and evil have been vanquished, then 'there was no longer any sea' (Revelation 21.1). Creation divided the sea. God's power restrains it now. At the end of historical time, and only then, the sea will be finally overcome.

In the biblical use of these symbols, there are not (as in the Babylonian story) many gods who arise from the primal Deep and engage in a vast cosmic battle in which humans have a relatively late and minor role. There is one creator God whose power is unchallenged, and who has a purpose for creation which gives human beings a role and dignity founded on the fact that they are made in 'the image and likeness' of God. This is an importantly new theme in Middle Eastern religion. It is the foundation of a fully biblical theme of creation. But what of the serpent and the sea?

The serpent crops up in the Genesis story as unambiguously created by God, and as 'more crafty than any of the wild animals' (Genesis 3.1). Not only is the serpent subtle. It deceives Eve into disobeying God, and, by God's decree (Genesis 3.15), becomes the enemy of humankind. Literalists presumably think that at one time snakes had legs, and spoke to people. Most theologians, however, have always taken a symbolic interpretation, and seen the serpent as a spiritual being or reality which, though created by God, encourages disobedience to God and so frustrates God's purpose.

The creation of conflict and suffering

This is the mystery, that God creates something – sea or serpent or spiritual power – which has the capacity to frustrate God's purpose. If the Great Deep is not a sort of uncreated principle of formlessness, but is, as later theologians were to affirm, created by God, why should God create what frustrates the very purpose of creation? Does this point, in veiled and metaphorical ways, to the fact that conflict and destruction is in some way essential to development and creation, even in a universe that is 'very good'? Perhaps it is only by conflict and competition that more developed forms of life can come to exist, and only by striving against opposition can excellence be achieved.

This thought raises doubts about the possibility of heaven, for if excellence can only be achieved by conflict, it does not seem that there can be a heaven, a human state of excellence without conflict. On reflection, however, it is clear that while excellence may need to be achieved through conflict, and with the possibility of failure, once achieved it can be sustained and enjoyed without conflict. After years of hard practice and intense competition, a violinist can achieve world eminence, and may then enjoy the excellence of playing well, though long beyond the need to prove anything further. Perhaps Paradise is a state in which hard-won excellence can be enjoyed in a serenity beyond striving. Or perhaps, as theologians like Gregory of Nyssa have suggested, there will always be an infinite journeying into God, but without the restless searching and estrangement which marks our present earthly lives. Perhaps human lives must begin with striving and opposition, before they come to a spiritual maturity that is beyond striving, but not beyond endlessly new enjoyments and relationships.

There are many indications in modern physics that support such a view. The second law of thermodynamics states that all things in this physical cosmos inevitably lose energy and tend towards formlessness. It is a law of inevitable long-term decay. Yet it is that law which gives time a direction, and so which makes the evolution of life and consciousness possible. If atoms did not decay, energy would not be released to form more complex substances. From the explosions of stars the complex element of carbon is formed from hydrogen and helium, without which life as we know it could not evolve. The progress of evolution takes place only because earlier generations die to make way for their mutated offspring. Only by competition for scarce resources do 'fit' forms of organic life evolve, which give rise eventually to consciousness and intellectual thought.

In all these ways conflict, decay and destruction are essential parts of the complex interplay of forces that enables our universe to exist. Perhaps universes with completely different characteristics, with completely different sorts of beings in them, could exist. But a universe like this, in which conscious beings live in communities in an environment which is challenging yet provides opportunities for creative change, and have evolved through generations of striving and endeavour – in which, in short, *we* exist – depends upon the existence of a few fundamental physical principles which have to be what they are. We could not change the basic physical constants and laws of our universe, and still have a universe of this general character at all. So perhaps the elements of this universe, both destructive and creative, are interconnected in ways that are necessary to its existence.

It is very easy for us to say that 'God can do anything.' Job does say this, when confronted by God; 'I know that you can do all things; no plan of yours can be thwarted' (Job 42.2). But he says this precisely after he has suffered in the most terrible ways, though he had done nothing to deserve suffering, and though every justification of suffering offered by his friends had been rejected as superficial or even blasphemous.

Was it God's purpose that Job should suffer, and did God cause that suffering for no reason? That does not seem a plausible interpretation of the goodness of God. At the beginning of the book of Job, Satan, the Adversary, appears as one of the 'sons of God' in the heavenly court, and God gives him permission to test Job by inflicting suffering: 'everything he has is in your hands' (Job 1.12). God has created the Adversary, the prosecuting counsel against humans, and though God does not intend Job to suffer, God allows the Adversary, even encourages him, to inflict suffering on Job. The book of Job demolishes any idea that God only inflicts suffering on the unjust, as a punishment for wrong-doing. God 'sends rain on the righteous and the unrighteous' (Matthew 5.45). It seems to be Satan who produces suffering, in a similarly indiscriminate way, but he does so as a 'son of God', and with the permission of God.

The book of Job is a notoriously difficult text to interpret, but it seems to teach that God does not primarily *intend* suffering and harm to come to creatures. It is not God's will that they should suffer. But God is 'incited by' Satan (Job 2.3), and gives Job into Satan's destroying power. In this notion of divine permission-to-act of a destructive power which God has created, and which has some ability to 'incite' God, we catch a glimpse of a secondary aspect of God's causality. God creates destructive powers and allows them to operate, until they are finally, but only in a new heaven and earth, restrained completely – 'the devil . . . was thrown into the lake of burning sulphur' (Revelation 20.10).

It is hard to avoid the conclusion that 'testing' by suffering is something that God has to allow, at a certain stage in the history of the universe, even though it is not what God primarily intends. A remote analogy may be this: a father may encourage his child to enter gymnastic competitions, on the ground that this will develop great athletic skills. But the father will then have to allow that the child may lose competitions, or suffer injury, or undergo long periods of unpleasant training. That is part of the acceptance that developing athletic skills is worthwhile. The father primarily intends that athletic skills should be developed, and that the child should be happy in developing them. But that entails a certain degree of suffering for the child, and it may result in a great degree of suffering if things go wrong.

I stress that this is a remote analogy. God is not really like a human father in this respect. In particular, it may be meaningless to say that God could refuse to create a universe anything like this one. Since all things exist 'in Christ', in the mind of God, the possibility of conflict, opposition, destruction and chaos may exist by necessity in the idea of any created universe containing free rational creatures. God necessarily creates the destructive power symbolized by Satan, the serpent and the sea, but intends that it should be opposed, contained and eventually defeated by the renewing and reconciling power symbolized by Christ, the eternal Wisdom of God.

The Bible does not tell us whether or not this is so. But it is suggested by two central biblical doctrines. First, that God is the creator of all things without exception – 'I form the light and create darkness, I bring prosperity and create disaster; I the Lord, do all these things' (Isaiah 45.7). Second, that God wills good – 'Every good and perfect gift is from above, coming down from the Father of the heavenly lights' (James 1.17). These two doctrines can only be held together if we accept that God creates things God does not positively intend. They presumably arise from the divine being as a necessary implication of what God is or what God does will, but not as positively intended.

If this should be thought to undermine the omnipotence of God, we should bear in mind that the statement in Job, 'You can do all things', is not a technical statement in a philosophy textbook. It is an expression of awe and submission before the might of the creator God, of whom Job says, 'now my eyes have seen you. Therefore I despise myself and repent' (Job 42.5–6). Just as it should not be thought that Job has a character that really ought to be despised, just because he uttered that thought when faced with God, so it should not be thought that God can do anything we think we can imagine, just because Job bowed before God's overwhelming power.

We might wish to say that God is the source of all beings and of all powers. There is no possible being that is more powerful than God, or that is an external limit to the divine power. But certain things are impossible even for God: 'It is impossible for God to lie' (Hebrews 6.18). Again, 'he [Christ] cannot disown himself' (2 Timothy 2.13). God cannot die, change in character, or be untrustworthy. These are necessities of the divine nature, though they are not external limitations. As later theologians were to put it, God is necessarily what God is.

The mystery of divine love

Now we cannot know what the inner nature of God is – 'no-one may see me and live' (Exodus 33.20). So it might be – we can only guess at this – that the nature of God as creator necessarily contains all possibilities, both good and bad. It might be that God as creator necessarily brings some of these possibilities into actuality, makes them existent, 'creates' them, as an expression of the divine being. After all, if God is necessarily what God is, and God creates the universe, it seems as if the creation of the universe must be a necessary outflowing of the being of God.

Christian theologians have not usually said this, preferring to think that God need not and might not have created any universe. That is because they wanted to magnify the absolute freedom of God. At the same time, most theologians have developed the view that freedom and necessity are ultimately compatible. For a being to be free is not for it to be absolutely undetermined by anything. It is for it to act in accordance with its own nature. In this sense, God is absolutely free if the divine nature is to create and to love, and if God necessarily acts to realize that nature. We can therefore see the act of creation as both necessary and free.

The Bible does not, I think, decide on this thorny issue of whether some creation is a necessary outflowing of the divine being. But if 'God is love' (1 John 4.8), there is some reason to think that love does not really exist unless it expresses itself in relation to an 'other' who is the object of love, and who can return (or reject) love. So a God who is love will create others with whom a relationship of love can be established, and such creation will be necessary, not as a limitation of God, but as a natural and inevitable expression of the divine nature.

Theologians have noted this point, and some of them have supposed that the doctrine of the Trinity, of a communion of loving 'persons' within God, is indeed a natural implication of the New Testament idea of God as love. However, we might think that a love that remains enclosed within the divine being itself, which does not move out in risk to others who really can reject God, is a relatively restricted sort of love, though it may indeed be real and important.

The Christian picture of the love of God is given by the New Testament, and it seems most adequately expressed in such parables as that of the Prodigal Son, who leaves his father's house, but is accepted in love when he returns (Luke 15.11–32). Such love, which bears rejection, which suffers with and which reconciles those who are estranged, is a sort of love that cannot be found within the life of the Trinity, where love is necessarily accepted and returned, without the possibility of journeying to a far country.

There is some plausibility in seeing Jesus' teaching on love as involving the possibility of rejection, loss, suffering and reconciliation. If so, the creation of a universe in which such a possibility can be realized will also be a natural and inevitable expression of the divine nature as love, not a restriction of it. In that sense, the possibility of suffering and evil will necessarily exist in any universe that manifests this sort of love.

This doctrine is not explicitly taught in the Bible, but it is biblically based at every step. The first step is to see that God has certain essential, necessary characteristics. The second step is to see that God must hold all possibilities, good and bad, in the divine mind. The third step is to see that God's love naturally leads to the positing of objects of that love. The fourth step is to see that the character of divine love, revealed in Christ, is such as to risk rejection and extend itself in compassion to reconcile all things to itself.

The final step of the argument is to suppose that the creation of such a universe will involve the creation of those negative possibilities of suffering, conflict and destruction, which are conditions of rejection, loss and reconciliation, and thus of manifesting the wholly self-giving love of God – 'God demonstrates his own love for us in this: While we were still sinners, Christ died for us' (Romans 5.8). God's love opens itself to the risk of rejection, and goes to the furthest limits to reconcile those who reject God. Such a love can only exist in a world in which rejection is a real possibility.

The manifestation of this 'agapistic' love involves the possibility of love rejected as well as of love reconciled. So the story of this universe, which is one chapter in the story of the limitless love of God, is a story of how love works through creating freedom, through striving and diligence, to unite things that have been estranged and lost once more within the divine life.

Was that story necessary? The letter to the Ephesians says that 'he [God] chose us in him [Christ] before the creation of the world' (Ephesians 1.4). It sounds as though the eternal decree of the divine love already includes us, even before the first moment of creation. But was rejection and alienation, the journey to the far country, necessary? I think we can only say that it was always possible, in the creation of the universe, or of any universe that has such created beings in it. Its real possibility probably entails the actual occurrence of some degree of conflict, destruction and suffering. For without that, without the tempting serpent and the encircling sea, there can be no growth towards the maturity of wisdom and no knowledge of the cost of love, which demands commitment, fortitude and resolution before it can become established in the human heart.

And is this universe 'very good'? It is not without some suffering, and the possibility of much more (a possibility which has, of course, been realized with disastrous consequences). But without such a universe as this, agapistic love could not be realized, the divine nature as love could not be fully expressed, and the final reconciliation of all things to God could not be accomplished. On a Christian view, the physical cosmos must be seen as an elegant and efficient means to produce just the sort of goods it does produce – the goods of free, creative, intelligent communities of self-aware beings.

It is very plausible to see it in that way. The genesis of a complex world of persons by successive stages of emergence from blind primal energy, through the development of stable atomic compounds, self-replicating complex molecules, the development of cells within highly structured organisms, the formation of central nervous systems, culminating in conscious, free and responsible life-forms, seems to be a miracle of elegant design. Its beauty is breathtaking and its final purpose, revealed in Christ – the transfiguration of all of this into the life of God – is of absolutely overwhelming value.

The scientific world-view fills out our understanding of the way in which conflict and harmony, death and renewed life, enters into the warp and woof of the universe. It expands our appreciation of the glory of the Creator, who holds billions of galaxies in being, and whose power extends infinitely beyond them all. The Genesis creation stories, written long before this world-view became possible, are inspired poetic creations whose symbolism expresses the place of humanity as a creature of dust made in the divine image, raised to partake of the divine nature, and called to responsible care for the garden of the earth. Thus those stories are of inestimable spiritual value, but it degrades and misinterprets them to take them as literal records that compete with modern scientific accounts.

In the light of these considerations, the power of God needs to be seen as always qualified by the agapistic love of God, a love that leaves created persons free, calls them to strive to overcome self and learn to fashion communities of love, companions with them in their pilgrimage towards the love that moves the sun, and assures them of final participation in the divine nature, which is completed and limitless love.

All this is the 'eternal purpose which he [God] accomplished in Christ Jesus' (Ephesians 3.11). Out of the interplay of darkness and of light, by the suffering of the cross and the joy of resurrection, and in the hope of participating fully and consciously in the life of God, human beings are parts of a vast cosmic process of creation, both necessary and free, in which the purpose of God is realized. What the Bible teaches is that God is the one and only creator of all things, of weal and woe, that creation realizes an eternal purpose that is very good, and that human beings are called to help in realizing this purpose by caring for the earth from which they sprang. The serpent and the sea are parts of this creation, springing from the unfathomable depths of the divine being. They become the adversaries of humanity, and against them only divine help can prevail. That help comes, in the form of an eternal love that accepts suffering and death and so paradoxically defeats them. The history of humanity is the history of that struggle, and the Christian gospel is that victory is assured in Christ, in whom God 'predestined us to be adopted as his sons' (Ephesians 1.5). So it is that, despite all the destruction, conflict and suffering in the world, the created universe, perhaps flowing by inner necessity from the divine being, is indeed, seen in the light of its final destiny and goal, very good.

6

Interpreting Biblical Teaching about Sin and Grace

Original sin

We have seen that fundamentalists often claim that the Bible should be taken literally, and that this can lead them into conflicts with modern science. At the same time, strangely enough, they go to great lengths to avoid literal interpretations of some key passages of Scripture. There are also many biblical texts that fundamentalists simply ignore, as if they were not there at all. I shall now consider a range of such texts, beginning with one that ought to be inescapable for anyone who reads the Bible carefully: 'For as in Adam all die, so in Christ all will be made alive' (1 Corinthians 15.22).

This short sentence is one of the most mysterious in the New Testament. It summarizes in a few words the central teaching of the gospel, as it was understood by Paul. But it has proved very difficult to interpret. What is meant by all dying 'in Adam'? Does this happen whether people know it or not? And how could it happen if Adam lived thousands of years ago?

Exactly the same questions can be asked of all being made alive 'in Christ'. Does this really mean, as it plainly says, 'everyone'? Does it happen without people knowing it? And how can it happen if people do not realize it?

It must be emphasized that the word 'all' refers to the same group in both cases. The sentence does not say that everyone dies in Adam, but only a few shall be made alive in Christ. It says that everyone dies, and everyone will be made alive. This immediately challenges the widely held view that only a few humans will be saved, while the rest are doomed to some other fate. We have all died in Adam, and we shall all be alive in Christ.

What sort of death is being talked about here? A very literalist view would say that no beings before Adam, the first male human, died, and that death is a punishment for Adam's sin. If he had not sinned, humans would not have died, and perhaps there would have been no death in the animal kingdom at all. 'The wages of sin is death' (Romans 6.23).

Such a view contradicts everything we know about organic life on earth. Dinosaurs died long before humans existed, and death is necessary if there is to be the generation of new individuals, without radically overpopulating the earth. Death is necessary if there are to be mutations to new forms of life over many generations, through the processes of evolution.

But it also contradicts what the Bible says about death and life. According to John's Gospel, Jesus says, 'here is the bread that comes down from heaven, which a man may eat and not die' (John 6.50). Taken literally, this would mean that those who eat the flesh of Christ will never die and be buried. But that is not the meaning. As Jesus says just a little later, 'Whoever eats my flesh and drinks my blood has eternal life, and I will raise him up at the last day' (John 6.54). The faithful will die, but they will hereafter have 'eternal life'. Moreover, when Jesus says, 'Unless you can eat the flesh of the Son of Man and drink his blood, you have no life in you' (John 6.53), he is not saying that such people are physically dead.

Dying and living have a spiritual meaning in John's Gospel, not a physical one. To die, or to be without life, is to be without the life-giving presence of Christ within. John's Gospel even spells it out explicitly: 'this is eternal life: that they may know you, the only true God, and Jesus Christ, whom you have sent' (John 17.3). Knowing is much more than having a purely theoretical belief. It is an apprehension of, an immediate acquaintance with God, which transforms human life. To know Christ, to drink his blood and eat his flesh, is to assimilate the life of Christ into our own life, so that Christ lives within as the true life of the soul.

The wages of sin is death, inasmuch as sin is a turning against God, and so rejects the life of Christ, leading the soul to the way of spiritual death. To be spiritually dead is quite compatible with existing forever, but in a state of separation from God, the true source of all life. The sin of Adam, so John's Gospel would suggest, is not something that causes humans to die physically. It is something that cuts them off from the life of Christ, the divine Wisdom, whether they are physically alive or dead.

By now we should expect that Adam is not the name of a historical individual who lived a number of years ago. The Hebrew word *Adam* can mean 'man' or 'person', and can be read in the sense of 'human being'. This reading makes the phrase, 'In Adam all die' much more comprehensible. It means: in so far as creatures are human beings, and share in human nature, they are cut off from the life of God.

With the creation stories in general, stories about origins are ways of seeking the essential natures of things. So the Genesis story about the origins of sin is in fact a way of saying what the essential nature of sin is, and how all humans are affected by it. In the biblical story, God plants a tree of knowledge in the garden of Eden, and says, 'you must not eat from the tree of the knowledge of good and evil, for when you eat of it you will surely die' (Genesis 2.17). The serpent, however, points out that the tree was 'desirable for gaining wisdom' (Genesis 3.6), and that eating its fruit will open the eyes, so that 'you will be like God, knowing good and evil' (Genesis 3.5).

This is symbolism, not a sort of biology that we have now forgotten about, for which eating fruit made you wise. Humans, like Dr Faust in the German legend, desire wisdom. They desire to know good and evil, to experience all that the world has to offer, and to have power over it. Such wisdom, however, is dangerous if it comes too soon. Many early Christian theologians – Irenaeus most famously – supposed that Adam and Eve were like children, innocent and naive, and they needed to grow to maturity before they could assume responsibility for caring for the earth. Too much experience too soon would be harmful. It would bring power without responsibility, knowledge without wisdom.

So God says, 'I will destroy the wisdom of the wise' (1 Corinthians 1.19, quoting Isaiah 29.14), for 'the world through its wisdom did not know . . . God' (1 Corinthians 1.21). The wisdom being referred to here is worldly wisdom. We sometimes speak of people being 'worldly-wise', meaning that they have a lot of experience, which has often made them cynical and suspicious, and they know how to manipulate things to their advantage. If the fruit of the tree of knowledge is eaten in defiance of God's command, it is worldly wisdom that we shall obtain. And that is spiritual death.

It was not just one human ancestor who desired worldly wisdom, when tempted by a snake. Virtually all humans, when they see the pleasures and rewards of fame and success, are tempted by the thought that they might taste those rewards without having to pay the penalty of losing the knowledge of God. The sin of Adam is the sin of Everyman. We each walk by our own tree of the knowledge of good and evil, offering experience of selfish desire and luxury. We each meet our own serpent, who whispers to us that we can taste such experience without disaster. We each taste the fruit, and we each die, as we cast out from our hearts the life of God which was, if we could only have realized it, the only source of true wisdom without selfish attachment. 'In Adam', sharing in the human nature that is common to us all, a nature tempted by selfish desires and filled with longing for mastery of the ways of the world, we die to God. That seems to be the core meaning of what Western Christians call 'original sin'.

Morality and grace

We might want to claim exemptions from this gloomy belief in universal spiritual death, to say that not everyone need fall victim to temptation, even though to be subject to such temptation seems part of human nature. There might be people who do not share the death of Adam.

Paul, however, does not share this view. 'There is no-one who does good', he writes, 'not even one' (Romans 3.12). It is indeed so written in Psalm 14.3. It is worth recalling, however, that Jews have no doctrine of 'original sin', so that, whatever this verse means, it has never been interpreted by Jews (and it is a Jewish Psalm!) to mean that nobody ever does any good thing. It is rather a cry of despair, arising from a particular mood, not a general truth about the world.

There are many statements in the Psalms of this sort. When the Psalmist writes, 'The righteous will flourish like a palm tree' (Psalm 92.12), he expresses a confidence in the moral government of the universe that is undermined by the book of Job, which seems almost expressly written to undermine any easy view that the righteous flourish and the wicked are punished. We cannot infer from that verse that the righteous will always flourish. We might want to say that there is a general connection between goodness and human flourishing, and – we hope – an ultimate vindication of goodness, if only after death. The Psalmist, we have to say, is exaggerating a general hope that divine justice will be expressed somehow in the universe.

So, in saying that no one is righteous, the Psalmist is expressing a general lament at the injustice of human beings. But for the Hebrew Bible there certainly are righteous men. Psalm 37 advises: 'Consider the blameless, observe the upright; there is a future for the man of peace' (Psalm 37.37). It does not add, 'By the way, there are no blameless men.' In fact the general teaching of the Old Testament is fairly clear, that each person will be judged according to what they do, and many will be declared righteous by God. Thus the prophet Ezekiel, protesting about the immorality of his generation, says, 'even if these three men – Noah, Daniel and Job – were in it [the land], they could save only themselves by their righteousness, declares the Sovereign Lord' (Ezekiel

14.14). At least three men, according to Ezekiel, were righteous, and delivered themselves by their righteousness.

This suggests that the Psalmist in Psalm 14 is, like Ezekiel, bemoaning the evil of the people of his own generation, but not declaring that there have never been any righteous people. The Old Testament view may be that there are very few righteous people, but there are some, and it is possible to do what God requires of us. Adam and Eve, in the Genesis story, were punished for their sin (Genesis 3.16–19), and all their descendants share in the consequences of that punishment. But there is no idea of 'original sin', an inherent and unavoidable sinfulness, in the Old Testament.

If we take seriously Paul's statement that 'all have sinned and fall short of the glory of God' (Romans 3.23), it seems at first that he is contradicting the general teaching of the Old Testament. But by now we know that, rather than speaking of contradictions, it is better to say that some biblical teachings are sublated by others. We cannot just take whatever the Bible says, wherever it says it, as true. We need to read the Bible over the whole of its range, and exercise judgement and discrimination to discover what teachings are sublated, and why – and in such matters there will almost certainly always be differences of interpretation that cannot finally be decided just by appeal to the Bible itself.

The Bible resolves none of our perplexities about moral freedom and human sinfulness. What it does is to challenge our thinking about these matters, leading us to see matters from different perspectives, and to explore them ourselves. This generates an important insight into the nature of biblical revelation. The Bible gives no systematic doctrine – that is for theologians to attempt, and their attempts are always tentative and revisable, whether they are Calvin, Maximus the Confessor, or Aquinas. What then does the Bible do? It upsets our preconceived ideas, puts in question our over-neat systems of doctrine, presents paradoxes and conflicting viewpoints (compare the stark pessimism of Ecclesiastes with the easy optimism of some of the Psalms). But above all, it turns the mind to God, in reverence and praise rather than in comprehension and explanation. What it reveals is mystery beyond human comprehension ('the revelation of mystery', Romans 16.25), but mystery that transforms our lives by conveying to us the presence and power of God. In a word, the Bible evokes faith, obedient trust in God. It does not teach systematic doctrines. It is more like a great work of art, opening the human mind to transcendence, than like a textbook of philosophy.

So the Bible teaches that we shall be judged by our deeds. But then it puts a great question mark against this teaching, and states that moralism is not enough. The teaching of personal moral responsibility needs to be sublated by a deeper insight into the tragedy of the human condition. The perplexing thing is that Paul seems to sublate not only the Old Testament but also the Gospels. This is particularly clear in the case of the Gospel of Matthew, where the parable of the Sheep and the Goats (Matthew 25.31–46) makes a sharp distinction between the 'cursed' and the 'righteous'. The righteous are those who feed the hungry, take in strangers, clothe the naked and visit the sick and those in prison. The cursed call the King 'Lord', but are led to 'eternal punishment' because they did not do any of those things.

There is no mention in this parable of faith. Those who inherit eternal life are those who act charitably, and those who inherit eternal punishment are those who do not, however much they profess to have faith. Matthew puts it very clearly elsewhere: 'Not everyone who says to me, "Lord, Lord," will enter the kingdom of heaven, but only he who does the will of my Father who is in heaven' (Matthew 7.21).

It seems that, according to Matthew, people will be judged by how they act, not by what they believe. Believing alone is not enough: 'faith without deeds is dead' (James 2.26). At these points the Bible teaches that some people will be judged as righteous, and inherit eternal life, because of their charitable actions, not because of their faith.

Matthew's parables are, however, parables of the Kingdom of Heaven. The Kingdom is not something people can bring about by their own efforts. It comes by the grace, the loving act, of God. Jesus' teaching is that the Kingdom is 'near at hand', and we know that in fact it comes near to people in the person of Jesus. As Luke's Gospel puts it most dramatically, 'But if I drive out demons by the finger of God, then the kingdom of God has come to you' (Luke 11.20).

As the Kingdom draws near to people in Jesus, their reaction to him – whether of faith or of rejection – determines their relation to the Kingdom. At a time when the eternal Christ could not yet live 'within' them, because Christ stood before them in the person of Jesus, the gift of the Kingdom is the gift of the presence of Jesus, whose teaching they can either accept in faith or ignore.

What Matthew is saying, therefore, is not that deeds without faith is enough to determine human destiny. He is saying that faith without deeds is not sufficient for salvation. Paul adds to this that works without faith are not sufficient for salvation – 'no-one will be declared righteous in his [God's] sight by observing the law' (Romans 3.20). Taken together, the New Testament teaching seems quite unequivocal – both faith and good deeds are necessary for salvation. Neither, taken alone, is enough. When Paul sublates the apparent moralism of much of the rest of the Bible, he is emphasizing the necessity of faith as well as righteousness. It is necessary for salvation that human nature is united by grace to the divine nature, and that humans obey the will of God by doing what is right.

That is not a point the prophets or Matthew would have denied. What is often said to be the most important commandment of the Torah is, 'Love the Lord your God with all your heart' (Luke 10.27). Such love demands more than obedience; it demands a union of heart and will. Paul is not really contradicting the prophetic teaching about judgement, even though he does literally contradict some specific statements in the Old Testament. He is emphasizing what is already implied in the notion of a divine covenant with humanity, that divine grace must come first, raising humanity to union with the divine. Moralism is not enough, without that transformation of the heart that only divine love can bring about.

The universality of sin

Because of his own experience of the grace of God in Christ, Paul has a new concept of how divine grace is given – through the person of Jesus, and through an inner union of humanity and divinity by the interior action of the Spirit. And he has a new concept of its range and extent – it is given to Gentiles as well as Jews. The new covenant is for all humans without exception.

The way in which Paul sublates the Old Testament teaching that all people will face the Judgement of God is to add that no one can stand in that Judgement who does not accept the grace of God which is freely offered to all. A person can only be held morally responsible for things that are in their power to do, but which they are not compelled to do. This agrees with the statement in Ezekiel that 'the soul who sins is the one who will die' (Ezekiel 18.20). Children shall not be punished for their fathers' sins, Ezekiel says, and any person who repents and turns from sin shall live, 'For I take no pleasure in the death of anyone, declares the Sovereign Lord. Repent and live!' (Ezekiel 18.32). It is bluntly stated here that no one should be punished for another's sin, and that it is possible for sinners to repent, or for the righteous to fall into sin. These things are in our power, and our power alone, and we shall be judged according to what we do.

The Bible is full of passages calling on people to repent, warning of judgement if they do not, and offering forgiveness if they do. One of the best examples is in the book of Jonah, in which Jonah prophesies destruction for the city of Nineveh, but the people repent, and God does not destroy it, much to Jonah's displeasure. 'When God saw what they did and how they turned from their evil ways, he had compassion and did not bring upon them the destruction he had threatened' (Jonah 3.10).

Such passages imply that God will punish evil, but it is in the power of people to repent. What God will actually do depends to some extent on the people's response. As Moses said to the people of Israel, 'I have set before you life and death, blessings and curses. Now choose life' (Deuteronomy 30.19). It is up to the people what they will choose. What God does is to set before them the possibilities of life and death, but God does not compel them to act in a specific way.

It looks as though anyone is free to choose life, and that is what most of the Bible teaches. But Paul sees something else. 'In Adam' all choose the way of death. Human nature is oriented towards death, away from fellowship with God, and nothing humans can do will restore that relationship. One way to approach this thought is to see the great extent to which humans are shaped by the web of social relationships within which they are born and reared.

For Jews this is very clear. You do not choose to be a Jew (unless you convert to Judaism). You are born a Jew. You are brought up as a Jew. You are taught Torah, and your whole life is shaped by the sense of being separate from the *Goyim*, the Gentiles. It is possible for you to renounce faith, but it is almost impossible to stop being, and feeling, Jewish, in some very basic sense.

As Ezekiel said, you should only be punished for your own sins. But your whole outlook on life, your values and goals, will be shaped by your family and society. This will impose both opportunities and limitations upon you, from which you cannot escape. In one of the earliest creeds of the Bible, God says, 'I, the Lord your God, am a jealous God, punishing the children for the sin of the fathers to the third and fourth generation of those who hate me, but showing love to [thousands] who love me' (Exodus 20.5–6). This may seem unjust, but it is a simple statement of the fact that what parents do and think will have effects on their children. If I bring my children up to steal and lie, and to think such acts are natural and even commendable, they will probably suffer the fate of criminals, though that will largely be my fault. If I bring my children up to pray and read, they will have the advantages of a thoughtful and cultured person, though they may make no notable moral decisions about such matters.

In addition to the area of morally responsible conduct, then, there is also an area of the cultivation of personality, which shapes the capacities, values and propensities of human beings. This is not strictly a moral area, in the sense of an area over which people have full control. It is an area of basic orientation and outlook.

We know that children, with great difficulty, can sometimes escape their upbringing. And whatever people are like, there is always some area of moral responsibility within which they can choose right or wrong. But what people cannot change is the basic set of relationships within which they exist, and which limit the possibilities and choices of their lives. If the parents of a young child die, the absence of that relationship will make a great difference to the life of the child. Of course the child can make moral choices, can have a happy life, and can find love in other human ways. But the child will still be deprived of a central sort of human relationship, which is important to many people.

Paul sees that the human situation is one in which human beings are deprived of the knowledge and inner experience of the love of God which might have been and which should have been theirs. As later theologians were to put it, the natural capacities of human nature should have been directed and fulfilled by the supernatural gifts which give intimate knowledge of God and the capacity naturally to do God's will. Humans should have been the instruments and experients of the divine life. But they are not. They might have all the natural capacities, including the moral capacities, which are proper to human nature. But they lack those supernatural gifts that could give humans a share in the divine nature, and so orient the natural to a supernatural end.

We know much more about human nature now than Paul did. But he knew that 'I myself in my mind am a slave to God's law, but in the sinful nature a slave to the law of sin' (Romans 7.25). 'The sinful nature' or flesh (*sarx*) is, we would now say, that nature which the evolutionary process has left us with. We are lustful, aggressive and hostile to unknown tribes, because those are the qualities that have enabled us to become the dominant species on the planet. It is quite natural for us to have those propensities, and no blame attaches to us for that.

The flesh, of course, also provides us with good propensities – to love our families, care in a limited way at least for others, and develop artistic culture and scientific understanding. It provides us with a moral sense, for all 'show that the requirements of the law are written on their hearts, their consciences also bearing witness' (Romans 2.15). We do have a choice between right and wrong, and can be held responsible for making it.

In all of this, however, there is no mention of God. And that is the trouble. If there were a deep and meaningful unity between human and divine nature, then lust would be, perhaps gradually over the course of generations of pre-human life-forms, but inexorably nonetheless, moderated into loving desire and sensual delight in a fully personal relationship of love. Aggression would be moderated into the courage to face affliction and to compete with others without rancour. In short, the natural human affections, generated by evolutionary competition, would be transformed into spiritual capacities of love and vitality, interwoven at every point with divine power and wisdom.

The story of the eating of the fruit from the tree of knowledge is a symbol for the failure of humanity to accept the divine–human unity that would have made that transformation possible. Humans grasped at knowledge without unity with the divine, indeed in opposition to and in fear of the divine – Adam and his wife 'hid from the Lord God among the trees' (Genesis 3.8).

We might now say that at the beginning of the evolutionary leap to *Homo sapiens*, those early humanoid beings had the freedom to turn to God or to turn away. They had the capacity to choose the way of life or the way of death. They chose death. And since that time, a time lost in prehistory, humans have lived 'in Adam', in the flesh, a purely natural existence alienated from the divine source of all life.

Salvation is the fulfilment of human life by its union with the divine. That is why salvation can be attained, 'not because of righteous things we had done, but . . . through the washing of rebirth and renewal by the Holy Spirit' (Titus 3.5). However many good and charitable deeds we do, we cannot of ourselves establish that divine–human unity which is the true human vocation. Only God can do that, by the power of grace freely given, renewing human nature and liberating it from the grip of decay and death.

Paul sublates the teaching that we shall be judged by our deeds, and that on Judgement Day the righteous will be separated from the wicked once and for all. In its place he puts a picture of human beings as separated from God and from the divine life, because they are members of a community that has chosen separation and exile from God as their path. The moral law remains binding, but it can never unite humanity to the divine. Humans do not know God clearly, and their lack of knowledge of God, and the consequent lack of the divine power which such inner knowledge brings to aid their actions, makes moral conduct difficult if not impossible. What should have been a natural response to the impulses of love becomes a set of absolute commands of the moral law, set against natural human inclinations.

Original sin is not some sort of innate guilt we are born with, even before we have done anything. It does not mean that we are guilty because of something that some remote ancestor did long ago. It is our sharing in the separation of human existence from its divine source, a separation that darkens our spiritual knowledge and disables our moral will. That separation occurred early in the prehistory of the human race, and it has been reinforced by the acts of millions of humans throughout many generations. It leaves us in a state of spiritual death, of separation from God. So it defines an important element of our human mode of being in the world. That is the important truth conveyed by Paul's statement that 'in Adam all die'.

The universality of life in Christ

However there is another side to Paul's picture. Where humans fail, and death reigns, God steps in to make possible what is impossible for human agency alone: 'What is impossible with men . . . is possible with God' (Luke 18.27). Jesus says this just after having said that it is harder for a rich man to enter the Kingdom than for a camel to go through the eye of a needle. He also says it just after having told the rich young man to obey the commandments of God and to give up his goods. The requirements of the law – a law of perfect love – are too hard for most of us to bear. It is at that point that divine grace offers forgiveness and the free gift of eternal life, of union with the divine nature.

To whom is this gift given? Paul is clear about that – to the same people for whom death is the wage of sin, that is, to all humanity. 'For God', says Paul, 'has bound all men over to disobedience so that he may have mercy on them all' (Romans 11.32). God sees all humans as sharing in Adamic nature, in the separated condition of humanity. But God also sees all humans as sharing in Christic nature, in the reconciled condition of redeemed humanity.

We need know nothing about any historical Adam to share in the humanity that is estranged from God. We are estranged, whether we know it or not. What the Christian gospel reveals is the fact of our estrangement, that all is not well with us, however morally good we may think we are, that we still lack what is necessary for the true fulfilment of human existence.

Similarly, we need know nothing about the historical Jesus to share in the humanity that is reconciled to God. We are reconciled, whether we know it or not: 'just as the result of one trespass was condemnation for all men, so also the result of one act of righteousness was justification that brings life for all men' (Romans 5.18). What the Christian gospel reveals is the nature of our salvation (that it lies in inner union with the divine nature), and the means of our salvation (that it comes through the sacrifice of Christ and the interior action of the Spirit).

But surely we are not actually reconciled to God, without knowing anything about it? And surely we need to do something to be reconciled – at least, repent and believe the gospel? That is true. The full reconciliation of humanity to God lies in the future; all we have are foretastes of its realization, and the assurance of its realization, in the future. And reconciliation does require repentance – a turning of the mind from selfish desire to the gracious love of God – and faith – acceptance of the divine love, shown in Jesus.

Reconciliation requires faith. But what exactly is faith? According to the New Testament, it cannot be confined to Christians, or to an explicit belief in Jesus as Lord. The letter to the Hebrews, chapter 11, gives a list of examples of faith, none of whom are Christian. Abel, Enoch, Noah, Abraham and many others are cited as people who had exemplary faith. There seem to be three main elements to the faith that is described in that chapter. First, there is belief that God exists, as the spiritual source of all reality – 'By faith we understand that the universe was formed at God's command' (Hebrews 11.3). Second, there is a disciplined commitment to 'try to find', to know and love God – 'throw off everything that hinders . . . and let us run with perseverance the race marked out for us' (Hebrews 12.1). Third, there is a resolute hope that God will fulfil the divine promises – 'She [Sarah] considered him faithful who had made the promise' (Hebrews 11.11).

The writer of this letter is referring to the heroes of Israel, and points out that 'none of them received what had been promised' (Hebrews 11.39), whereas in Christ God has truly been brought near. There is a quality of Christian faith they did not possess. But they are still heroes and exemplars of faith, and their faith is in the reality of God, in the possibility of union with God (the 'country' they search for, Hebrews 11.14), and in the ultimate realization of the divine purpose.

If humans are created in order to have a fulfilling personal relationship with God, then it is obviously necessary that they should believe there is a God, that personal knowledge of God is possible, and that they can come to know and love God fully – 'anyone who comes to him [God] must believe that he exists and that he rewards those who earnestly seek him' (Hebrews 11.6). If faith is assenting to the existence of God, trying to find God, and committing ourselves to believing that God will be found, then faith is indeed necessary to salvation.

The Bible does not teach that we must believe Jesus is the Son of God in order to avoid eternal punishment or to achieve the bliss of heaven. It teaches that moral striving and even moral success is not sufficient for salvation – for the attaining of the proper goal of human existence. Moral striving is necessary for salvation, but we must also strive to know and love God, and commit ourselves absolutely to the belief that God will make such knowledge and love possible. If we do not, we miss the mark of human existence. We are still bound to the way of death, for we have not found the way of eternal life.

What the Bible teaches is that those who strive for righteousness and have faith in God will be saved, and that it is Christ who saves them, whether they know it or not (Abraham surely did not know it, despite Augustine's rather desperate suggestion that Abraham and the prophets had miraculous foreknowledge of Christ, and so really believed in Christ).

People are not, strictly speaking, saved by their faith. That would turn faith into a sort of human achievement, or even make our eternal salvation turn upon our capacity to believe certain things – which is hardly in our power. People are saved by the freely given love of God. What it is in our power to do, as human persons, is to accept or reject this love. Faith must therefore be seen as the human assent to the love of God, an assent that does require commitment, persistence and striving, but which is always a matter of relationship and response, not of solitary moral achievement.

Faith is commitment to the utter reliability of another. Faith in God is staking our whole life on God's power and promise, and that is only possible when God appears as a spiritual presence, whose appearing holds the promise of future fulfilment.

The biblical vision is something like this: God creates the universe in order that finite persons should evolve, capable of loving relationship with one another and with God. In such a creation, the inner nature of the divine being as love can be realized in a particular way, a way that involves the risk of rejection and the destruction of relationship. Creaturely freedom is a condition of genuine loving relationship. God initiated a personal relationship of loyalty and love with human beings, but humans rejected this relationship, choosing instead the sort of autonomy that seeks knowledge without wisdom, and power without responsibility (Genesis 2.4—3.20). From that point on, humans were born in a society estranged from the knowledge and love of God, though still with a natural desire to seek the God whom they had lost.

The evolutionary account of human origins does not compete with this. On the contrary, it is very helpful in exploring the story of the 'fall' of humanity. It explains how lust and aggression are natural dispositions of an evolved species, which could form plausible temptations to egoistic desire. And it suggests, as theologians like Irenaeus did, that humans could have developed dispositions of love and courage if they had co-operated with the Spirit of God, to grow into the likeness of the divine power and freedom. But it was not to be. Sharing in a world cut off from knowledge of the divine presence, 'in Adam all die'.

God, whose nature is unlimited love, did not leave humans to their self-destructive fate, but sought in many ways to draw them back to unity with the divine being. The Old Testament tells the story of how God chose one people, the children of Abraham, to be the mediators of this unity to the world (Isaiah 49.6 – 'I will also make you a light for the Gentiles, that you may bring my salvation to the ends of the earth'). Not much is said about Gentiles, or about the ways in which God related to the other peoples of the earth.

There are some clear statements, however, that show that God's love and God's concern are not limited to Jews. One is the remarkable passage about Melchizedek, king of Salem (Genesis 14.18–20). This King was no Jew, no child of Abraham. On the contrary, he blessed Abraham, thereby assuming priestly authority over him, and is described as 'a priest of God Most High'. There are priests of God who are not Jews, who serve God and can bless in the name of God. Another example is Jethro, 'priest of Midian' (Exodus 3.1), with whom Moses lived in the desert. It is completely alien to the Bible to limit worship of God to the children of Abraham, be they Jewish, Christian or Muslim. As the prophet Micah says, 'All the nations may walk in the name of their gods, we will walk in the name of the Lord our God' (Micah 4.5).

Muslims reckon their descent from Abraham through his son Ishmael. The covenant passed from Abraham through Isaac to Jacob, who was re-named Israel. But Abraham's other son Ishmael, who was not one of the people of the covenant, was sent off into the wilderness because of the jealousy of Sarah. He was also blessed by God, who said, 'I will surely bless him; I will make him fruitful' (Genesis 17.20). Muslims are included in the blessing of God – 'God was with the boy' (Genesis 21.20) – and that is quite consistent with God having a special covenant with the children of Isaac and Jacob. That means that being children of the covenant does not mean that you are the only people loved by God. It rather means that God has a special vocation for you that it is your obligation to fulfil.

There is no thought in the Old Testament that only Jews will be saved. Jews do have a special vocation given by God. But the Noahide Covenant (Genesis 9.1–17) is for all human beings. Jews have always assumed that God would judge the nations of the earth by the light that is in them. I see no reason to think that the New Testament alters this view of God's universal care for all the earth. John's Gospel states that Christ is 'the true light that gives light to every man' (John 1.9). In his letter to the Romans, Paul says, 'To those who by persistence in doing good seek glory, honour and immortality, he [God] will give eternal life' (Romans 2.7). Moreover, the Lord 'is patient with you, not wanting anyone to perish, but everyone to come to repentance' (2 Peter 3.9). Since the vast majority of humans have never heard of Jesus, this entails that all must have a chance of repentance and salvation, whether or not they have heard of Jesus.

The good news of the free gift of divine grace

It is at this point that many people ask, 'What is the point of the gospel, if people can be saved anyway, whether they have heard of it or not?' From the biblical point of view, that is like saying, 'God has invited me into a relationship of close personal love which will fulfil all my deepest desires and bring the greatest happiness. But why should I accept? Or why should I tell other people about it, since God will come to them in time anyway?' There would be something wrong with anyone who said that. What God offers is no less than a restoration of the primal relationship of love of the eternal, filling life with vitality, compassion and happiness.

Such a relationship cannot be established by moral effort, however great. It requires a disclosure of the divine presence and love. When such a relationship is established, obedience to the moral law becomes natural and effortless – 'We know that anyone born of God does not continue to sin' (1 John 5.18). So Jesus was 'tempted in every way, just as we are – yet was without sin' (Hebrews 4.15). Sin was impossible for him, since he was begotten of God in a unique way. We are begotten by adoption and by the Spirit, and our adoption is as yet incomplete, so that we still remain under the obligations of the moral law.

Because our obedience to the moral law is incomplete, each person 'will receive God's abundant provision of grace and of the gift of righteousness' (Romans 5.17) by the power of the love of God which is given in Christ.

The picture is not that everyone is condemned, however hard they try to live morally, except for a few who are chosen by some inscrutable divine decree (not because of their goodness) to inherit eternal life. The picture is rather that it is good and necessary to strive for righteousness, but moral success is not enough to establish the loving relationship to God from which the human race long ago turned away. In the situation of necessary moral striving, and virtually inevitable moral failure, God steps in to offer, freely and to all, the gift of eternal life, forgiveness for moral failure and the gradual sanctification which finally will enable us to be 'set free from sin' (Romans 6.18). As in Adam all die, so in Christ will all be made alive.

The gospel is that God wills to save everyone. How that is accomplished is not for us to say. But Christians affirm that the eternal Christ, present fully and decisively in Jesus, is in fact the means of human salvation. Christians know that they have been 'marked in him with a seal, the promised Holy Spirit, who is a deposit guaranteeing our inheritance, until the redemption of those who are God's possession' (Ephesians 1.13–14). But they know that they share this salvation with Abraham and the Patriarchs and prophets of Israel (Romans 4.16 – 'Abraham . . . is the father of all of us'). They know that there will be 'glory, honour and peace for everyone who does good' (Romans 2.10).

In the same letter in which Paul says that no one can be saved by righteousness, he also says that all who do good will have eternal life. There is only one way in which this makes sense. God must give eternal life as a free gift to those who try to do good, even though their deeds do not strictly deserve it. And that does seem to be Paul's teaching.

It is tragic that some Christians have taken Paul's words as distinctly bad news – we can never deserve eternal life, so we will not get it unless we manage to believe exactly the right things in exactly the right way, and with enough fervour and sincerity. On this reading, eternal life becomes a virtually impossible goal. We can never be sure your faith is enough, or that it is the right sort of faith (Catholic or Protestant? Calvinist or Arminian? Which is the right faith?). All this leads to Christians agonizing about whether they are saved, and sometimes even despairing at the thought they might be damned, however many good deeds they do.

How far from this the biblical teaching is! What Paul is saying is not bad news, but good news, especially for the morally weak. It is that eternal life is God's free gift to all. God freely forgives, and God gives eternal life to those who do not deserve it. There is no need to agonize or despair. The gift is there for the taking. Of course it must be taken. There has to be repentance – a turning away from selfish desires and attachments – and there has to be faith – a desire to love God and to receive the life God gives.

Christian theologians have usually taught that the desire to love God may, however, be implicit. Consider someone who thinks God is a monstrous tyrant, or who thinks religion is all superstition. Such a person may be committed to goodness, and we may say that, if they could truly see what God is really like – a being of unlimited love – they would desire God. We can speak of an implicit desire for God in people who, through no fault of their own, do not even believe in God, and have not had that desire rightly evoked by a disclosure of the true God.

Christians think that Jesus does disclose the true God, but there are many reasons why others may not see the disclosure that we do – we may put them off, for a start! The notion of implicit desire is the only notion that gives a consistent reading of the letter to the Romans. So it is what the Bible really teaches. All who try to do good, and have an implicit desire for God will be saved by the free gift of grace. That grace comes through Jesus Christ, and in the end everyone will realize that fact. But they need not know it now, and we may not even know that they have such an implicit desire for God until they encounter the final revelation of Christ in glory.

Human beings are free. Humans are enslaved to sin. They are rewarded according to their deeds. And they are freely given the gift of eternal life. The Bible simply lays these assertions alongside one another. If we read the Old Testament on its own, we would probably agree with the first and the third assertions. If we read the New Testament on its own (ignoring the earlier parts of Romans and the letter of James, which Luther called an 'epistle of straw'), we would probably agree with the second and fourth assertions. But how can anyone agree with all of them at the same time?

One obvious possibility is this: humans are free in two senses. They are free to accept or reject the love of God – that is spiritual freedom. And they are free to do what is right or to do what is wrong – that is moral freedom. In both senses, however, human freedom is greatly restricted. Each person begins life in estrangement from God. Without a disclosure of God, they cannot accept or reject God, but live without God, and so in a state of spiritual death. Largely because of this, their moral freedom is also very restricted. While being responsible for many choices, they are usually unable ever to obey the moral law fully, and so remain enslaved to egoistic desires. It is impossible for us to tell how far particular individuals are enslaved, and how far they are free and responsible. Only God knows that, which is surely why Jesus tells us not to judge others (Matthew 7.1). So humans are free to respond to God's self-disclosure to them, and to make many important moral choices. But this freedom is never sufficient to unite them to God – only God can do that – and it is never sufficient to enable them to obey the moral law fully. Even slaves may be free within limits, and that freedom may be very important. But it cannot free them from slavery. So it is with human existence – we have spiritual and moral freedom within the limits of our knowledge of God and our moral capacities, but it is not sufficient to give us a deep and intimate love of God, nor can it free us from slavery to desire.

Only God, who knows the secrets of all hearts, is able justly to reward and punish the free and responsible acts of human persons. The New Testament is clear that God will do so. 'If any man builds on this foundation using gold, silver, costly stones, wood, hay or straw . . . his work will be shown for what it is . . . the fire will test the quality of each man's work . . . If it is burnt up, he will suffer loss; he himself will be saved, but only as one escaping through the flames' (1 Corinthians 3.12–15). So people will suffer appropriate punishment for wrong-doing and for their rejection of love, and appropriate reward for good works and their openness to love. Yet God adds to that punishment and reward a gift whose value is worth more than any moral reward, the gift of eternal life. Wrong-doers will be saved, though 'as one who has gone through the flames'. The righteous will receive far more than they could possibly deserve, as the love of God floods their hearts.

So the Bible teaches that humans have real but limited spiritual and moral freedom. For their use of that freedom they will reap appropriate consequences. Over and above that, however, humans are enslaved by selfish desire and ignorance of God, which makes all their choices fatally inadequate. The gospel, the good news, is that humans are also offered the gift of eternal life, of freedom from desire and knowledge of God. Perhaps their final freedom is to have the power to accept or reject that gift. The final freedom, in other words, is not moral but spiritual freedom, the freedom to say 'yes' to God when at last God appears as God truly is, rather than in the inadequate forms by means of which people often think of God.

Paul's sublation of the biblical themes of individual freedom, responsibility and judgement, is that all these things exist within the wider, tragic reality of human ignorance of and estrangement from God. The gospel of Christ is that this estrangement is overcome, in principle and decisively, if not yet in fact and completely. God enters into the human situation and reconciles humanity to the divine in the person of Jesus. Such reconciliation is for all, and though it requires individual assent, none of us can say how or under what conditions individuals make or withhold that assent. We can only say that, although human nature is estranged from God, it is also reconciled to God. No one is without the grace of God, whether that grace is recognized or unknown. The gospel is not that all are lost unless they meet certain stringent conditions of belief. That is bad news for most people. It is that all are reconciled and united to God in love forever, unless they explicitly, finally and irrevocably reject God. That is good news indeed, and it is what the Bible really teaches.

7

Interpreting Biblical Teaching about the Sacrifice of Jesus

Fundamentalists are often unhappy with the thought that God can redeem absolutely anyone, whatever they believe about Jesus. That is partly because they read the Bible as saying that human sin leads to death, that Jesus died for our sins, so that only if we accept Jesus' sacrifice can we be saved from sin and its consequences. In a way, this is quite right. But it often goes along with a misinterpretation of biblical teaching about sacrifice, and with a misunderstanding of what the sacrifice of Jesus accomplishes. The misinterpretation is that the death of a man (or of an animal, in the Old Testament) can somehow literally take away the sin of someone else. The misunderstanding is that only those who believe in this doctrine can be saved. I shall show that the biblical teaching about sacrifice is really quite different from this. And I shall show that Jesus' sacrifice is for the whole human race, and not just for a few people with special beliefs. This should be clear from texts like this: 'we have put our hope in the living God, who is the saviour of all men, and especially of those who believe. Command and teach these things' (1 Timothy 4.10–11).

God is not the saviour only of believers, much less only of Christians. God is the saviour of the whole human race. Since God wishes all people to be saved, God will make it possible for all to be saved. The writer of the first letter to Timothy says that God is *especially* the saviour of believers. That entails that God is not the saviour only of believers, but that believers have a special place in the economy of salvation. Perhaps this is because believers know by whom it is that they are saved, whereas many, possibly most, humans do not know the God of our Lord Jesus Christ by name. God comes to them incognito, and they may not even realize that God wills their salvation, and is doing something to help them realize it.

Fundamentalists are right in thinking that, in a special sense, it is the death of Jesus that is the supreme divine redemptive act by which God redeems the world. 'Christ died for our sins according to the Scriptures' (1 Corinthians 15.3).

The death of Jesus is a fact so surprising that Muslims, honouring Jesus as a prophet, cannot bring themselves to believe that Jesus died. They hold that he ascended immediately to heaven, and was not crucified. They cannot believe that a true prophet could die the death of a criminal. But the major part of each Gospel is an account of the passion and death of Jesus on the cross. Since the Gospels are the only accounts we have of the life of Jesus which contain eye-witness testimony, it must be accounted one of the most certain things we know about Jesus that he was crucified and died and was buried.

The New Testament writers seek to understand the significance of the death of Jesus in many ways. But the idea of sacrifice became one of the most important clues to its meaning. The letter to the Hebrews develops this idea at length, concluding that 'Jesus also suffered outside the city gate to make the people holy through his own blood' (Hebrews 13.12). Just as the High Priest in ancient Israel offered sacrifices for the atonement of sin, so Jesus offered himself as a sacrifice for the atonement of sin.

The biblical idea of sacrifice

The idea of sacrifice is central to the Bible. In the Torah, the rules for the great sacrifices that were to be offered in the central sanctuary were elaborated in detail, especially in Leviticus 1—7. It is important to see what was involved in these sacrifices. Sometimes Christians have misunderstood the biblical idea of sacrifice, thinking that it is a ritual of killing in order to appease an angry God, or that all sacrifices are offerings to take away, or expiate, sin. This is completely mistaken.

The main sacrifices of the Old Testament are offerings of praise and thanksgiving to God, expressing adoration of the Creator, submission to the divine will, and gratitude for the great goods God gives. An analogy might be the way in which people bring a small gift to a party. They do not do so in order to appease the wrath of an angry host; that would be absurd! They want to express their thanks by a small sacrifice, which costs them a little – not too much – and which honours their host, celebrating and cementing friendship.

So the Israelites were asked to pay for a beast in good health – a 'male without defect' (Leviticus 1.3). The writer says it will be 'an aroma pleasing to the Lord' (Leviticus 1.13). The meaning of the Hebrew is that it will cement the covenant relation with God. The offering will please God, but not because it is some sort of payment. It will please God because it expresses the desire to honour and thank God, and gives a reasonably costly commitment to doing God's will.

The blood of the sacrifice, poured out on the altar, does not actually do anything because of its own intrinsic properties. It has value only because God says it has. There is no law of nature that says that God feels pleased if animals are killed. It is God who lays down the conditions for sacrifice, who sets out its rules. God could no doubt have set out any rules God chose. The reason for obeying the rules is simply that God laid them out, so that in obeying them – whatever they are – we show our obedience to God. According to the biblical view, we do not sacrifice because we think it is a very reasonable thing to do, or to accomplish some purpose by magical means. The blood of an animal is not something that compels God to do what we want – the Bible absolutely rejects such magical views of sacrifice, classifying them as idolatry. We sacrifice just because God asks us to give something up and offer it to God in order to show our devotion to God. God tells us what to give up, what to offer, and how we should do it. Apart from God's command, sacrifice has no importance or effect at all.

This point becomes clear when the prophets criticize in the harshest terms rituals of sacrifice, however correctly carried out, which do not really express devotion to God. 'I hate, I despise your religious feasts; I cannot stand your assemblies. Even though you bring me burnt offerings . . . I will not accept them', says Amos (Amos 5.21–22). Rather, the prophet asks that justice should flow like a river, and integrity like an unfailing stream. The prophet is not recommending that sacrifices should stop. He is saying that sacrifice without justice and integrity is empty and not pleasing to God.

The sacrifice does not accomplish anything of itself. But if we are committed to the pursuit of justice and to devotion to God, then it is God's wish that we should offer the sacrifices God has ordained. To do so renews the bond of fellowship between God and Israel. It is not enough to do good alone. It is not enough to offer sacrifice alone. We must do good and sacrifice to God, to express our love and devotion, to give thanks and also to renew and extend fellowship within our human community. Many sacrifices are communion sacrifices, in which many, and especially the poor and widows, share in the meal that follows the offering. Sacrifices are feasts and festivals, not gloomy or fearful occasions.

But why should animals be killed? Why should God choose that way in which the Israelites should honour God? One simple answer may be that for a poor nomadic people to eat meat was both a necessity and a luxury. To eat it after it had been offered to God sanctifies the acceptance of food at God's hands. Eating becomes a symbol of the reception of life itself at God's hands, and to eat sacrificed meat is to remind ourselves of the divine source of life.

But there is also the point that, symbolically speaking, 'the life of every creature is its blood' (Leviticus 17.14). For that reason it is forbidden to Jews to eat meat with blood in it. The blood symbolizes the life. So in offering the blood of the slain animal to God, we are offering the life of a 'perfect creation' to its Creator. As we lay our hands on the head of the animal to be sacrificed, we identify ourselves with it, as if to say, 'This is my life offered to God.' So the point is made, at a deep symbolic level, that what God requires is an offering of self. The gift of the animal is a substitute for the gift of ourselves, and if we eat the flesh of the sacrifice, we receive back from God a renewed self, reborn in fellowship with our Creator. In this way, the biblical sacrifices are effective symbols of the offering of self to God, and the renewal of self in a covenant relation with God. These are symbols, because they have no efficacy of themselves, without a divine decision to use them to renew a covenant relation between God and Israel. They are effective, because God chooses to accept our devotion and renew our relationship by these means that God has ordained as appropriate symbols.

As well as sacrifices of praise, thanksgiving and communion, there are sacrifices for sin in the Old Testament, even though they do not take the primary place. But one thing that is sometimes overlooked by Christians is that these sins are ritual offences that have been unknowingly committed. There is no sacrifice that can take away deliberate sin: 'Anyone who sins defiantly ... blasphemes the Lord and that person must be cut off from his people' (Numbers 15.30). For some offences, like fraud, a sacrifice can be offered, as long as reparation is made – money must be paid back plus a fifth, usually (Leviticus 5.15–27). In other words, the biblical view is that all sin must be punished, and reparation must be made wherever possible. Only when that has been done, can a sacrifice be offered to bring back the sinner into relationship with God. Biblical sacrifices for sin do not pay the punishment due to sin, nor do they remove such a punishment. They renew relationship for those who have paid, or who are prepared to pay, the proper price. If we remember this biblical principle, we shall be less likely to get into accounts of the death of Jesus that see it as taking someone else's punishment, or removing the punishment due to human sin. It will rather be seen as a way of renewing a personal covenant relationship with God, for those who are prepared to accept the proper punishment for their sin themselves.

Even on the Day of Atonement, when a goat is sent into the wilderness that shall 'carry on itself all their sins to a solitary place' (Leviticus 16.22), the faults and sins in question are ritual faults or non-deliberate sins. All that stands between the people and God is wiped away by this complicated ritual, but the punishment for sin is not removed.

It would be extremely odd to think that estrangement with God could actually be removed by sending a goat into the desert. We must abandon any attempt to seek a mechanical explanation of this ritual. That would be a descent into magic. We should probably regard this as a divine reformulation of an ancient tribal rite, turning the rite into a sign of obedience that God promises to honour by restoring relationship with those who perform it. What matters is not the exact rite, but the preparedness of the people to do whatever God commands, and the promise of God to restore broken relationship as a result of such obedience.

Sacrifices for sin should be seen, not as rituals which have objective efficacy in removing sin in some magical way, but as rituals that God ordains to enable the faithful to express obedience to the divine will, an obedience which God promises to honour by restoring a living relationship of knowledge and love with God.

Perhaps at some ancient time it was thought that sin could be transferred to an animal and disposed of. But I suspect that interpretation may be too literalist for ancient forms of human thought. Literalism in religion is a rather modern movement that only really began to exist after the rise of science in the sixteenth century. It is not a characteristic of primal religions, which are actually much too sophisticated to fall for it. It is more likely that the rite was always symbolic of a putting-away of sin, a genuine repentance of heart, and an obedient believing in the promises of God, or of some primal spiritual being. In the Levitical code, this rite was reinterpreted in the light of the fully personal covenant relation between Israel and God. On the Day of Atonement, the people's turning from sin was expressed by the ritual of the scapegoat, and their belief in God was expressed by their performance of the rite at God's command, believing that God would renew a personal relationship with them.

The efficacy of the sacrificial rite does not lie in any transaction with blood, any magical connection between the shedding of blood and the removal of sin, or any literal transference of sin from one being to another. It lies solely in the command of God, which makes the rite a test of the repentance and obedience of Israel, and the means by which the divine–human relationship of covenant would be renewed.

God could have commanded almost anything to be such a test of faith and means of renewal. This is what God did command for Israel. It is easy to imagine how other cultures might have other means of expressing a turning away from hatred, greed and ignorance, other ways of expressing faith in the possibility of relationship with God, and other ways in which God might renew human lives. Jewish sacrifices are rituals specifically meant for Jews. Yet the Jewish sacrificial system is normative for how humans are truly related to God, because it shows what the character of God is, and therefore what true relationship to such a God is. But it is not exclusive, in the sense that it excludes other people from having any saving relation to God, which might be expressed in different ways.

Jesus as a sacrifice

How does this biblical understanding of sacrifice apply to Jesus, and in particular to his death? It applies, in the first place, in a very direct and obvious way to the person of Jesus itself. What Jesus offers is not an animal-substitute, but himself. He offers not blood but his own life. He expresses the heart of true sacrifice, the total offering of a life to God. This does not in itself entail that Jesus should die. But Jesus was prepared to face death as the price of his obedience to the divine will in a world that has turned from God. The death of the cross is the final, most complete expression of Jesus' self-offering to God. It is not that the shedding of blood was necessary before humans could be united to God. That would be to revert to a magical transaction view of sacrifice. It is rather that his whole life, and his loyalty to his vocation even to death, was a full offering of humanity to God, so that God could unite humanity to the divine completely in him.

God did not just require that Jesus die – as though the whole of Jesus' life was just a prelude to the important thing, his death. God required that Jesus live a wholly surrendered life, in full obedience to the divine will. That obedient living is what unites humanity to divinity, and thus makes God and humanity one. Such obedience has a double significance. It exposes the hostility of the 'world' (the world which rejects God) to God. And it expresses the sharing by God of the suffering of that estranged world. Because the world rejects God, it rejects Jesus, the incarnation of God. The cross represents what the world does to God.

Jesus, in freely accepting obedience to God's will, becomes the expression of God's suffering, accepted at the hands of disobedient humanity. Jesus' obedience draws upon himself the disobedience of estranged humanity. In this sense, God does require that Jesus dies – but only because God knows that a complete obedience, in a disobedient world, will inevitably lead to rejection and death.

The prophets were not strangers to such rejection and suffering. Jeremiah was beaten and thrown into prison (Jeremiah 37.15). He was then thrown into a cesspit, where he sank into the effluent, and would have died if he had not been rescued by friends. The word of God can be disturbing for tyrants, and the suffering of Jesus in Jerusalem repeats what had happened to Jeremiah in the same city centuries before.

To the question, 'Can a true prophet of God die?', the Christian response is: yes, a true prophet can suffer injustice at the hands of sinful people, and the exposure of the depths of human rebellion is shown by the killing of God's anointed one (the Christ). God foreknew this, and in that sense the death of Jesus was willed by God (not that God desired or required it to appease the divine anger, but that God desired an obedience which would inevitably lead to suffering and death in a fallen world).

But though a true prophet can be put to death, death cannot be the end for a true prophet. The resurrection of Jesus from the dead is the divine vindication of his Messiahship, and it is also the expression of the sublation of suffering and evil in the reality of the divine being. It was because of his obedience, which led to death, that Jesus 'was declared with power to be the Son of God by his resurrection from the dead' (Romans 1.4). His death is the way to his unending life, a life that becomes for all humanity the source of divine redemption.

So the death of Jesus is not the placation of an angry God. It is the opposite. It is the expression of the unrestricted love of God. It is the full expression of human obedience to the divine calling, and at the same time of the divine humility that shares the human condition.

It is the demonstration of the depth of human hostility to God. So it becomes an expression of the love of God which bears this hostility, and which transforms its power by bringing about a new power of life, resurrection life, beyond the grasp of time and suffering. The death of Jesus is the means of human redemption, because it is the way to the resurrection life of Jesus, through which the redemptive power of divine love is shown and mediated in its true form and power.

Because the human was united to the divine, Jesus is beyond the power of death. 'By his death he might destroy him who holds the power of death – that is, the devil' (Hebrews 2.14). Jesus, in whom humanity is united to divinity, receives his human life back from God in resurrection. So Jesus is able truly to offer himself as a perfect sacrifice, which God honours by the gift of eternal life.

Jesus does not only offer the sacrifice of himself, in order to receive new life from God. He offers himself for the sake of others. 'Christ was sacrificed once to take away the sins of many people' (Hebrews 9.28). Here the offering of devotion is combined with the atonement offering. Jesus is both wholly devoted to God, and also, like the High Priest offering the sacrifice of atonement, he offers himself in order to re-establish the relation of 'God's people' with God that has been broken by sin.

We do not need to think of a magical connection between the shed blood of Jesus and the removal of sin. Following the Old Testament pattern, God ordains that Jesus' offering, which expresses complete obedience to the divine will, shall be the means of restoring a living relationship with God, for all who accept it as a free gift. Jesus prays that people should be united to God in knowledge and love. His self-sacrifice is a perfect prayer. God answers that prayer by uniting people to God by the inner gift of the Spirit. That gift is offered, and may be accepted or rejected. But God decrees that the gift is definitively offered in response to Jesus' sacrifice.

Christ as the Passover lamb

It is arguable that the main Old Testament pattern that is used to interpret the death of Jesus is not that of the Levitical sacrifices, but the Passover ritual of the slaughter of a lamb. John's Gospel declares that John the Baptist said of Jesus, 'Look, the Lamb of God, who takes away the sin of the world!' (John 1.29). There are a number of important implications of this short phrase. First, it is clearly using symbolic, not literal, language. Jesus is not literally a lamb. The lamb sacrificed at Passover was to have its blood smeared on the doorposts of the Israelites, so that the Angel of Death would pass over them, and not kill their firstborn (Exodus 12). This symbol is overtly brought out in the first letter to the Corinthians, where Paul says that 'Christ, our Passover lamb, has been sacrificed' (1 Corinthians 5.7).

The Passover lamb was not thought to take away sin, particularly. Its significance lay in the blood that was smeared on the doorposts, which averted death for the children of Israel. The sacrifice was the culmination of a period of fasting, and part of a ritual that commemorated the deliverance of Israel from Egypt. This is a rite of liberation. It commemorates God's act of liberation, and in making that act present it renews the Israelites as a liberated community, freed from evil to serve God.

The most natural way to read John the Baptist's statement has no implication that the death of Jesus was an appeasement for sin. It implies that Jesus' death, and more importantly the offering of his life (the blood), will be a means of liberating the world from sin. It is the whole world that is to be liberated. No longer is one group of people to be freed from a world that remains fallen. Rather, the world – which in John is always in opposition to God ('the world did not recognize him', John 1.10) – is itself to be freed from sin. So we could interpret the phrase 'the lamb of God who takes away the sin of the world' like this: 'the person whose life, fully offered to God, liberates the whole world from its enmity to God'. Jesus is not the appeaser of an angry God. Jesus is the liberating act of a loving reconciling God, who liberates through the life of Jesus precisely because that life is a true sacrifice, an offering of devotion and obedience. There is no magical immolation to satisfy a rigorous and inflexible divine justice here. There is the total transparency of a human life to God, which enables God to act decisively for the liberation of the world from evil.

The Bible teaches that Jesus is a sacrifice that takes away sin. The imagery of sacrifice covers the offerings of praise and thanksgiving that express total commitment to God. It covers the Day of Atonement requirement of repentance and faith to which God responds by setting aside all that makes fellowship with God impossible. And it covers the Passover liberation of the world from evil. Sacrifice is not killing for the sake of God, so that a few may escape divine wrath. It is a joyful losing of the self in God, a turning from hatred, greed and ignorance, and a faithful dependence upon the liberating activity of God to free the world from evil.

Why was Jesus necessary to this process? To understand that we have to understand first that God willed to unite the human nature of Jesus to the divine being of the eternal Word. Jesus' human nature became the vehicle and manifestation of the eternal Word. It thus became a prototype of what human nature is when it is wholly united to God. This is what Christians call the incarnation. Because human nature was united to the divine in this unique way in Jesus, only he was fully able truly to give his life completely to God and so become the vehicle of liberating divine activity. That was the nature and uniqueness of his sacrifice.

Fundamentalists are usually very clear that Jesus is the unique incarnation of God. That is one of their great witnesses to Christian truth.

What they do not always realize is that this is a belief that is not explicitly spelled out in the Bible itself. When you read the first three Gospels, you could be forgiven for not knowing whether Jesus was divine or not. In two of the Gospels, it even looks as though Jesus is not thought of as one with God. Jesus says, 'Why do you call me good? No-one is good – except God alone' (Mark 10.18; Luke 18.19). Like most of Jesus' sayings, this is very hard to interpret. It could be a hidden pointer to Jesus' own divinity ('If you recognize that I really am uniquely good, you will recognize that I am God'), but it looks at face value as if it is making a distinction between all humans, including Jesus, and God. In these Gospels Jesus is certainly given supreme authority over demons, over nature and over disease. He is recognized as the Messiah, the Christ, the Anointed One of God. But he is never explicitly said to be the eternal Word of God (the expression 'son of God' does not imply divinity, and was used in the Bible of David and Solomon also, and in Luke's Gospel of Adam – Luke 3.37).

It is only in John's Gospel that Thomas explicitly affirms Jesus' divinity – 'My Lord and my God!' (John 20.28). Even then, the relation between Jesus, who is the Word of God, and God is not spelled out. It took hundreds of years before the Church came to formulate the doctrine of the incarnation at the Council of Chalcedon (AD 451), when it was agreed that Jesus was a unique person in whom human and divine natures were both fully present, indivisibly yet not confused with one another.

It took even longer for belief in the Trinity to be worked out in the form in which most fundamentalists would now accept it. The Trinity is classically defined in the so-called Athanasian Creed (not, incidentally, composed by Athanasius). It affirms that the Father and the Son and the Holy Spirit are all co-equal 'persons' of the one God, equally divine and uncreated, and all co-operating in every divine act. It is an implication of beliefs about Jesus that is even further from the biblical texts. For nowhere in the New Testament can that doctrine of the Trinity be found. Matthew's Gospel ends with the exhortation to 'go and make disciples of all nations, baptising them in the name of the Father and of the Son and of the Holy Spirit' (Matthew 28.19). But there is no mention that Father, Son and Spirit are all co-equal persons of the one God. The relation of the Son to the Father is left obscure, and the relation of the Spirit to both of them is never discussed.

So it was quite possible for Bible-believing Christians in the early centuries to deny that Christ was co-eternal with God, or to deny that the Holy Spirit is actually identical with God, or to deny that Christ was co-equal with God. Such Christians even had biblical texts to support their views – Christ is described as 'the firstborn over all creation' in Colossians 1.15, and in Greek it sounds even clearer that Christ is in some sense created. In John's Gospel, Jesus speaks of 'the Holy Spirit, whom the Father will send in my name' (John 14.26), which sounds as if the Spirit is subordinate to the Father. And in the same long discourse Jesus says, 'the Father is greater than I' (John 14.28).

It was only after long discussion – and sometimes heated arguments – that these texts were held to be sublated by others, or were explained in a sophisticated way which made them consistent with what came to be the 'orthodox' doctrine of the Trinity. For instance, the Father was said to be greater than Jesus in respect of Jesus' human nature, though not of his divine nature. Whatever we think of all these arguments now, it is pretty clear that the Bible does not itself establish a clear doctrine of the Trinity. Those who believe in Trinity and the incarnation are giving high authority to the Councils of the early Christian Church, and accepting their interpretations of the Bible, which develop and systematize biblical teachings in important ways.

I am not saying that a belief in the Trinity and in the incarnation is not present in the Bible. Belief in Incarnation is present in John's Gospel, and most Christians think it is implied in many other places. But the belief is certainly not clearly and explicitly set out. Years of reflection and argument had to take place before the belief that Jesus was both fully God and fully human was generally agreed – and to get that agreement ideas and words had to be used (like 'nature' and 'person') which were not in the Bible at all. So if we believe in the incarnation we are accepting the results of long theological discussion, and not simply reading it off from the Bible. The importance of this is that it shows how the most central Christian beliefs have arisen from theological reflection on the Bible. It shows the vital importance of theology. It shows the need to understand the history and development of biblical interpretation. It shows that the Bible does not just speak for itself. While the Bible will always be the main evidence and the ultimate test for Christian beliefs, those beliefs are often based on reasoning and experience, and not solely on the Bible itself.

Theories of atonement

So when we are thinking about the sacrifice of Jesus on the cross for the sins of the world, theological thinking has developed well beyond the biblical texts themselves. The usual fundamentalist view is called the substitutionary theory of the atonement. That is one of the 'five funda-mentals' with which the movement began. What I mainly want to stress is that it is a theory. It is not in the Bible itself, but was developed out of it over many hundreds of years by theologians. In fact it is a rather late theory, and it is not explicitly formulated until the sixteenth cen-tury, by the French theologian John Calvin.

Christians are entitled to hold this theory. It has neither been endorsed nor condemned by Church Councils. It has to be assessed pre-cisely on its adequacy to express Christian experience of forgiveness in Christ and the development of moral insight in the Church, as well as on its capacity to interpret the biblical material in a consistent, coher-ent and spiritually enlightening fashion.

For the substitionary theory, all human beings deserve the death penalty for their sins. But Jesus pays the penalty in their place. His death on the cross substitutes for the deaths of every human being. So humans are freed from the penalty of death, and can live with God for-ever, as long as they put their faith in Jesus' substitutionary sacrifice.

I do not reject the death of Jesus on the cross for the salvation of the world, but I do reject this theory of what is going on, or of how it works. I reject it most basically because it seems to misrepresent the biblical idea of sacrifice. The sacrifice of Jesus was the offering of his whole life to be the vehicle of God's action, not the payment of some punishment, which really should have been paid by other people anyway. Even if Jesus' sac-rifice had been an attempt to take someone else's punishment, it would not have worked, on biblical principles. For no sacrifice could remove another's guilt – 'the soul who sins is the one who will die' (Ezekiel 18.4). The Christian gospel is that God can indeed forgive sins, and not impose the penalty of death. God can be, and is, merciful. But God does not do so by requiring that somebody else dies in my place. In biblical faith, it is never the case that an animal or human sacrifice can remove the guilt either of myself or of anybody else.

There was no magic in the sacrifices of the Hebrew faith. But the means God chose were deeply symbolic of the spiritual realities of repentance, commitment and liberation that they are meant to express. So it is with Jesus. In the New Testament there is one decisive command for those who would follow Jesus: 'do this in remembrance of me' (1 Corinthians 11.24). As in the Old Testament, so in the New. We are to do it simply because God commands it. Just as the repeated Passover ritual re-presents, actually makes present the original liberating act of God in Egypt, so the repeated sacrifice of the body and blood of Jesus makes present the original liberating act of God in him.

It should not need saying that the sacrifice of Christ is not repeated in the sense of causing Jesus to suffer again and again. But Paul says, 'Who has bewitched you? Before your very eyes Jesus Christ was clearly portrayed as crucified' (Galatians 3.1). If we are to avoid distorting the text, this is a pretty clear reference to a visible setting-forth of the crucifixion in a Christian community. From the earliest times, each celebration of the eucharistic liturgy was seen as a setting forth of Jesus' death: 'For whenever you eat this bread and drink this cup, you proclaim the Lord's death until he comes' (1 Corinthians 11.26).

Proclaiming the Lord's death is the Christian sublation of the Levitical sacrifices. Then, the life of an animal was offered to God, with the prayer that God would respond by offering a renewal of life in the covenant community of Israel. Christians offer bread and wine, with the prayer that God will respond by offering divine life to the community of the Church. That offering of bread and wine is explicitly associated by Jesus with his body and blood, which was broken and poured out on the cross. What was offered on the cross was a life fully obedient to the divine will, and a self fully open to the divine love, in an estranged world that tried to destroy a life that challenged its very existence. That death happened once in the history of the earth. But there is an even deeper mystery implied by the Christian insight that Jesus is the divine Son, both humanity and divinity united in one person, so that this self-offering is at the same time the self-offering of God. As God's self-offering was fully expressed in the self-offering of Jesus' life, so it continues to be expressed in the eucharistic sacrament.

How does God offer the divine being itself? And to whom is the offer made? These questions have confused some Christian thinkers, who have been misled by phrases like, 'The Son of Man [came] . . . to give his life as a ransom for many' (Mark 10.45). Gregory of Nyssa thought that since Jesus was a ransom, the ransom must be paid by God to the Devil. But, as Anselm pointed out a few hundred years later, God owes the Devil nothing; and, in any case, the ransom was not really paid, since Jesus defeated the Devil by escaping his clutches at the resurrection – the ransom was taken back, and God deceived the Devil! This is a good example of what happens when symbols are taken too literally, and pressed to what seems their logical conclusion – which turns out in this case, as Anselm claimed, to be the moral absurdity that God owed something to the Devil, which God only pretended to pay, so that God was both a debtor and a deceiver.

The idea that Jesus was a ransom for the freeing of humans from the power of sin can be an emotionally effective one, reminding us both of

Jesus' self-giving love and of his liberating power. But of course the ransom was not paid to anyone. The crucial point the symbol of 'ransom' makes is that Christ liberates from the power of sin, and that this liberation is costly – 'you were bought at a price' (1 Corinthians 6.20).

To understand the cost to God of sin and of liberation from sin, we have to consider three major qualities attributed to God in the Bible – anger, compassion and delight.

The anger of God is often referred to in the Bible. It is anger at immorality and injustice, at the harm done to creation by created beings. God says, 'I was enraged by his sinful greed' (Isaiah 57.17). Anger is not natural to God, for it is destructive, and it represents a sort of defeat of the purpose of creation. Anger is the divine reaction to the frustration of the divine purpose. The cost of sin to God is that it causes God to be destructive and to accept a frustration of divine purpose.

But divine anger is never the last word in the Bible. It is allied with compassion, loving-kindness, a steadfast love that is likened to the love of a husband for his wife, a passionate and healing love. So the prophets insist that the Lord 'will have compassion on his afflicted ones' (Isaiah 49.13). They speak of a loving personal relationship between God and Israel: 'your Maker is your husband' (Isaiah 54.5). And they are sure that love will replace anger in the end: 'my unfailing love for you will not be shaken' (Isaiah 54.10).

It may seem odd to speak of compassionate love as a 'cost' to God. But compassion can only exist where suffering exists, and loving-kindness, in the biblical context, is about accepting back into relationship people who have turned away. Forgiveness and compassion are costly, because they require the acceptance of the hurt of rejection, and a patient kindness in bringing about reconciliation.

The Bible rarely speaks about the grief of God, but it does speak of the delight God has in a fulfilled loving relationship: 'I will rejoice over Jerusalem, and take delight in my people' (Isaiah 65.19). Where God feels delight in love established, God will feel frustration at love rejected. The frustration of the delight that should exist between God and creatures is a cost, and it can truly be spoken of as a sort of suffering – though, in the case of God, not a suffering that can ever come to despair, or impair the divine perfection.

Sin, we might well say, causes a change in the divine nature – the realization of anger, even when transformed by compassion, the frustration of divine purpose, and the frustration of joy. These are costs that God bears wherever sin impairs a possible divine–creaturely relationship. The crucifixion of Jesus, in so far as it is the act of God as well as the self-offering of a human life, is the particular and definitive historical expression of the universal sacrifice of God in bearing the cost of sin. Sin is a harm done to God, inasmuch as it causes God to know, and to share, the suffering and reality of evil. The 'ransom' God pays is to accept this cost, to bear with evil, in order that it should be redeemed, transfigured, in God. The ransom is not paid to anyone. The offering God makes is accepting the harm done by humanity, in order that it might be transfigured, accepted yet overcome, in the divine being itself.

The Suffering Servant

The Song of the Suffering Servant, in Isaiah 53, has always, and rightly, been taken as the supreme biblical expression of God's acceptance of the cost of sin. In its Old Testament context, the 'servant of God' is almost certainly Israel. Growing up in the wilderness, despised and rejected among the nations, suffering not for her own sins but because of the sins of the nations, Israel yet offers herself to God, praying for God's world and for the healing of the nations. The point of the Song is to promise the vindication and triumph of Israel, who had suffered because of the sins of the world, yet who continued to intercede for the transgressors: 'For he bore the sin of many, and made intercession for the transgressors' (Isaiah 53.12).

The Song is sublated in the New Testament by being applied to Jesus, who is, as man, the suffering servant of God, and as divine, is God in human form. Jesus suffers, not because of his own sins, but because of the sins of others. Jealousy, hypocrisy, religious exclusivism and hatred all play their part in causing the torment and crucifixion of Jesus. We can truly say, 'he was crushed for our iniquities' (Isaiah 53.5), and 'the Lord has laid on him the iniquity of us all' (53.6).

Yet in the midst of his suffering, Jesus offers himself as an *asam*, a sin-offering. An innocent victim, he offers his life as a prayer that his persecutors might be forgiven ('Father, forgive them, for they do not know what they are doing', Luke 23.34). God answers his prayer by vindicating his servant, raising him from death and making him the mediator of the gift of divine life to all who believe in him – 'by his knowledge my righteous servant will justify many' (Isaiah 53.11).

For Christians there is an added dimension to this picture. The suffering servant is God. The prophets had spoken of God as angry, compassionate and joyful. The Christian belief that Jesus manifests truly what God is leads us to add that God suffers. 'Surely he took up our infirmities and carried our sorrows' (Isaiah 53.4).This sentence, originally applied to Israel, now applies to Almighty God. God does not only have a dispassionate knowledge that humans grieve and suffer. God shares in that grief and suffering, as God responds to creatures with empathy and inward passionate knowledge.

God is the sin-offering; that is, the suffering of God, God's preparedness to share in the sufferings of the world, becomes the means by which God's own life is given to liberate the world from sin. The patience of God, bearing the cost of sin, takes the life and death and resurrection of Jesus as its own self-manifestation, and makes it the means by which the liberating life of God is made available in its essential form to the world.

What has sometimes gone wrong in interpreting the Servant Song is the reification of metaphor. The metaphor of the servant who suffers and redeems (transfigures suffering into joy) is turned into an exact literal description of an object. Then absurd questions are asked about that object, which lead to absurd answers and miss the whole point of the original metaphor.

This happened with the metaphor of Christ as a 'ransom'. The point of the metaphor was to say that the occurrence of sin, and the divine decision to permit it and transfigure it is costly for God – causes a harm to God, even though it is a harm that God has the power to make the occasion of good. But if we reify the metaphor, and say a real ransom has been paid by God, we get led into absurd questions about to whom the ransom was paid, how much it was, and what happened to the ransom after it was paid. Anselm of Canterbury pointed out that all this leads to morally unsatisfactory beliefs about God deceiving the Devil.

Unfortunately, Anselm himself fell into a very similar trap. He took metaphors like 'the Lord has laid on him the iniquity of us all' (Isaiah 53.6) and reified them. So, he thought, there is something called 'iniquity', like an object which each of us has. But God takes our iniquity away, and places it on Jesus, who then literally has all our iniquities. Now we have the question: what is this iniquity, this object we all have? Anselm's answer is basically that it is a debt of honour we owe to God. We all owe God total obedience and devotion, but we do not and cannot pay this debt of honour, however hard to try. What God does is to live out a perfect human life, which is so obedient that it builds up an infinite amount of surplus honour. That surplus can then be given to us, to wipe out our debt. So Jesus takes our debts, pays them off, and we can start with a clean balance sheet.

There is something appealing about the thought that Jesus clears all our debts to God. In John Calvin's rather similar interpretation, what we owe God is the punishment due to our sin. This is the substitutionary theory, defended by fundamentalists. Jesus takes on himself so much punishment that God can declare us acquitted of guilt. Calvin speaks of the debt of punishment, whereas Anselm spoke of a debt of honour, but the basic thought is the same. We owe God a debt we can never pay, and Jesus pays it for us. Jesus takes my sin away, and I am free, acquitted, guiltless. As a metaphor this has appealed to many devout Christians, and if handled with care and sensitivity, it can speak powerfully to the condition of many who are burdened with a sense of guilt and failure.

But if taken as the one true account of how God reconciles the world to himself in Jesus, it is quite inadequate. The moral problem is that it is quite unjust for an innocent person, however well intentioned, to pay the debt of a guilty person. And it is a very unjust God who can say, 'You owe me a debt which must be paid, but I do not mind if someone else pays it.' Further, there is something very odd in the idea that God pays a debt to God. It would be much simpler if God simply remitted the debt, which God presumably has the power to do.

But the real problem is that Scripture is often being misinterpreted by such accounts. When Isaiah says, 'he took up our infirmities and carried our sorrows' (Isaiah 53.4), this cannot mean that our infirmities are literally taken away from us and that Jesus has them instead. Human sorrows are not removed, and Jesus cannot literally have the sorrows we have (the sorrow for sin, for example, which Jesus cannot have, since he never sinned). The natural meaning, in its Christian attribution to Jesus, is that God in Jesus shares the sorts of griefs and sorrows that belong to the human situation. Further, this points to the fact that God is affected by all human griefs and sorrows, and does not remain unmoved by them.

In a similar way, when Isaiah says that 'the Lord has laid on him the iniquity of us all' (Isaiah 53.6), he does not mean that Jesus somehow becomes a sinner, and we cease to be sinners. The natural meaning – again in its Christian sublation – is that God in Jesus shares the sorts of sufferings that result from sin. Indeed, his sufferings directly result from the human sin of those around him. This points to the fact that God is affected by all human sin, which causes real hurt to God, which God freely bears.

The Anselmian interpretation is most obviously inadequate, however, in that it focuses on death and guilt, rather than on life and liberation. It is true that God suffers because of human sin. Jesus suffers because humans try to efface the challenging presence of God in their midst.

Jesus' obedience to God, by which he offers his whole life, including his sufferings, to the Father, enables his human self to lose itself in the divine. This in turn enables the divine life to be poured out through his person, now raised to the glory of the resurrection life, to the whole world. God's patient bearing of suffering is turned into a means of giving the Holy Spirit to the world in a new way, because Jesus' risen life becomes the means of liberating the world from hatred, greed and ignorance – from sin.

The cross is vitally important to Christianity, and for Christians it gives a distinctive insight into the being of God. It shows that God is a suffering, passionate God, who shares in the human condition in order to take humanity into the divine being. But the cross is important because it is the path to the resurrection – Jesus 'for the joy set before him endured the cross, scorning its shame' (Hebrews 12.2). The self-offering of Jesus makes possible the liberating gift of the Holy Spirit through his risen life. That should be the emphasis of any 'theory of atonement' we might have. Liberation from the slavery of sin, and new life in the power of God – that is the good news of the gospel.

When Christians gather together to offer the sacrifice of bread and wine, in obedience to God's command, they do not present a dead body to God, or repeat the pain of the crucifixion. They make present at a particular moment of time the life of the one who 'always lives to intercede for them' (Hebrews 7.25). Jesus offered himself for the sins of the world, and he continues, as human, to pray for the salvation of the world and, as God, to bring it about. But that self-offering needs to be appropriated by humans, and by the community of the disciples of Jesus. In offering bread and wine, the Church makes present in its own community the prayer of the eternal self-offering of Jesus. As Jesus' self-offering on the cross released divine power into the world, so he is present in a special way at the eucharistic offering to bring the same power to the community which celebrates it. In the liturgy it is not so much we who offer Christ, as Christ who takes us into his self-offering, and incorporates us into the power of his risen life. Both sacrifice and liberation are combined in the eucharistic rite. This is well summed up in Paul's statement, 'Now if we died with Christ, we believe that we will also live with him' (Romans 6.8). The cross is not some event far off in time and space. The sacrifice of Jesus, the total loss of his self in God, is eternal, and is made present in the Church's obedience to his command to 'do this' in memory of him. Under the forms of bread and wine, Jesus is really and truly present, and communicates his divine life to us. In offering bread and wine, we seek to die to the egoistic self, and in eating and drinking bread and wine, we seek to receive the life and love of the divine self.

So the sacrifice of Christ stands at the heart of the Christian gospel. It is a death that occurred because of human sin, in order to liberate humans from sin and unite them to God. The *kenosis* or self-emptying of Jesus, which expresses in historical time the *kenosis*, the long-suffering of God, is the sacrifice which makes possible the *theosis* or raising to God of human life, enabling it to share in the eternal life of a God of limitless love. Precisely because that is the God who is revealed on the cross, the significance of the cross is not, and can never be, confined to a few people who have a special set of beliefs (who explicitly believe that Jesus is Lord, for example). It is the exemplary pattern for the whole world of what human salvation really is, and it makes effective in history in a divinely sanctioned way the path to that salvation which, in the end, often after following many different ways, all humanity is destined to follow.

♦ 8 ♦

Interpreting Biblical Teaching about Resurrection

The salvation of humanity is connected with the resurrection life. We are saved by Christ from hatred, greed and ignorance of spiritual truth. But ultimate salvation is from destruction and death, and it comes as human lives are united to the reality of God forever. This eternal union with God – eternal life – has always been portrayed in Christian tradition as the resurrection of the body, of the whole person who lived on this planet earth. Biblical teaching about the resurrection is explicit and clear. The extraordinary thing is that fundamentalists systematically misinterpret it and even contradict what it plainly says. In particular, they often speak about the resurrection as though it is the reassembling on earth at some future time of the physical bodies we have on earth. This strange idea gets us into all sorts of difficulties about how old the body will be, how its individual atoms can get reassembled when they have scattered all over the universe, and how all the bodies that have ever lived will fit onto an overcrowded planet. Such problems disappear as soon as you see that the Bible quite unambiguously denies that these physical bodies will ever be reassembled: 'When you sow, you do not plant the body that will be' (1 Corinthians 15.37).

Christians believe that God is disclosed in the life and teachings of Jesus. The death of Jesus, crucified as a criminal, is of particular importance, as it discloses the passionate love of God that will go to any length, even to death, to liberate humans from the grip of sin that imprisons them. But without the resurrection of Jesus, none of this would make sense. The absolute uniqueness of Jesus does not lie in his teaching, wonderful though that was. It does not even lie in his death, for millions of people die and are forgotten. It lies in the fact that he was raised from death by God, and lives forever in the presence of God. That is what gives Jesus a crucial significance in human history. The resurrection is the foundation stone of Christian faith, without which it would never have come into being.

But what exactly is the resurrection? I have been asked countless times, on radio and television, 'Do you believe that Jesus physically rose from the dead?' My response has usually been to ask, 'What do you mean by "physically"?' But this goes down like a lead balloon. Either the resurrection was physical, or it was fantasy, they say. People find it very hard to see any alternative.

Yet the Bible clearly teaches that there is an alternative, a different way of understanding the resurrection. It is hard to see how any reader of the Bible can miss this fact, and yet many seem to. The central biblical teaching about resurrection is given in Paul's first letter to the Corinthians in chapter 15. If any one thing is clear about that teaching, it is that the resurrection is not physical. It is not the resurrection of the same flesh-and-blood body that dies. Paul puts it bluntly: 'Flesh and blood cannot inherit the kingdom of God' (1 Corinthians 15.50).

If the body that is raised from death is not flesh and blood, what is it? Again Paul's teaching is very clear: 'It is sown a natural body, it is raised a spiritual body' (1 Corinthians 15.44). The words in Greek are *soma psychikon* and *soma pneumatikon*. A literal translation is difficult, but might be 'a mind-body' or a 'soul-filled body' and 'a spirit-body' or a 'spirit-filled body', which is probably not very helpful.

The word *psyche* is Greek for mind or soul. Paul almost certainly accepted the traditional Jewish understanding of the soul, which is based on Genesis 2.7: 'God formed the man from the dust of the ground, and breathed into his nostrils the breath of life'. For Old Testament thinking, the soul is not a substantial reality specially created by God. It is the breath of life, which makes dust live.

There was little importance given to any idea of life after death in the Old Testament. *Sheol* was the 'world of the dead', and was not a desirable place at all. The book of Job puts the general attitude very forcibly: 'the land of deepest night, of deep shadow and disorder, where even the light is like darkness' (Job 10.22). And the Psalmist says, 'It is not the dead who praise the Lord, those who go down to silence' (Psalm 115.17). In *Sheol* there were just the shadowy remnants of people, living in darkness. It is not surprising that Hebrew religion was not concerned with life after death. It was much more interested in life in this world, and for a person's children.

The idea of resurrection comes into the Bible quite late. The book of Daniel says, 'Multitudes who sleep in the dust of the earth will awake' (Daniel 12.2). Here there is at least the sketch of an idea that the shadowy figures of the dead, whose state might be likened to sleep, will come back to life. If the soul is a breath that makes dust live, then the breath cannot exist on its own. It must have some dust to animate. The idea seems to be that in *Sheol* some very thin dust remains of past people, and it can be reanimated by God, life breathed into it again. Ezekiel the prophet writes of his vision of a valley of dry bones, upon which God puts sinews and flesh, and puts breath in them so that they live again (Ezekiel 37.1–11). Admittedly this is a parable for the bringing back to life of the land of Israel, but it provides an idea of the bringing back to life of the dead.

By the time of Jesus, belief in a resurrection of the dead was common in Israel. But it was not shared by the most orthodox and traditional Jews, the Sadducees (Matthew 22.23), and even today Jews do not have to believe in resurrection, though probably most do.

Jesus certainly believed in the resurrection of the dead. To the Sadducees who questioned him, he said, 'He [God] is not the God of the dead but of the living' (Matthew 22.32). This reply implies that Abraham, Isaac and Jacob, to whom Jesus explicitly refers, were not dead, but alive. As to where and in what state they were, Jesus is silent. But he once told a parable in which a rich man went to Hades, which is a Greek term for *Sheol*, though in Luke it is described as 'a place of torment'. Meanwhile a poor man, Lazarus, went to 'Abraham's side' (Luke 16.22). Perhaps we should not take a parable too literally. Nevertheless, there does seem to be an acceptance that Abraham, at least, was not in Hades, but somewhere else, where he was capable of meeting and comforting at least some of the dead. It looks as though, by the time of Jesus, *Sheol* had got divided into Hades, a place of torment, and somewhere else – possibly Paradise, where Jesus promised to meet one of those crucified with him ('I tell you the truth, today you will be with me in paradise', Luke 23.43).

The account of Jesus' transfiguration also speaks of Jesus talking with Moses and Elijah, who, according to Luke's account, 'appeared in glorious splendour, talking with Jesus. They spoke about his [Jesus'] departure, which he was about to bring to fulfilment at Jerusalem' (Luke 9.31). So Moses and Elijah, as well as Abraham, live in glory, are capable of speaking, and are concerned with events on earth. Paradise seems to be a state in which many of the dead have knowledge, and pursue an active life.

So there is a changing, developing view of life after death in the Bible. From the view of the Psalmist that none of the dead praise God, there develops a later Prophetic idea that the dead might be reanimated by God. Even later, and probably between the writing of the Old and New Testaments, another change happens. We find that there is Hades, a place of torment for the wicked, and Paradise, a place where the penitent or the good live in conscious awareness of God and of one another. Both these places precede the resurrection, however, since Jesus is 'the firstfruits of those who have fallen asleep' (1 Corinthians 15.20). We might conclude that those who have fallen asleep in their earthly bodies are awake in some other form, either in Hades or in Paradise. The resurrection is a state still to come, though Jesus' resurrection is a foreshadowing of it.

The resurrection body

What sort of body is resurrected? Is it exactly like the body in which we die? At one time the Roman Catholic Church taught that we will be resurrected in the same flesh in which we now live, and fundamentalists commonly still hold this. Today Catholic teaching is more guarded. The Catholic Church affirms that we will be the same persons, the same 'psychosomatic unities', and that we will have a truly corporeal existence – bodily resurrection is not just a metaphor. But it is also clear that these bodies will be very unlike our present ones.

Even in medieval theology there were said to be four ways in which the resurrection body differs from our present 'natural' body. First, it will be impassible (at least in the case of the blessed), without suffering pain or discomfort. Second, it will be 'shining', as Jesus' body shone at the transfiguration. Third, it will be 'agile', having the capacity to move at will or pass through material objects with perfect freedom. And fourth, it will be 'subtle', under the complete control of the soul.

Obviously the physical properties of such bodies are quite different from those that belong to objects in this physical cosmos. Any realm in which such bodies exist will be quite different from this physical world. So it may seem rather odd to insist that bodies will look rather like our present bodies (though dead infants will be resurrected as they would have looked at 30, according to Augustine). It may be better to admit that, as Paul says, 'How foolish' it is even to raise the question of what resurrection bodies will be like (1 Corinthians 15.36). But it does seem that the biblical teaching stresses the difference of the resurrection from the natural body much more than the similarities.

Jesus says that 'At the resurrection people will neither marry nor be given in marriage; they will be like the angels in heaven' (Matthew 22.30). Like most of Jesus' sayings, this is infuriatingly cryptic. But at the least it entails that marriage relationships will not exist for those who are resurrected. That in turn implies that our bodies will be very different – they will not be inclined to sexual activity, and that entails a major hormonal and structural difference in the body. In addition, angels do not have physical, flesh-and-blood bodies, so there is an implication that our bodies will not only be different in their chemical make-up, they will be bodies of a different sort altogether.

Paul certainly confirms this impression. 'You do not plant the body that will be' (1 Corinthians 15.37). Paul uses the analogy of a seed, nothing but a small hard lump. When sown in the ground, it generates wheat, strong and tall, blowing in the wind. The 'natural body', the lump of dust filled with the breath of life, which we are, dies. And from it grows, in the fullness of time, something quite different, though it had always been potential in the physical body.

We might call that 'body of Spirit' an angelic body. It does not look like our physical body, it is not made of the same stuff, and it does not have the same physical constitution. Paul says, 'The body that is sown is perishable, it is raised imperishable' (1 Corinthians 15.42). The spiritual body is not subject to corruption – that in itself shows that it is not physical, since all physical things are subject to the law of entropy, of decay.

Why then should we call it a body at all? A body is what enables us to communicate and live with others in a community, what enables us to express our thoughts and feelings, and act in a common world. The physical bodies we have are carbon-based compounds, made of the dust of dying stars, and subject to all the laws of this space–time universe. Could we, the very people we are, with all our thoughts and feelings, not have different sorts of body, bodies not made of carbon, and not part of this space–time universe? Could we live in another universe, another environment, where our thoughts and feelings could be expressed more fully, and where we could act in freer and more communal ways?

That is exactly what the Bible teaches – that we can and will live in such another universe, a spiritual universe of incorruptibility, glory, and power. 'Then I saw a new heaven and a new earth', says the visionary John (Revelation 21.1). In that new universe, there will be no more sea, and no sun, moon or night. Even allowing for the poetic metaphors, this is obviously quite a different universe. Nature will be different, and its laws will be different. 'The wolf and the lamb will feed together, and the lion will eat straw like the ox ... They will neither harm nor destroy on all my holy mountain, says the Lord' (Isaiah 65.25). According to the prophet there will be animals, not just humans, in the resurrection universe. But the digestive systems of predators will be completely different. In fact they will not be predators any more. Their lives will truly be made new, refashioned in a way we can hardly imagine.

So Paul's teaching is that there will be a renewal of the universe, and we will live in it in a renewed, quite different, form. If we have a truly biblical view of resurrection, we must never think of it in terms of bodies climbing out of tombs, or of the resuscitation of our physical bodies. The resurrection will not be in this universe at all. It will be the creation of a new universe, and we will be strange new creatures, related to our present selves and bodies as wheat is related to its seed. We will be products of our lives on earth – which makes these earthly lives of eternal importance – but we will be quite different sorts of being, spirit beings 'like the angels in heaven'. We will be able to act and communicate, to create and share experiences. We will know the people we used to be, and how we have been changed 'in the twinkling of an eye' (1 Corinthians 15.52) into beings glorious, imperishable and immortal. That is the hope and the destiny the Bible sets before us.

This amazing vision is produced by one amazing fact, the resurrection of Jesus. But if this is our account of resurrection, then the resurrection of Jesus too is not a 'physical' resurrection at all. Jesus died, and his body was sown in the earth. Then he became the firstfruits of the resurrection universe. He assumed his spiritual body, imperishable and incorruptible, as his proper form of transfigured humanity. The uniqueness of Jesus is not that he lived after death – according to the Bible, we all do that (God is the God of the living, not the dead). Jesus' uniqueness consists in the fact that he is in his own person a foreshadowing of the new creation. His form of life is as far beyond our ordinary human form as the wheat blowing free in the sun is from the seed buried in the dark soil. This is no body that climbed laboriously out of a tomb and walked around Jerusalem. It is a blazing, glorious spiritual form that foreshadows, makes present, the glory of God's future when this whole physical universe has passed away. It is what Paul saw as a 'blazing light' on the road to Damascus, which convinced him that he had indeed seen the risen Lord. It is what is prefigured in Jesus' life at the transfiguration, recorded in the three Synoptic Gospels, when Jesus appeared to Peter, James and John, and 'His face shone like the sun, and his clothes became as white as the light' (Matthew 17.2).

The implication is that the resurrection body of Jesus did not just come into being after the death of his physical body. Paul writes that 'Though outwardly we are wasting away, yet inwardly we are being renewed day by day' (2 Corinthians 4.16). The 'earthly tent' is destroyed, but 'we have a building from God, an eternal house in heaven' (2 Corinthians 5.1). What is mortal is being swallowed up by life. The picture is of the earthly body decaying and moving towards death, while at the same time a spiritual body is being built up which will endure with God forever. So the spiritual body of Jesus existed at the same time as his physical body. It manifested at the transfiguration, and swallowed up the physical body entirely in the garden tomb. To understand the resurrection in its biblical sense we have to give up all ideas of physical bodies climbing out of their graves, or of physical atoms being reassembled into their old bodies. Instead, we have to think of the transfiguration of the whole material cosmos into a vast spiritual realm, like the emergence of a butterfly from a chrysalis. That is what Jesus prefigures, because he is, as the Christ, a primarily spiritual being. 'The first man was of the dust of the earth, the second man from heaven' (1 Corinthians 15.47). Adam was first dust, physical, and became a life-giving spirit. But Christ is a spiritual being, the eternal Word of God, before he is a human being. 'And just as we have borne the likeness of the earthly man, so shall we bear the likeness of the man from heaven' (1 Corinthians 15.49). Of Jesus, and Jesus alone of all humanity, Wordsworth's words were true, that even as an infant he came 'trailing clouds of glory' (from 'Intimations of Immortality'). The resurrection body of Jesus is his real, spiritual body. It was clothed for a while in the physical body of Adamic humanity. But when that body of dust suffered physical death, it was transfigured finally and completely into its spiritual substratum. That transfiguration in Jerusalem prefigures, is a prototype of, the destiny of the whole cosmos to be similarly transfigured from decay into glory, from darkness to everlasting light.

The resurrection of Jesus

If we approach the gospel records of Jesus' resurrection with this in mind, what might have seemed odd and inexplicable is illuminated in a marvellous way. If we try to think of resurrection as the reanimation of Jesus' physical body, we are faced with insuperable problems. For a start, how did the body get out of the tomb? Perhaps it simply walked out – but Matthew tells of how an angel came and rolled away the stone (Matthew 28.2), which entails that Jesus left the tomb while the stone still covered the entrance. The Gospels are unanimous that Jesus' body was not in the tomb. This leaves only two possibilities. Either it walked out, or it dematerialized, ceased to exist as a physical body of flesh and blood, being instantaneously transfigured into a different, spiritual form. The account of resurrection I have just given compels us to accept the latter, 'spiritual transformation' view. That would be compatible with Matthew's account, since a spiritual body would not properly belong to this space–time universe at all. It would not be constrained by the laws of this universe. It could manifest in physical form or not, as it chose. This would also account for how it was that Jesus could appear to the disciples when they were behind locked doors (John 20.19), how after talking with them for a while he simply disappeared from their sight (Luke 24.31), and how he was not recognized on a seven-mile walk (Luke 24.16).

No one could say that the accounts of the resurrection in the Gospels are all entirely accurate, in their literal details. Whereas Matthew has an angel roll the stone from the tomb entrance, the other Gospels record that it had already been rolled away. The Gospels disagree on how many women visited the tomb and found it empty – though they all agree it was women who went, and that the tomb was empty. The implication is, as elsewhere in the Gospels, that these are not literal accounts dictated without error by God. They are records of memories treasured in the early Christian community, and different memories, as always in human life, give slightly different versions of the same events. That is exactly what we would expect, after a gap of 30 years or so, and with memories passed on orally in different groups with different characteristics and interests. This does not impugn the reliability of the gospel witness to the resurrection. But it does mean that we should not place too much stress on specific details of the accounts, since they cannot all be correct in detail.

My judgement would be that Matthew's report of an angel rolling the stone away is probably a piece of exaggeration on Matthew's part, since only he gives this account, and he does tend to emphasize the miraculous more than the others. Nevertheless, the report of the empty tomb and the nature of Jesus' appearances – brief, intermittent and mysteriously abrupt in their beginnings and endings – does strongly support a 'spiritual transformation' account of resurrection.

There is one text that seems to put such an account in question, and it is always quoted by fundamentalists, who often do not seem to realize its true purpose in Luke. That is Luke's report that Jesus said, 'A ghost does not have flesh and bones, as you see I have' (Luke 24.39). Just to rub it in, Jesus then ate a piece of broiled fish (Luke 24.42). In assessing this text, we must remember that it begins with the sudden appearance of Jesus among the disciples – not something a physical body could manage – so that they supposed that they 'saw a ghost' (Luke 24.37).

In this context a ghost would be a hallucination or a visual appearance of a dead person, without solidity or the usual causal connections with its surroundings. What Luke was concerned to say was that the appearances of Jesus were not those of a ghost. Jesus was not just dead like other people, even like Abraham, living in Paradise. Jesus was a new reality, a prototype of the resurrection world, with the power to bring others into that world through relation to him. In other words, Luke wants to stress, not the ordinariness of Jesus, but his absolute extra-ordinariness. This was not an ordinary physical body, which had presumably been hiding behind the door all the time, and had picked up some clothes from somewhere in Jerusalem. It was a totally extra-ordinary spiritual body, with the power to manifest itself when and where it chose, and to communicate nothing less than the divine life to those to whom it appeared. So it could indeed manifest in a body of flesh and bones, and eat fish. It could, in other words, become a real physical body intermittently and at will. It could truly appear in the physical world, taking physical form, but it was not in its true nature physical.

It was not less than physical, like a spirit. It was more than physical, a complete transfiguration of the physical world into a greater spiritual reality, with the power to appear as a physical form for the sake of those who found it hard to believe such a transfiguration had happened or could happen.

This parallels the account in John's Gospel where Thomas the Twin was invited to put his hand into the wounds in Jesus' side (John 20.27). These physical manifestations of Jesus were real and, like the empty tomb, validated in a convincing way the belief that it was Jesus who was appearing to them in a new form, and not just some supernatural spirit or angel sent from God, or possibly from the Devil. Thomas' response is the only place in the Gospels where divinity is explicitly ascribed to Jesus: 'My Lord and my God!' (John 20.28). The proper response to Jesus' invitation is not to say, 'Ah, I see that you are an ordinary physical human being after all.' It is rather to say, 'You have power over all things, even the physical forms of the universe. But you transcend them all in the power and reality of your being.'

When Jesus finally ascended into heaven, Acts has an angel say to the disciples, 'Why do you stand here looking into the sky? This same Jesus, who has been taken from you into heaven, will come back in the same way you have seen him go into heaven' (Acts 1.11). This account is unintelligible if we think of a physical body soaring through the clouds to some distant galaxy, and then coming back through space like a rocket at some future time. It makes sense when we see Jesus' ascension as the final removal of his spiritual body from the physical realm, the final transfiguration of his material life into the life of eternity. The disciples are told not to look to that spiritual realm, neglecting the affairs of the physical world. For at some time Jesus 'will come back in the same way' – that is, as a spiritual presence. It will not be a physical return. It will be the final breaking-in of the spiritual into the remnants of the decaying physical cosmos. The sentence can be very reasonably interpreted to mean, 'Jesus will come as a spiritual reality, as you have seen him go.' The spiritual will finally transfigure the material itself. A new heaven and earth, a new cosmos, will come into being, even as the physical passes away. The reality of spirit will be established as something that has grown out of this ambiguous existence in the physical world. That is the biblical vision of resurrection – this physical world is a preparation for the creation of a spiritual kingdom, and what the resurrection of Jesus manifests and prefigures is the transfiguration of time into eternity. 'My kingdom is not of this world', says Jesus to Pilate (John 18.36). But neither is it a kingdom that is simply and totally different from this world. It is rule in a world transfigured, taken through the experience of the cross into the experience of glory.

The resurrection took the disciples by surprise. According to Mark, Jesus told the disciples that he would rise from death, but 'they kept the matter to themselves, discussing what "rising from the dead" meant' (Mark 9.10). Even those who believed there would be a resurrection thought that it would be at the end of time, and that all the dead would rise together. So how could Jesus rise from the dead, when time had not come to an end, and when there were still people living normal lives in the world?

This perplexity partly accounts for the early Christian belief that the cosmos would perish within a generation. What was needed, and what was slow to come, was an appreciation that Jesus' resurrection was a prototype of a general resurrection far in the future of the cosmos, unimaginably far for them. Israelite religion had begun with a strong emphasis on God's commands for living well in this world. Only gradually did the hope for resurrection spring up, as the prophets realized how far from knowledge of God almost all humans were, and how much God longed to give creatures the joy of the divine presence. 'When I awake, I shall be satisfied with seeing your likeness', sings the

Psalmist (Psalm 17.15). Such awakening, it was gradually realized, could only fully come after death. The idea of life after death did not originate, in Judaism, with a longing to prolong this earthly life as much as possible. It arose from a longing to see God more clearly, from the hope for a complete transformation of life, from the thought that 'you will fill me with joy in your presence, with eternal pleasures at your right hand' (Psalm 16.11).

The hope for eternal life is hope for life in the presence of the eternal God. It was only slowly that the biblical writers moved to the clear formulation of such a hope, and Christians would say that it was only with Jesus that it achieved a definite form. For Jesus is Immanuel, 'God with us', and he is in his own person the unity of temporal and eternal in which human hope is grounded.

The resurrection of Jesus is a miracle, but it is not a 'breaking of natural law', as some have misleadingly defined miracle. It is actually a revelation, an unveiling, of the truth about all reality. The truth is that the fundamental reality, from which all else springs, is the reality of spirit. 'God is spirit' (John 4.24), and the whole material world is subordinate to that reality.

The miracle of resurrection

Miracle is a transformation of the material by the spiritual, a disclosure of the real (the spiritual) that reveals the true function of the material to manifest its spiritual basis. John's Gospel typically describes miracles as 'signs' (*semeion*), material events that point beyond themselves to disclose something of the spiritual basis that underlies them. According to the three Synoptic Gospels, Jesus never used miracles as proofs of his power and spiritual status to the general public ('no sign will be given to it [this generation]', Mark 8.12). Remarkably, this assertion occurs in Mark's Gospel, immediately after his account of the miraculous feeding of four thousand people. According to the Gospels, Jesus did perform miracles. But they were symbols of his nature as the eternal Wisdom of God for those who had eyes to see, not overwhelming proofs for everyone.

Jesus' miracles unmistakeably mark him out as a person imbued with divine power and authority. He walks on the water (Mark 6.48), which resonates with the Psalmist's celebration of God cleaving and ordering the Great Deep ('Your path led through the sea', Psalm 77.19). He transforms water into wine (John 2.1–11), symbolizing the transformation of Jewish ritual into the sacramental celebration of new life in him.

He stilled the storm, raised the dead, exorcised demons and healed many who came to him in pain and despair.

All his miracles seem to show his supreme power over death and destruction, but he never uses that power destructively. When his disciples James and John ask him to call down fire on a Samaritan village that would not receive him (as the prophet Elijah had once done), Jesus 'turned and rebuked them' (Luke 9.55). Some ancient manuscripts add that he said, 'You do not know what kind of spirit you are of, for the Son of Man did not come to destroy men's lives, but to save them.'

Jesus' miracles are saving miracles, symbols of the will and power of God to heal those who turn to him in faith. Mark records that in his home town, when people took offence at him, 'he could not do any miracles there' (Mark 6.5). The healing power of God is to some extent conditional on the receptivity of human lives – the sanctity of Jesus allows divine power to work through him in an unparalleled way, whereas the obstinacy of the crowd can impede even the working of God's power.

The life of Jesus shows the power of the spiritual realm breaking into the material. It never does so destructively, and it never does so in such a way as to give conclusive evidence even to those who do not care for God. It manifests the power of Spirit to heal and give life, and to those ready to perceive it, the reality of the invisible God is made visible in the acts and person of Jesus.

Eternal reality cannot be defeated by death. So if Jesus really was, as he is claimed to be, the act and image of the eternal God, the resurrection is simply the declaration – again, for those prepared to receive it – that eternal 'love is as strong as death' (Song of Songs 8.6). We should not see the resurrection as an odd event that breaks natural laws. We should see it as a disclosure of the spiritual reality that underlies all natural laws, and of the real function and purpose of the material cosmos, which is to mediate and express the eternal.

The Christian view stands between views that see this material universe as the only thing there is, and views that see spiritual reality as lying in complete separation from the material. The biblical position is that the physical cosmos is where persons originate. Persons are truly parts of the physical world. Their decisions help to make that world what it is, and also shape their own characters as they grow and develop. But the physical world itself is to be transformed by God into a spiritual world, which will be the fulfilment as well as the transformation of its possibilities and its actualized states. As Paul puts it, 'the whole creation has been groaning as in the pains of childbirth right up to the present time' (Romans 8.22).

Because of the human choice of estrangement from God, the whole universe has become a realm 'subjected to frustration' (Romans 8.20), and yet it has been 'subjected . . . in hope'. Life on earth has become a way of death and decay, as humans become slaves to hatred, greed and ignorance. Human creatures realize all the negative possibilities that lie in the mind of God. The creation is radically flawed, and does not realize God's original intention.

Yet those negative possibilities do not completely overwhelm the original goodness of creation, and humans still have the responsibility to realize understanding, beauty and companionship in their lives. What God reveals in the resurrection of Jesus is that the negative, the evil, will be transformed by integration into a wider goodness, and the beauty will be more fully and gloriously realized, in a spiritual realm beyond this cosmos.

'The Lord Jesus Christ . . . will transform our lowly bodies so that they will be like his glorious body' (Philippians 3.20–21). We look, not for a reassembling of our earthly body, but for a complete transformation of life: 'what we will be has not yet been made known. But we know that when he appears, we shall be like him, for we shall see him as he is' (1 John 3.2). We cannot yet see or even imagine the glorified body of Jesus, but we believe that we shall be like him, transfigured and redeemed by God. And this process begins even during earthly life: 'we, who with unveiled faces all reflect the Lord's glory, are being transformed into his likeness with ever-increasing glory' (2 Corinthians 3.18).

The New Testament teaching is that our earthly life is something like a growth from seed, or like a birth from the womb. What we do on earth is of eternal significance, for what will be built on in eternity is what we have begun on earth. But what we do on earth is not the end, for the evil will be transformed and the good fulfilled, as we share in the mind of God, which includes and reconciles all earthly experience, good and bad, into the divine life.

The resurrection of Jesus is the appearing in time of the transfigured future, a prototype of the glory of God that brings all creation into the divine life, and enables creatures to share in it. So is the resurrection physical? No, the Bible teaches that it is spiritual. But it is a transformation of the physical, it is the foretaste of God's glory, and it is the transfiguration of time into eternity. It is the disclosure of the real basis and the future destiny of created beings. In that sense it is deeply natural, because it reveals the original purpose for which the whole universe was created, the participation of all things in God (2 Peter 1.4). Only when we begin to understand this can we truly share the Christian hope, and be freed from thinking that the resurrection is just a very odd and absolutely singular physical event, when it is in fact the disclosure of the true nature and fulfilment of the whole created reality. One of the tragedies of fundamentalism is that it misses this vision of a transfigured universe, and of the glory of God that wills all humanity, and perhaps all conscious beings, to share in that new creation. It replaces it with a mean-spirited and niggardly offer of an extension of physical life on earth for a few like-minded folks. Such a limitation of vision is a betrayal of what the Bible teaches, and a tragically restricted view of the unlimited love and power of God.

♦ 9 ♦

Interpreting Biblical Teaching about Judgement, Heaven and Hell

The Christian view of the world is that it was created in order to realize new forms of goodness, especially the goodness of shared experience and the creation of beauty, friendship and understanding. But the human world was disordered by passion and attachment, so that it realized instead those negative possibilities of hatred, greed and ignorance that led into a far country, away from the presence of God. God resolved in love to enter that far country in order to draw humanity back to the divine. The way was prepared in many forms, but especially by the prophets of Israel, and the manifestation of the divine life itself occurred in the person of Jesus the Christ, whose life of healing and reconciliation was completed in his self-sacrifice on the cross and his raising to resurrection life. The destiny of humanity is now to be attained by accepting the free offer of divine grace, and learning to grow into the life of Christ, both in his humble self-giving and in his joyful resurrection.

This is indeed a gospel, 'good news', for it offers to all forgiveness of sins and eternal life, a liberation from hatred, greed and ignorance into a life of love, joy, compassion and wisdom, which will be completed with Christ in a new creation beyond the historical time of this cosmos, and which will never fade or decay.

This is a gospel of limitless hope, especially for those in this world whose lives have been crushed by the brutality and hatred of others. Christ, God in human and personal form, shares with them the alienation of human life, in order that they should share with God the endless companionship of divine life. The gospel of God's unconditional love simply *is* the Christian gospel.

And yet many fundamentalists reject it. They deny that God's love is unconditional and unlimited. Indeed they sometimes place extremely severe limits upon it. The 'good news' of salvation in Christ is sometimes replaced by the very 'bad news' of eternal hell for almost everyone, unless they happen to have a very specific and explicit set of beliefs about Jesus – and they cannot even be sure that even then they are safe. A gospel of grace and love is changed into a message of fear and despair. It does not quite seem to fit a Jesus who said, 'I did not come to judge the world, but to save it' (John 12.47). Note that it is 'the world' he came to save, not just a few favoured believers. Just in case you think that even if Jesus judges no one, God the Father does, Jesus also says, 'The Father judges no one, but has entrusted all judgment to the Son' (John 5.22). That looks conclusive. The Father gives all judgement to the Son, who prefers to save rather than to judge.

Where then does all this fundamentalist talk of judgement come from? Fundamentalists do not make it up. What they do is to find bits of the Bible that do speak of judgement and condemnation, and allow them to overrule all the bits that speak of salvation and unlimited divine love. There is a lot in the Bible about God's anger and about judgement. But a great deal of historical sense is needed to put it in context. The early Hebrews did not believe in life after death in any real sense, so they were certainly not talking about eternal hell. They had no such idea – and in fact, the word 'hell' does not occur anywhere in the Bible in the original languages in which it was written. It is a later invention – so it is very ironic that fundamentalists, who claim to believe only what is in the Bible, so often believe in hell, which is not in the Bible!

The God of the Old Testament is certainly a God who lays down strict moral rules, and judges human evil severely. But without life after death, God's judgements must be played out on earth. God says, 'I, the Lord your God, am a jealous God, punishing the children for the sin of the fathers to the third and the fourth generation of those who hate me, but showing love to thousands who love me and keep my commandments' (Exodus 20.5–6). This may seem rather harsh to our ears, but it is a simple statement of the fact that the descendants of those who reject God will suffer because of their ancestors' hatred and greed. None of them suffer torment forever, but sin brings its own natural punishment, by the very nature of things. Those who love God, however, will be loved by God and attain happiness and wellbeing. Obviously these are generalizations, and they are not true in every case. The ancient Hebrews tried to see this world as a realm in which the rewards and punishments of justice were on the whole realized by the structure of the laws of history. To speak about 'God's anger' was to speak about the torment and vanity of a life without God, in a world which the rejection of God makes much more bleak and cruel than it would otherwise be.

But writings like the book of Job show a realization that even if there is a moral structure underlying history, it is a very blunt instrument. The innocent suffer, and the evil are quite often rewarded, or so it seems. So there developed, quite late in the Old Testament, talk of a Day of Judgement, when the wrongs of history would finally be ended. In the writings of the major prophets, judgement was conceived in terms of historical catastrophe. The Judgement Day was a day in the future when the great military powers would be overthrown and Israel would live in peace (Zechariah 14.12–14). The primary emphasis was not on a judgement beyond death, but on a historical judgement on oppressors and a historical liberation of the peacemakers. The idea of a moral law underlying all the events of history was replaced by the idea of a decisive Day of Judgement, followed by a Messianic rule of peace ('the day is coming; it will burn like a furnace. All the arrogant and every evildoer will be stubble, and that day that is coming will set them on fire . . . But for you who revere my name the sun of righteousness will rise with healing in its wings', Malachi 4.1–2).

When human existence is confined to life on earth, it hardly makes sense to speak of the 'unlimited love' of God. We can speak of God's loving-kindness (*chesed*), but equally apparent in this world is God's anger, for this world sets itself against God. God's anger will be shown against all the oppressive powers of the world, and the righteous will be rewarded. But all that is set in the future, as something to look forward to, probably for your descendants, but not for you.

As religious thought developed in Israel, it came to seem insufficient that God would postpone justice to far future generations. Each individual person acts and suffers, is happy or sad. If God is truly just, surely the wicked and the good would not go down alike to *Sheol*, where the dead no longer praise God. The Psalmist sings, 'you will not abandon me to the grave, nor will you let your Holy One see decay' (Psalm 16.10). The Psalmist may only be thanking God for not letting him die yet. But the idea begins to develop, and is then partly based on texts like this, that there will be different destinies for the wicked and for the good, there will be both the 'Outer Darkness' and the Presence of God.

If there is a personal life beyond death, it becomes possible for the first time to speak of God's unlimited love. For in a world beyond death the wicked can be both punished and corrected, and the good can learn ever more and more of the infinite love of God. This seems to be the teaching of the letter to the Romans. Paul stresses that since 'all have sinned' they 'are justified freely by his [God's] grace' (Romans

3.23–24). All who have sinned, and received the wage of death, are also justified by the free gift of God (not just given to some, but to all). Even more clearly, 'as the result of one trespass was condemnation for all men, so also the result of one act of righteousness was justification that brings life for all men' (Romans 5.18).

This should be sufficient to settle the issue of who gets saved. Everyone does, for God does not limit the divine love to just a few. Whatever else Paul says must be consistent with this. It immediately follows that there must be a life after death (and of course that is no surprise, since Paul's whole Christian faith is based on belief in resurrection). For most people do not get saved during this life – the fundamentalists are right about that. But what fundamentalists do not see is that most people must therefore get saved after death. As Paul puts it, 'I am convinced that neither death nor life . . . will be able to separate us from the love of God that is in Christ Jesus our Lord' (Romans 8.38–39). Death is not a barrier that prevents the saving love of God from operating, and it is the firm Christian belief in resurrection that for the first time makes salvation possible for all without restriction.

All Israel will be saved

What begins to go wrong, for fundamentalists, is that they try to twist Paul's statement that Christ brings life for all, and make it mean that he only brings life for some, sometimes for very few. They do this because they read the remarkable passage of Romans chapters 9 to 11 as a set of statements about what happens to individuals after they die. But in this passage Paul is not thinking primarily about the salvation of individuals. He speaks in typical prophetic language of future historical events. He says little at that point about life after death. His problem is about the future history of the Jews, not about what happens to people after death. Once we see this, it all falls into place quite neatly.

Paul's problem is that the Jews as a whole did not accept Jesus as Messiah, and seem to have been replaced as the covenant people by largely Gentile Christians. So has God's calling of Israel into the covenant failed (Romans 9.6)? Paul's first response is to say that God has at least kept a remnant of Israel, those who have become disciples of Jesus. 'God has mercy on whom he wants to have mercy, and he hardens whom he wants to harden' (Romans 9.18). That is, God calls those whom God wills to follow Christ, and hardens the hearts of others. It is no use complaining about this, Paul says, for God may have a purpose in it we cannot easily see. He suggests that purpose is to allow the Gentiles to hear the gospel, and thus turn Christianity into a world-faith instead of a continuation of a Torah-based Judaism.

'Did God reject his people? By no means!' (Romans 11.1), he exclaims. Not only did God keep a remnant of Israel, but even those who reject Christ play a part in God's purpose, for 'because of their transgression, salvation has come to the Gentiles' (Romans 11.11). Paul's final conclusion is that 'Israel has experienced a hardening in part, until the full number of the Gentiles has come in. And so all Israel will be saved' (Romans 11.25–26). Just to be sure we have got the point, that Israel has not been rejected, but that all Israel will be saved, he adds, 'they too have now become disobedient in order that they too may now receive mercy as a result of God's mercy to you' (Romans 11.31). And to be quite certain we have not evaded his meaning, he returns to the totally universal statement about God's unlimited mercy with which he began his letter: 'For God has bound all men over to disobedience so that he may have mercy on them all' (Romans 11.32).

How anyone can turn this remarkable passage into a doctrine that all Jews are damned, or that only a few people will be chosen for salvation, is hard to understand. Some fundamentalists have even misused Paul's question that 'What if God, choosing to show his wrath and make his power known, bore with great patience the objects of his wrath – prepared for destruction?' (Romans 9.22). What it means is that God patiently endures the rituals of Judaism, which are ultimately destined to be sublated in a higher form of worship, in order that Gentiles may be admitted to the realm of grace, and the world without God shall be judged as futile and empty. What some fundamentalists make the passage mean is, incredibly, that a God of love creates some 'vessels' in order to destroy them, and shows divine anger in simply destroying them, or even sending them off to be tortured for ever in a special vessel-torturing place. Apart from the fact that such an interpretation flatly contradicts Paul's statement that God will have mercy upon all (Romans 11.32), it absolutely contradicts any belief that God's love is unlimited or even half-way charitable – and that is deeply anti-biblical.

This whole passage in the letter to the Romans is not about individual destiny beyond death, in heaven or hell. It is about God's calling for the Jewish people, and its point is to assure Jews that God still has a purpose for them, and that in the end all Israel will all be saved. Of course this does have implications for individual lives. If we are thinking about individual life after death, and if 'all Israel will be saved', then it follows that every Jewish individual will be saved. That will have to be after death, if salvation is the knowledge and love of God as revealed in the face of Jesus Christ. God can only be unlimited love, and it is only possible for God to have mercy upon all people, and to save every Jew (and everyone else too), if there is a life beyond death, in which such salvation can be effected.

Paul is committed to life after death, as anyone who believes in resurrection is. But we are not quite talking about resurrection here. We are talking about the Jewish ideas that developed out of the idea of *Sheol*, ideas of Paradise, a place for the Patriarchs and the saints, and of an Outer Darkness, or place of punishment and correction. These are ideas that fundamentalists usually ignore altogether, or change into ideas which do not allow any repentance or development or liberation after death.

Biblical metaphors of hell

I have said that there is no word for Hell in the Bible, and I need to make that clearer.

In the Old Testament, *Sheol* is sometimes referred to as *Beer*, the Pit or Well ('But you, O God, will bring down the wicked into the pit of corruption', Psalm 55.23). That is clearly not meant to be pleasant. The picture is of a deep underground well or cavern, where all is gloom or darkness. Jewish commentators have either taken it to be just a metaphor for death, or less commonly for some shadowy post-mortem state rather like the Greek Hades – which is a word found in the New Testament for the world of the dead. In the book of Revelation, the time spent in Hades is said to be finite – 'death and Hades gave up the dead that were in them, and each person was judged according to what he had done. Then Death and Hades were thrown into the lake of fire' (Revelation 20.13–14).

So this gloomy world is where the dead stay until the time of judgement. In Jesus' parable of the rich man and Lazarus, the rich man is said to be in Hades, and to be 'in agony in this fire' (Luke 16.24), so Hades has become a place of flames and torment. Just as Hades is not literally a pit under the ground, so there is no reason to think it contains literal flames. The flames are more likely to be those of passion, desire and greed, and the torment is the anguished realization of a life wasted in indifference and luxury. We are not told what happens when the rich man is given up for judgement. But we are told that at least for a time, and probably for the duration of the age (*aeon*) before the Day of Judgement, there is a place of torment and anguish for those who have failed to obey God's law.

Another term used in the New Testament for this state is *Gehenna*, which is the rubbish pit in the valley of Hinnom outside Jerusalem. There the fires burn continually, and rubbish thrown onto them is burned and destroyed. So the letter of James says, 'The tongue also is a fire . . . set on fire by hell (*Gehenna*)' (James 3.6). The metaphorical usage is clear, for 'the tongue is a fire' is not literally true. It depicts the way in which speech can be used to destroy and ignite destructive passions. Similarly, being 'set on fire by *Gehenna*' is not describing anything literally. It depicts the way in which those who have destroyed reputations by gossip will find themselves tormented by their own malice.

In the teachings of Jesus a metaphor recurs of a great Feast in the Kingdom of God, from which many will be excluded, and being in outer darkness, will weep and gnash their teeth (Matthew 22.13). Sometimes Jesus uses a different metaphor, of weeds burned in a great fire after the harvest has been gathered into the barns, where again 'there will be weeping and gnashing of teeth' (Matthew 13.42).

Jesus teaches that there is a state of anguish, sadness and regret after death for those who have turned from God and have refused to repent. But the New Testament is unclear about whether this state follows immediately after death, as in the parable of Lazarus and the rich man, or whether it comes 'at the end of the age' (Matthew 13.40).

There is a similar unclarity about the fate of the righteous. In some parables, it is not until the close of the age that 'the righteous will shine like the sun in the kingdom of their Father' (Matthew 13.43). But Lazarus was carried straight to Abraham's side when he died. And Jesus promised the penitent thief that 'today you will be with me in paradise' (Luke 23.43).

Those who want all biblical texts to be consistent at any price will have to twist and turn to try to find a way in which all these statements can be true at once. The plain fact is, however, that they are not consistent. And the reason is simple – metaphors and parables do not have to be consistent in all their details. Metaphors differ but they do not contradict. What the Bible teaches, by exhibiting these unclarities about the state of life after death, is that it is speaking in metaphors, not in literal descriptions. It is a fundamental misunderstanding to press a metaphor too far. What is needed to understand a biblical metaphor properly is to see its central spiritual point, and to avoid literal-mindedness like the plague.

We have metaphors of one great universal Judgement Day, metaphors of Paradise and the Pit, metaphors of a feast, a garden, a fire

and Outer Darkness. The central spiritual point is that what we do in
this life matters, and will carry great spiritual consequences for us as
well as for others. Happiness, the ancient Greek philosopher Aristotle
said, consists in the unimpeded exercise of virtue. Misery consists, by
contrast, in the rule of unrestrained excess. After death each of us will
reap the happiness or misery that results from a clear unambiguous
knowledge of our slavery to passion or our creative freedom. That is
what may be called heaven and hell – not a place or a state that can be
literally described, but a condition in which we receive the appropriate
consequences of our earthly actions.

The idea of purgatory

Many of the biblical metaphors for life after death speak of a state in
which change and development is possible. The first letter to the
Corinthians says, each man's 'work will be shown for what it is . . . the
fire will test the quality of each man's work . . . If what he has built . . .
is burned up, he will suffer loss; he himself will be saved, but only as one
escaping through the flames (1 Corinthians 3.12–15). Here, what we do
is compared to erecting a building. There are rewards for good work,
but a certain sort of loss for those who have not built well. The strong
suggestion is that after death there will be punishments of some sort,
which will serve to purify rather than to destroy completely.

A similar suggestion can be found in Jesus' parable of the unforgiv-
ing servant, where 'his master turned him over to the jailers . . . until he
should pay back all he owed. This is how my heavenly Father will treat
each of you unless you forgive your brother from your heart' (Matthew
18.34–35). In the course of the Sermon on the Mount, Jesus also says,
'Settle matters quickly with your adversary' or 'you may be thrown into
prison. I tell you the truth, you will not get out until you have paid the
last penny' (Matthew 5.25–26).

These are parables and metaphors, and should not be taken literally.
Yet there is the suggestion that there will be a penalty for wrongdoing,
and that it is a penalty which can eventually be paid.

Such a suggestion fits well with the idea of a truly loving God, who
would surely not punish people without end and without any hope of
restoration. It seems fitting that there should be appropriate punishments for evil, but that they should not be infinite. That seems to be the
teaching of these New Testament passages.

Upon them was based the medieval doctrine of purgatory. According
to the French scholar Jacques LeGoff, purgatory was invented in 1170.

At least that is when the word first appears in literature. There is little doubt that the idea of purgatory, a state of purgative suffering that would lead inevitably to Paradise in the end, developed over hundreds of years in the Church. Is it a biblical teaching? Fundamentalists seem united in affirming that it is anti-biblical. But the biblical evidence does not seem to support such a negative view.

The Bible does not have a clear and explicit teaching on this matter – as it does not, in fact, on the Trinity, the atonement, the precise nature of the incarnation, or the divinity of the Holy Spirit. But the passages already cited do quite definitely suggest a finite time of corrective punishment. More importantly, this is the view of punishment which is most consistent with the idea that God is a being of unlimited love, who will go to any lengths to redeem those who are lost ('There will be more rejoicing in heaven over one sinner who repents than over ninety-nine righteous persons who do not need to repent', Luke 15.7). We might well expect that God will constantly seek to bring sinners to repentance, and will thus use corrective or reformative punishment rather than purely retributive punishment that has no possible good consequences.

There are clearer indications than this in the Bible of the possibility of redemption from sin after death. The second book of the Maccabees records that Judas, General of the Jewish army, prayed for those who had died in battle. Not only that, 'he made atonement for the dead, that they might be delivered from their sin' (2 Maccabees 12.45, Revised Standard Version. This book is in the Apocrypha, and is not translated in the New International Version). Fundamentalists might well not accept this as Scripture, because it is part of the Apocryphal books, so I would not press it as decisive. But it does show that sacrifices for the dead were offered in Judaism between Old Testament and New Testament times, and were approved of at least by many pious Jews. Prayers for the dead were not unknown in Jesus' time. Paul refers to a similar practice that was apparently current in the early Church, of being baptized on behalf of the dead. Paul writes, 'Now if there is no resurrection, what will those do who are baptised for the dead? If the dead are not raised at all, why are people baptised for them?' (1 Corinthians 15.29). Paul does not condemn this practice, which he easily could have done if he had wished. He simply mentions that it happens. The implication is that people could be made members of the Church after they had died, and that things we do on earth can have effects on those who have died. Overall, the evidence is quite strong that those who have died can be liberated from sin, both by undergoing corrective punishments (the 'purifying fire'), and by being prayed for by those on earth – and of course, above all by the sacrificial self-offering of Jesus on their behalf.

The most remarkable, and most neglected, New Testament teaching on this subject is found in the first letter of Peter. It does seem to require an enormous amount of tampering with the plain meaning of the text to avoid. The writer says that Jesus died, 'put to death in the body but made alive by the Spirit, through whom also he went and preached to the spirits in prison, who disobeyed long ago when God waited patiently in the days of Noah' (1 Peter 3.18–20).

Here is a plain bit of biblical teaching: Jesus died in his body of flesh and was raised in his 'spiritual body'. There he went and preached to others who also had spiritual bodies of some sort, who had disobeyed God and been drowned in the Great Flood. Of them, the book of Genesis had said, 'the earth was corrupt in God's sight . . . all the people on earth had corrupted their ways' (Genesis 6.11–12). So Jesus preached to corrupt souls, which God had destroyed from the face of the earth, and who were 'in prison', in *Sheol*, serving their time of punishment.

What was the point of Jesus preaching to corrupt souls, enduring the just punishment of God? Was it just to reinforce their guilt and despair, to tell them that the time of hope was past, and they had nothing to look forward to but endless torment? Not at all. The writer says, 'this is the reason the gospel was preached even to those who are now dead, so that they might be judged according to men in regard to the body, but live according to God in regard to the spirit' (1 Peter 4.6). These people had been judged, destroyed and punished by God. But now Jesus preached the gospel, the 'good news' that repentance was possible for them, and they could live 'in the spirit'. So the Bible teaches that repentance is possible even after death. Those millions who die without having heard of Jesus are not deprived of the possibility of salvation, for the gospel was (and is) preached even to the dead. As John's Gospel says, 'a time is coming and has now come when the dead will hear the voice of the Son of God and those who hear will live' (John 5.25).

The Bible teaches that after death there is life in Paradise, with the Patriarchs, prophets and all the saints. Or there is life in 'prison', where humans are tormented by anguish, regret and the flames of passion, but where the gospel of salvation in Christ is still preached, and from which they can be liberated by the grace of Christ if they repent and accept the gospel. God never terminates the offer of salvation, or closes the door forever. It is only those afflicted with the spirit of vindictiveness who say, 'It is too late. You have had your chance. You must suffer forever, and I will not care, for I will be in Paradise, thank you very much.' The God who is revealed in Jesus Christ says, 'It is never too late for you to repent and believe. I will go to any lengths, even descending into Hades, to try to liberate you from your sins. And if you accept, there will be great joy in Paradise.' That is the authentic voice of the Christian gospel of the universal, non-vindictive, costly love of God.

The Day of Judgement

What has happened, though, to the idea of one great Judgement Day, and of the resurrection of the dead? We need to recall what was said about the resurrection of Jesus, which is the model for all Christian ideas of resurrection. The resurrection is the transfiguration of the physical into the spiritual. It involves the final destruction of all pain, suffering and evil. It is the creation of a new and glorious spiritual universe, which has no place for sea or sun – that is, for the abyss of chaos or for a source of light other than God. The resurrection therefore coincides with the Day of Judgement, the acceptance of the just into the Kingdom of God, and the rejection of evil forever.

In Paul's letters the resurrection and judgement are usually spoken of in the context of the return of Christ in glory with the saints, the transfiguration of believers into his spiritual form, and a decisive judgement on and destruction of evil. So Paul says, 'wait till the Lord comes. He will bring to light what is hidden in darkness and will expose the motives of men's hearts' (1 Corinthians 4.5). The coming of Christ, which is the final spiritual transfiguration of the material cosmos, is the time at which the hidden purposes of every heart will be disclosed. At that time there will, the Bible suggests, be a great division among the free rational creatures that God has created. 'This is the verdict: Light has come into the world, but men loved darkness instead of light' (John 3.19). Christ comes as the light of the Spirit, flooding into the world. Those who love darkness, because they do not want their deeds to be manifest, flee from the light. But 'whoever lives by the truth comes into the light' (John 3.21).

This great division is symbolized by Paul as what is sometimes called 'the Rapture'. 'The Lord himself will come down from heaven with a loud command . . . and the dead in Christ will rise first. After that, we who are still alive and are left will be caught up with them in the clouds to meet the Lord in the air. And so we will be with the Lord for ever' (1 Thessalonians 4.16–17). In Paul's vision, all the dead, both in Hades and in Paradise, who desire to come to the light rise with Christ. Those who are on earth are also united to Christ, being changed and transfigured into spiritual form 'in the twinkling of an eye' (1 Corinthians 15.52). But for those who flee from the light, 'the Lord Jesus is revealed from heaven in blazing fire with his powerful angels. He will punish those who do not know God' (2 Thessalonians 1.7). God's love will be hateful and threatening to their chosen way, and 'they will be punished with everlasting destruction and shut out from the presence of the Lord' (2 Thessalonians 1.9). This fate is *olethron aionion apo prosopou kuriou* – literally, age-long destruction from the Lord's person. It is exclusion from the life of God.

Who is excluded and who is accepted? Some fundamentalists think that only explicit believers in Christ as their personal saviour are accepted. But that is not the biblical teaching. When Peter preached his first sermon to the Gentiles, he said, 'I now realize how true it is that God does not show favouritism but accepts men from every nation who fear him and do what is right' (Acts 10.34–35). That does not stop Peter preaching that Christ Jesus was anointed with the Holy Spirit and with power, that he was 'the one whom God appointed as judge of the living and the dead' (Acts 10.42), and that 'everyone who believes in him receives forgiveness of sins' (Acts 10.43). This seems to be the authentic Christian witness – not that only those who believe in Jesus are saved. All who try to do right are acceptable to God, but Jesus brings the power and presence of God near, and he shows and manifests what the judgement and mercy of God really is. The judgement before the throne of God that takes place at the resurrection is not a judgement that rescues Christians and condemns all others. It is a judgement on the deeds that free moral agents have performed. What the Christian gospel adds to this is that, in addition, Christ offers forgiveness to all who turn to him, whenever and wherever they do so. It is therefore entirely possible that all, even those who have done great evil, will in the end, at the last day, turn to Christ. Perhaps when the evil have served their time in the prison of Hades, and Hades itself is cast into the lake of fire and destroyed, there will be no one left who excludes themselves from the forgiveness of Christ. That must be a possibility for anyone who really believes that, though God is just, the overriding message of Christ is that God desires everyone to be saved, forgiven and united to the divine life. For what God desires must be possible.

The final resurrection is therefore the closure of the history of this physical universe, the full manifestation in time of the true spiritual light that was seen on earth in the face of Jesus the Christ, the spiritual transfiguration of all who turn towards the light, and the exclusion from the spiritual realm of those who reject the light. That exclusion remains a possibility and a warning. But so does the universal salvation of all, and Christians may rightly pray that everyone will be saved by their final acceptance of the free gift of salvation in Christ.

The symbolism of language about judgement

Since New Testament teaching on resurrection, the Day of Judgement and the return of Christ are so closely bound together, our way of interpreting that teaching should seek to be consistent and true to the character of the biblical text as a whole.

In reflecting on biblical teachings about the return of Christ in Chapter 3 of this book, three major points emerged. First, they are best understood by reference to Old Testament prophecies, which reveal the character of such teachings as largely concerned with present or imminent historical events, depicted in disguised and highly symbolic ways. There is also an 'end of time' level of meaning in these prophecies, so that particular historical events are seen as prototypes of the ultimate future – manifestations in time of an ultimate state that is beyond historical time.

Second, since they are symbolic, they should not be taken at face value ('literally'), but we need to seek the spiritual teaching that is expressed, but also partly hidden, by the symbols. It is very misleading to try to find an exact literal interpretation for every detail of a symbolic picture or parable. Thus when Jesus says that the person who does not obey his teachings will be 'like a foolish man who built his house on sand' (Matthew 7.26), it would be absurd to ask what sort of sand it was. The whole point of symbols is that they can be interpreted in many ways, as people bring their own unique insights to bear on them. The meaning we find will be partly a function of our own level of spiritual insight. It will not be just obvious to anyone who hears or reads the words. As Mark's Gospel records of Jesus, 'He did not say anything to them without using a parable. But when he was alone with his own disciples, he explained everything' (Mark 4.34). Spiritual insight is needed to understand a parable or symbol, and there is not just one 'correct' meaning that such parables or symbols have.

Third, most New Testament writers clearly expected the return of Christ to occur within their lifetimes, which it equally clearly did not. So what the Bible itself teaches, if we take it with full seriousness, is that particular factual beliefs and predictions in the Bible cannot be accepted as inerrant. On the contrary, they need to be revised in the light of new circumstances, so that a deeper significance may be found in them which may seem to contradict the literal sense, but which is in fact a deepening and expansion of the spiritual sense.

If we apply these three principles to biblical statements about the Day of Judgement, we might expect such statements to depict historical events as prototypes of the ultimate future, to be framed in highly symbolic forms, not literal descriptions, and to invite sublation, or the possibility of cancelling their straightforward sense in order to reveal a deeper spiritual sense.

Once we see these points, they become almost blindingly obvious. When the Old Testament prophets talk about judgement (bearing in mind that they did not have a very clear belief, if any belief at all, in resurrection), they talk about a 'Day of the Lord' – 'The Lord, the Lord Almighty, has a day of tumult and trampling and terror' (Isaiah 22.5). The reference is to the punishment of Jerusalem for her sins by foreign armies, a punishment which will be followed by repentance and renewal, but which is in itself a day of terror and destruction. These historical events prefigure the ultimate destruction of evil and the renewal of God's creation, but their immediate reference is to the political situation of Jerusalem.

By the time of the prophet Malachi, this view is developed further: 'Surely the day is coming; it will burn like a furnace. All the arrogant and every evildoer will be stubble' (Malachi 4.1). It is the enemies of Israel, the arrogant powers of military oppression, who will be destroyed. But Isaiah's warning must not be forgotten, that Israel herself will be punished for arrogance and evil. Judgement is not just for others; it is, terrifyingly, upon oneself. Nevertheless, 'for you who revere my name, the sun of righteousness will rise with healing in its wings' (Malachi 4.2).

The same prophet who can speak of the destruction of the whole earth ('he will make a sudden end of all who live in the earth' (Zephaniah 1.18), can immediately go on to say, 'I will give you honour and praise among all the peoples of the earth' (Zephaniah 3.20). The prophet Zephaniah begins by saying, '"I will sweep away everything from the face of the earth," declares the Lord . . . "when I cut off man from the face of the earth"' (Zephaniah 1.2–3). Yet he ends by saying, 'Then will I purify the lips of the peoples, that all of them may call on the name of the Lord and serve him shoulder to shoulder' (Zephaniah 3.9).

It is useless to try to make consistent the claim that all the earth's inhabitants will be destroyed, and the claim that they will all praise Israel and Israel's God. These are not literal predictions. They are poetic depictions of an ultimate destruction of evil and redemption of good.

The later prophets of the Old Testament are vital for understanding New Testament language about Jesus as the Judge of the world. Then we can see that the prophets were speaking of God's providential rule of history, the rise and fall of empires, and the destiny of the Jewish people. But they were doing so by using cosmic symbolism of the destruction of the earth, the darkening of the sun and the fall of the stars from heaven. And their whole point was to call the people to repentance, so that God could heal them and unite them to the divine.

Is the judgement of which the New Testament speaks not also predicting (correctly) divine judgement upon the Roman Empire, and upon the state of Israel, for their arrogance and refusal to repent? The historical events of the fall of the Roman Empire and the destruction of Israel as a nation represent a judgement on human obstinacy and indifference. The birth of the Church represents the rise of a community that offers light and healing to the world – or so the early Christians saw it. So talk of judgement and redemption, in the New Testament as in the Old, is talk of the inevitable destruction of military might and oppression, and the divine promise of a community of compassion and love. And, in the New Testament as in the Old, the cosmic symbolism in which this is described also refers – though certainly not literally – to 'the end of time', God's ultimate destruction of evil and redemption of good.

The book of Revelation is a text that can only be understood in these terms. The Beast with 'ten horns and seven heads' (Revelation 13.1) does not depict any actual animal living in the depths of the sea. It is a symbol for a political empire, almost certainly the Roman Empire, which is at war with the Christians – as it was in the early Christian years. Another beast, also called 'the false prophet', whose number is 666, is a symbol to represent the powers of false religion and apostasy. What the visionary writer is conveying is that the powers of political might and of religious fanaticism will rise up against faith in the love and compassion of God, so that they will almost seem to overcome it. But in the end they will be defeated, and 'the beast and the false prophet ... will be tormented day and night for ever and ever' (Revelation 20.10). These words are terrifying indeed, but we need to remember that the beast and the prophet are not individual beings. They are symbols for political and religious structures of oppression. Their 'torment' does not result in feelings of pain, because structures of oppression have no feelings. The symbol of endless and unceasing torment in a lake of fire and sulphur is a vivid depiction of utter destruction.

Millions of words have been wasted trying to read literal correspondences into these poetic passages, identifying people to whom '666' might correspond, or correlating symbols with contemporary events in order to show that the world is about to end. Sadly, all those words are futile. There were historical events to which the symbols corresponded, but they were long ago, in New Testament times, and we have lost the key to interpreting many of them. The world did not end then, and it is not any more likely to end now. The book of Revelation does not give a timetable by which we can tell when the world will end. It constructs a cosmic myth, of a war between monsters and angels, whose inner meaning is to depict the nature and consequences of greed, hatred and ignorance, and the triumph of divine love. It is like a dream – in fact it is a visionary dream – in which fantastic beings present in mysterious form the inner desires, fears and hopes of the dreamer. These fears and hopes apply to every time in human history, and they relate every time to the ultimate fulfilment of the world in God, when every evil will be consigned to fire, to destruction, and every good will be transfigured under the rule of God.

Is the God of the Bible vindictive?

One of the most characteristic uses of language throughout the Bible is hyperbole, the use of exaggeration to express emotional intensity. Hyperbole is often used by Jesus. When he says that you should pull out your eye if it offends you (Matthew 5.29); that it is harder for a rich man to enter the Kingdom than for a camel to go through a needle's eye (Matthew 19.24); that faith can cause mountains to move from one place to another (Matthew 17.20); and that you should never refuse anyone who wants to borrow from you (Matthew 5.42), few would hesitate to say that these are not literally true statements. They are certainly memorable. If we wanted to put a literal meaning onto the recommendation that you should pull your right eye out if it offends you, I suppose it would be something like: it is a very serious matter indeed to allow our senses to lead us into immorality, to acts which destroy relationships of trust and loyalty and trap us in egoistic conduct. The whole point, however, is that there is no one correct literal meaning of such statements. Their very excess leads us to reflect for ourselves on what is morally required of us, with regard to our senses of sight and touch.

Remembering that interpretation of texts must be consistent, the second half of the Matthean statement should be interpreted in a similar way. It says that it is 'better for you to lose one part of your body than for your whole body to go into hell' (*Gehenna*, the town dump). We are not literally going to be thrown onto a rubbish dump. Though there is no one correct literal meaning, the sense is clearly that the consequences of sin are extremely serious, and involve some sort of torment and destruction – perhaps the torment of feeling the harm we have done, and the painful destruction of the evil impulses that led to it. The hyperbole lies in the thought of being burned alive on a rubbish dump. The spiritual meaning is that our sins must be burned away and that they will lead to self-destruction if persisted in.

That this is the right sort of interpretation is confirmed by the clear New Testament teaching that 'God is love . . . and sent his Son as an atoning sacrifice for our sins' (1 John 4.8, 10). Jesus said, 'I did not come to judge the world, but to save it' (John 12.47). We are commanded to 'Love your enemies, do good to those who hate you' (Luke 6.27). The reason for this command is that we will thereby be imitating God – 'Be merciful, just as your Father is merciful' (Luke 6.36).

If we are to do good to those who hate us, God cannot do less. We have the clearest warrant to think that God will love, save and seek to do good to everyone, however evil. When we set this belief alongside the parables about *Gehenna*, the Outer Darkness and the lake of burning sulphur, we have to get an interpretation that is consistent with the unlimited love of God. Unending torment is not consistent with such love. Forms of punishment that consist in oppressors coming to realize in their own experience the harm they have caused to others, but which could lead to repentance and reform (even if they do not do so) are so consistent.

This is because doing good to those who have immersed themselves in hatred can be seen to consist in leading them to see the real consequences of evil, and purging their characters of all that leads them to evil. This may well be painful, but the pain will not be a penalty imposed by God. It will be the pain of seeking to escape from the crippling disease of sin. Such escape may not be achieved, and in that sense the torment may be unending. The soul, as long as it exists, remains in the torment it has created for itself.

Beneath all the hyperbole, that the Bible teaches some form of judgement is clear, that God will always desire to save the lost is clear, and that final salvation is accomplished by turning to the Christ, the eternal Word which was truly in Jesus, is clear. But we have no clear literal accounts of what exactly will happen and when.

Will there be an actual Day of Judgement? No, no more than there ever were actually six days of Creation. Yet, just as all things come from God, so all things return to God. The Judgement is what happens when creatures are exposed to the full reality of God – and that is to them either the light of the sun with healing in its wings, or the inextinguishable lake of fire.

When does that happen? Not on any particular day, in the history of this universe. But each individual life will come to that moment, in a form of existence in which the idea of countable, measurable time has ceased to make sense.

There is undoubtedly a great deal of talk of judgement in the Bible. It never takes the view that, whatever you do, everything will be all right, because God will simply overlook it. On the contrary, Jesus warns that 'Everyone will be salted with fire' (Mark 9.49), and he warns in a parable that when the master returns, he will kill the servant who beat others and got drunk, will severely beat the servant who did not obey the master's will, and will lightly beat the servant who did not fully know the master's will (Luke 12.42–48).

There will be varying degrees of punishment appropriate to the wrongs that people have done. Sometimes these are portrayed in the severest terms. Matthew records that those who do not feed the hungry or visit the sick 'will go away to eternal punishment – *kolasin aeonion*' (Matthew 25.46). The punishment may be that of knowing we have lost eternal life, of finding ourselves in 'outer darkness', far from light and joy. It will, in other words, not be torture inflicted by an angry God, but a self-inflicted agony of mind and spirit that will indeed cause 'weeping and gnashing of teeth' (Matthew 25.30).

It is important to see that these are not predictions, but warnings. They place before people the terrible possibility of the loss of life and joy, of mental torment and decisive, 'eternal', loss. But the whole point of them is to bring people to repentance. The Bible is not 'bad news' promising hellfire for almost everybody. It is 'good news', promising deliverance for all who repent.

The outer darkness, the burning rubbish pit of *Gehenna*, the lake of fire and sulphur, the gloom of *Sheol* – these are the limiting possibilities of a life which finally rejects God and is entrapped in its own egoistic desires. It seems quite unbiblical to give these symbols a literal interpretation – it is impossible to see how we could be in darkness, in a lake of flames and in a rubbish heap all at the same time. The Bible licenses a spiritual interpretation of such passages in many places. A typical one is in the song of Zechariah, in the Gospel of Luke. The prophet blesses God for, he says, with the birth of Jesus God has kept his promise 'to rescue us from the hand of our enemies, and to enable us to serve him without fear' (Luke 1.74). It is just false that the Jews were delivered from fear of Roman domination, and allowed to live in peace. The nation was destroyed by Rome within a generation. The song has to be taken in a spiritual, non-literal, sense, so that it is spiritual enemies from whom we are delivered, and the fear from which we are free is the fear of abandonment by God. In a similar way, statements about the destiny of the wicked are to be taken in a spiritual, non-literal sense. It is not that we will be tortured forever, in a temporal way. Rather, the point is that our spiritual loss is final and decisive, and – unless we turn to God – it will lead only to destruction.

But that 'unless' is never removed. How do we know that? Because God desires all to be saved, and what God desires can never become impossible. Statements of ultimate destruction are placed before us precisely in order that we should avoid them, and turn to the God who wills everyone to be saved. As we saw earlier, the book of Jonah captures the meaning of such warnings exactly when God commands the prophet Jonah to go to the city of Nineveh and say, 'Forty more days, and Nineveh will be overturned' (Jonah 3.4). Then the people of Nineveh repented, and God 'had compassion and did not bring upon them the destruction he had threatened' (Jonah 3.10). Jonah was angry that God had not carried out his prediction. But God made the point that, though it sounded like a prediction, it had really been a warning, and it achieved its point by bringing the people to repentance. No one in Nineveh was destroyed.

May we hope that no one will finally be excluded from the great 'Feast of the Lamb', from the barn where the wheat is stored, from the presence of God on his throne? I think the Bible licenses us to hope that, and to pray for that. While the book of Revelation records that the destiny of the wicked 'will be in the fiery lake of burning sulphur' (Revelation 21.8), it also says that in the end 'No longer will there be any curse' (Revelation 22.3). As in the prophet Zephaniah, while all have been destroyed, strangely they are still there, singing the praises of God. Perhaps what burns, what is burned wholly away until it is no more, is part of us, the part that clings to self-will. And what is raised to glory is the part of us, of all of us, that has been transfigured by grace into the form and image of Christ.

One of the most subtle temptations of those who think themselves righteous is vindictiveness, the desire to seek revenge, without considering the ultimate wellbeing of the one who is punished for wrongdoing. Fundamentalists may not mean to be vindictive. They may feel themselves to be compelled to believe in the endless tortures of hell, because they think that is a biblical teaching. There is good reason to think that it is not. The key biblical teaching is that we should do good to those who hate us, because God does good to those who hate God. This means that any punishment inflicted by God must be compatible with the ultimate good of those who are punished. There cannot be any form of divine punishment that does not allow for the ultimate good of those who are punished, even if that ultimate good can only be achieved by the destruction of tendencies that are deeply rooted in corrupted human wills.

There is judgement, there is fire, outer darkness, prison and the rubbish dump. Without the grace and forgiveness of God, we might never escape from the state of inner destruction and despair to which such metaphors point. Perhaps there are those who will not accept the forgiving love of God. If so, their ultimate end is destruction, for 'the wages of sin is death' (Romans 6.23), and when death itself is 'thrown into the lake of fire' (Revelation 20.14), they will be consumed by fire; they will cease to be.

But we must never despair of the salvation of any. We must continue to work and pray for that salvation, even of those who have died. We must never desire the harm of anyone, and we must never believe that God desires such final unredeemable harm. That seems to be the clear entailment of the central New Testament teaching that God is unlimited love.

Some implications for interpreting the Bible

Nevertheless there are elements in the New Testament that do seem to be vindictive, and this raises a major question of interpretation. How are we to reconcile vindictiveness and unlimited love? I do not think anyone can. Either vindictiveness must be sublated by unlimited love or unlimited love must be sublated by vindictiveness. It is logically possible that the teaching of unlimited love could be sublated by the superior insight that God is vindictive. This is what fundamentalists claim. Despite the many statements that God wills to save all, that all will be forgiven who turn to Christ, and that love always seeks the good even of enemies, superior moral value is given by fundamentalists to the statement that Christ 'treads the winepress of the fury of the wrath of God Almighty' (Revelation 19.15).

What is being said is that the teaching of the unlimited love of God is cancelled by a deeper insight that God's anger will be poured out mercilessly on the wicked, who will be 'thrown into the lake of fire' (Revelation 20.15). The insight is, I suppose, that God's justice requires a harsh, even an infinite, penalty for sin. If people do not repent, but persist in sin, they deserve to suffer forever. Vindictive justice triumphs over mercy in the end. The problem is that this does not even seem to come up to the moral standard of the Old Testament rule of 'eye for eye' (Exodus 21.24). It asks for the whole body, tortured forever, for an eye. Many fundamentalists at least have the grace to say that they do not understand the justice of God, but simply bow to the divine revelation that this incredibly harsh treatment is what God requires.

But that is precisely the question. Is this really divine revelation? It is in the Bible. That is to say, there are specific sentences in the Bible that speak of vindictive divine justice. But also in the Bible is the teaching that God is love, and that love cares for the good of all, however wicked. One of these teachings must be sublated by the other. The only question is: which?

The principle of sublation is well established in the Bible. The whole teaching of the Sermon on the Mount is a sublation of parts of Jewish law. The prophet Ezekiel says, 'The soul who sins is the one who will die. The son will not share the guilt of the father' (Ezekiel 18.20). Thus he sublated the barbarous practice of killing whole families for the sins of the father – as in the case of Achan, whose sons and daughters, oxen and asses and sheep were all destroyed for his sin (Joshua 7.24–26). The doctrine of the resurrection of the dead is a sublation of the Psalmist's cry that 'It is not the dead who praise the Lord' (Psalm 115.17). There are many other cases of sublation in the Bible. We simply cannot take biblical statements in isolation and suppose that they are to be accepted just as they stand. We must interpret them in the light of the whole biblical teaching.

Why should the Bible be like this? Why should it not just consist of wholly adequate and true statements, without any development of human understanding? The fact that the Bible was written by many people over many centuries, with many varied and often developing views, shows something very significant about the nature of biblical revelation. Revelation is truly given by God, inspiring, 'breathing over' human minds and imaginations. But it is received by fallible, limited human beings in particular cultures, and those limitations often need to be corrected and amplified by later revelation. Revelation includes a difficult, often lengthy, process of reflection and interpretation. We do not just passively receive it, and assent. God calls us to reflect on it, pray over it, and attend to the judgements of many different people in different situations. The acceptance of revelation often means that we should be hesitant about our interpretation, listen carefully to the interpretations of others, and always try to allow it to extend and deepen our spiritual insight (not just contradict it).

So reading the Bible as God's revelation may involve a good deal of suspension of judgement, a readiness to learn from others of differing views, and a concern to take our understanding of revelation to new levels, under the guidance of the Spirit. Revelation is more like a living relationship to God, who speaks through the words of the Bible, but often asks us to see them in the light of the full revelation in Jesus Christ, and an increasing understanding of that revelation as the community of the Church continues to seek the guidance of the Spirit.

Within the Bible itself such a process is set out, as a model for us to follow. The Bible makes it clear that the apostles continually misinterpreted the teachings of Jesus. Jesus revealed the truth, but the apostles just did not get it. Luke reports that many people 'thought that the kingdom of God was going to appear at once' (Luke 19.11), and Jesus had to correct them. Two disciples on the road to Emmaus, after Jesus' death, said, 'we had hoped that he was the one who was going to redeem Israel' (Luke 24.21). Again Jesus had to instruct them what the redemption of Israel meant. The disciples argued about who would be greatest in the Kingdom, and Jesus had to tell them that 'he who is least among you all – he is the greatest' (Luke 9.48). James and John wanted to call down fire from heaven on a Samaritan village that would not receive Jesus. But Jesus rebuked them and said, 'You do not know what kind of spirit you are of' (Luke 9.55; some manuscripts only).

There are many other examples in the Gospels of human misunderstandings or limited understandings of Jesus and his message. In the book of Acts and the letters in the New Testament, records of such misunderstandings continue. Peter himself on some occasions refused to eat with Gentiles, and was confronted on the matter by Paul (Galatians 2.11–13). James the brother of Jesus apparently tried to make all Christians obey the Jewish law (Galatians 2.12) – which was later seen to be an unduly limited application of Jesus' teachings. And most obviously many early Christians continued to think the Kingdom might come at any moment, and had to revise their ideas as time passed.

Within the pages of the New Testament the apostles did not fully understand the teachings of Jesus or its implications. There is no reason to suppose that they suddenly came to a full and unrevisable understanding as soon as the New Testament canon was complete (the canon in its present form is first attested to by Athanasius in AD 367). The implication is that limited understandings of Jesus' teaching are present in the Bible. But there are also powerful statements of Jesus' teaching in the light of which those limited understandings can be seen for what they are.

Some passages in the New Testament depict God as a God of vindictive justice (that is, a form of retributive justice which insists on paying a penalty for wrong-doing, without regard to the future possible good of the offender). The question is whether this is a limited understanding of Jesus' teaching about the love of God and the necessity of repentance. Jesus himself talks of punishment, of fire and of exclusion from the Kingdom. That is not in question – he never teaches that God will ignore wrong-doing. The question is whether God, in the teaching of Jesus, will ever close the possibility of repentance, make it impossible for creatures to turn to God in mourning for their sins, or will impose a punishment that has no hope of ever bringing the guilty to the possibility of salvation.

Jesus said, 'love your enemies, do good to them, and lend to them without expecting to get anything back . . . and you will be sons of the Most High, because he is kind to the ungrateful and wicked. Be merciful, just as your Father is merciful' (Luke 6.35–36). This seems to me to be decisive. God is kind and merciful to the selfish. God will despair of no one. God will continue to love even those who have made themselves the enemies of God. Such a God can never close the door of repentance. Such a God cannot be vindictive, but when God executes retributive justice, God will always keep open and even point the way to the possibility of repentance, so that even retributive justice is never solely punitive.

Passages like the one in Paul's second letter to the Thessalonians: 'the Lord Jesus is revealed from heaven in blazing fire with his powerful angels. He will punish those who do not know God and do not obey the gospel of our Lord Jesus. They will be punished with everlasting destruction and shut out from the presence of the Lord' (2 Thessalonians 1.7–9), show a very limited understanding of the love of Christ. Paul's thought at this point is vindictive in so far as it threatens others with eternal exclusion from God, without hope of repentance, and thinks of Jesus as a vengeful warrior.

A sensitive reading of the passage may emphasize that 'not knowing

God' and 'not obeying the gospel' are not matters of simply not believing there is a God, or not living up to some rule of the Church. They apply only to people who turn away from God, from all apprehensions of goodness they have, and from selfless love of others. Such people exclude themselves from the presence of God, and their eternal destruction is the final disintegration of their personalities as they are consumed by their own hatreds, passions and obsessions. It is always possible for them to repent, in which case the fire of destruction is transfigured for them into the fire of divine love that will purify them for eternal life. It is, as many theologians have said, the same fire, appearing to those who reject God as punitive, but to those who love God as light and warmth. This same Paul was to write that 'God has bound all men over to disobedience so that he may have mercy on them all' (Romans 11.32). That is the higher, sublating insight – God will burn all selfishness away, and it will be excluded forever from the divine presence. But God will never cease to love those God has created, or make it impossible for them (even if as by fire, 1 Corinthians 3.15) to fulfil what God wants, their ultimate sharing in the divine life.

Vindictiveness is present in the Bible. It is caused by a limited understanding of the punitive justice of God, which has not fully appreciated Jesus' teaching of the unlimited love and mercy of God. It is decisively overcome by the cross, which shows God going to the uttermost limits to reconcile the whole world to the divine being. So what the Bible really teaches cannot be found in isolated texts, taken as completely true just as they stand. That could actually be misleading. Some texts are sublated by others, and the only question at issue is which ones are sublated, and which ones do the sublating. In view of this, it turns out that what the Bible really teaches is that human understanding of divine revelation is very often limited. The example of the apostles, who again and again failed to understand Jesus, is plain. But that limited understanding can be expanded and deepened by reflection on the life and teachings of Jesus, and what that implies when thought through. The Bible teaches that we must always seek greater understanding, more thoroughgoing application of Jesus' teaching to our own lives, and a more sensitive spiritual interpretation of its diverse and complex contents. The Bible teaches us to go on a spiritual search of self-discovery and deepening understanding of the revelation of God in Jesus. That will never be obtained by simply repeating a highly selective set of texts, read in isolation, while twisting or ignoring the meaning of other texts which put them in question. It may be obtained, always partially and provisionally, by wide and instructed reading of the Bible, and by prayerful reflection, discussion, and attention to the insights of others. It is in that way that 'the holy Scriptures . . . are able to make you wise for salvation through faith in Christ Jesus' (2 Timothy 3.15).

◆ 10 ◆

Interpreting Biblical Teaching about the Moral Law

Nowhere is a sensitive and careful reading of the Bible more important than in matters of morality. It is on such practical issues as sexual conduct, marriage, divorce, war and peace and social justice that fundamentalists appeal to the Bible in a way that turns out to be extremely selective and inconsistent. Fundamentalists often claim to derive moral certainties from Scripture. But as I shall show, what they claim can rarely be supported by the Bible, and it is often undermined by what the Bible teaches about the moral law.

The clearest case of this is the central ethical teaching of Jesus himself.

It would be widely agreed that this is to be found in the Sermon on the Mount (Matthew 5—7). It is truly remarkable how many people have been able to read that text, and believe that Jesus taught that the Jewish 'law', the Torah, should be abandoned. That is what I was taught as a new Christian, and it was some years before I realized that it is the exact opposite of the truth.

Matthew prefaces the Sermon, however, with an absolutely clear statement that the Torah is not to be abandoned until the end of time, 'until everything is accomplished' (Matthew 5.18). The Torah (the Hebrew word is best translated as 'Teaching', but the New Testament always calls it 'the Law') in its written form consists of all the commands and ordinances from Genesis to Deuteronomy. It is supplemented by the oral Torah, which was passed on verbally and was written down much later in the Babylonian Talmud, perhaps the most important document for present-day Judaism. There are a great many commands in the written Torah, and Jewish tradition puts the number at 613. Some are very important – like not killing unlawfully. Some seem fairly trivial – like not boiling a kid in its mother's milk. But orthodox Jews keep the whole Torah, because they believe it is given by God.

Many fundamentalists believe that Jesus abandoned the Law, or at least abandoned most of it. But Matthew reports that Jesus said: 'Anyone who breaks one of the least of these commandments and teaches others to do the same will be called least in the kingdom of heaven' (Matthew 5.19). On this account, Jesus was a totally orthodox Jew. He taught his disciples that even the most trivial commandment should be kept, until the end of time.

Some fundamentalist commentators have tried to argue that Jesus only said that the Law should be kept 'until everything is accomplished'. But, they say, everything was accomplished at the time of Jesus' death and resurrection, so that the Torah loses force then. But this interpretation is wildly implausible. The text actually says that nothing will disappear from the Law 'until heaven and earth disappear' (Matthew 5.18), and that certainly did not happen at Jesus' resurrection. What is being said is that the Torah is simply not to be abandoned.

The amazing fact is that the vast majority of Christians – including fundamentalists – ignore this clear command completely. Not only do they abandon Torah, they usually do not even know or care exactly what commands are in the Law. Yet according to Matthew, Jesus says that anyone who even relaxes the least of these 613 commandments will be least in the Kingdom. Even the iotas and dots of the Hebrew text, the tiniest little marks in the written script, must be preserved and observed. There could hardly be a stronger statement of punctilious legalism than this!

The reason many Christians reject this belief is that they simply cannot believe Jesus was a legalist. But Matthew, and therefore the Bible, plainly states that he was. Putative literalists are here caught in an inescapable dilemma. Either what Matthew says – that Jesus taught Torah should be kept in the fullest rigour – is false (so there are definitely false statements about ethics in the New Testament), or Christians do, and should, disobey the clear moral teaching of Jesus. Either way, it follows that some moral injunctions in the Bible, even if they are said to be issued by Jesus himself, are in fact not binding upon Christians. This is a principle with tremendous implications for the moral authority of the Bible.

Do the principles of spiritual meaning and sublation help here? They certainly do; and indeed they provide the only acceptable way of preserving a high sense of biblical authority with intellectual honesty and rigour. When we say that the statement that the Son of Man will come on the clouds is symbolic, we mean that it does not speak of a man flying through the air. It expresses the belief that at the end of history Jesus will be seen by all to express the presence and power of God, and that the eternal divine Wisdom (*Logos*) which is fully present in him will unite all human lives which assent to share in the divine life. So the statement that even the dots of Torah remain in force until the end of time can be taken symbolically to express the belief that the will of God for human fulfilment, truly expressed in the giving of Torah to the Jews, is unshakeable, and will always demand our total commitment. But the command that we should actually keep all the rules of Torah is sublated by statements like Paul's that 'The entire law is summed up in a single command: "Love your neighbour as yourself"' (Galatians 5.14). And that is a more profound understanding than one that thinks Christian obedience consists simply in keeping a list of rules, however long.

Christians usually see this point very readily. But they do not always see that the principles of spiritual meaning and of sublation that are so necessary at this point need to be applied throughout the Bible. And they do not always feel the force of the fact that, since the first century, Christians have not hesitated to disobey the literal commands of Jesus for what they felt to be good enough reasons.

Arguments about the moral law in the early Church

A great revolution in Christian belief occurred in the very first genera-tion of believers. In that generation a Jewish Messianic sect – which is what the disciples of Jesus were – turned into an almost completely Gentile universal Church. Biblical scholars disagree about whether Jesus is likely to have foreseen this development. In Matthew's Gospel, Jesus says, 'I was sent only to the lost sheep of Israel' (Matthew 15.24). At the Last Supper, Jesus said to the apostles, 'you' will 'sit on thrones, judging the twelve tribes of Israel' (Luke 22.30). It sounds as if Jesus was adopting the traditional Messianic role of calling Israel back to her true vocation, and of reuniting the twelve tribes of Israel in a renewed Davidic Kingdom. Matthew's claim that Jesus taught rigorous obedi-ence to Torah is certainly consistent with this view.

My own view is that this is probably correct, but that Jesus also fore-saw the rejection of his mission to Israel, and the subsequent coming into being of a radically new religious form of life, a 'new Israel'. Nevertheless it seems extremely unlikely that Jesus himself taught that the Torah would be given up in this new Israel. The strongest piece of evidence for this conclusion is that all the apostles who had known Jesus continued to keep Torah and to teach that it should be kept. If Jesus had taught renunciation of Torah, they would surely have renounced it, not opposed its renunciation, as they did. It was Paul, who had never met Jesus, who campaigned for freedom from Torah, and the New Testament leaves us in no doubt that the apostles resisted his campaign.

Acts 10.9–16 records that the apostle Peter had a vision of a sheet descending from heaven filled with all sorts of meats. He said, 'I have never eaten anything impure or unclean', but was told not to consider anything unclean that God had declared clean. This is a clear withdrawal of the Torah regulations about unclean foods, on what Peter took to be divine authority. But it was not the authority of Jesus. It is obvious that Peter had not been told by Jesus that all foods were clean, or he would not have been surprised by the vision, which apparently had to occur no less than three times before he was convinced. Indeed, Peter felt the need to excuse even his meeting with a Gentile, the centurion Cornelius, saying, 'You are well aware that it is against our law for a Jew to associate with a Gentile or visit him. But God has shown me that I should not call any man impure or unclean' (Acts 10.28). It seems that before that point Peter had been, if anything, overscrupulously Jewish. He and the Christians with him were certainly amazed when the Holy Spirit was poured out on some Gentiles (Acts 10.45). In view of this, it is hard to deny that the disciples of Jesus were at first rigorous observers of Torah and of Jewish separateness.

Arguments continued for some time after this, and Acts 15 records what is sometimes called the first Council of the Church in Jerusalem. There was a debate in which Peter, on the basis of his vision, supported Paul's request that the Gentile Christians should not be required to keep Torah. The very fact that there was debate shows that most disciples felt that being Jewish, and keeping Torah, were essential to Christian belief. In the end, a letter was sent to the Gentile Christians in Antioch. It was in effect a compromise, requiring Gentile believers still to keep at least some of the Jewish food laws ('abstain . . . from blood', Acts 15.29), but releasing them from almost all other obligations of Torah. Jewish Christians, however, were to continue to be observers of Torah (Acts 21.21–24).

What is happening here is that Jewish rigorism, taught by Jesus to his disciples, is being sublated as a result of the amazing success of Paul's preaching to Gentiles, by Paul's great discovery of the gift of salvation by pure grace, by the threefold vision of Peter, and by the undeniable fact of the gift of the Holy Spirit to Gentiles. These things led to an increasing realization that salvation is by faith in Jesus, not by obedience to Torah. Gentiles and Jews alike shall be saved 'through the grace of our Lord Jesus' (Acts 15.11). Here is a dramatic new perception, brought about by new spiritual experiences and by deeper reflection on the inner meaning of Jesus' own teaching. The apostles realize, only then, that they are saved by the love of God poured out in the person of Jesus, not by obedience to law, and that God's love is for all humanity, not for a limited group. The apostles grow in understanding, but their more limited views remain in the New Testament as well as their later realizations. It is as though Scripture is teaching us that we can never rest content with the ancient perceptions of others, however exalted those others may be. We need to be sensitive to new spiritual experiences, and to be ready to deepen and extend our understanding of ancient teachings, as we come to see what is implicit in them but needs to be made explicit by continued debate and reflection.

So the teaching of Jesus about obedience to Torah was a teaching given to Jews, whose inner meaning was that legal righteousness is not enough. The five 'Great Antitheses' of the Sermon on the Mount (Matthew 5.21–48) make this clear. Jesus says, 'You have heard . . .', and adds, 'But I tell you . . .'. In each case he does not rescind the law, but presses its demand to the limit. Not only should we not kill; we should not be angry. Not only should we not commit adultery; we should not look lustfully. Not only should we not swear falsely; we must be absolutely truthful. Not only should we conform to the demands of strict fairness; we must seek the good of those who harm us. Not only should we love our neighbour; we must also love our enemies.

What matters is the attitudes of the heart, attitudes of non-vindictiveness, self-control, honesty, mercy and benevolence. That is the innermost meaning of Torah, and that meaning can survive the abandonment of the Law's specific regulations. When the 'old dispensation' comes to an end, and the Kingdom is opened up to the Gentiles, we are in a totally new situation, and we have to ask anew, 'What is appropriate for non-Jews? Must they become Jews?' The answer to this question was not obvious to the apostles. James, the brother of Jesus, who was to be head of the church in Jerusalem, thought they should. He sent men to Antioch to call for circumcising Gentile converts, and his men even frightened Peter into drawing back from eating with Gentiles for a while (Galatians 2.11–14).

But Paul won the day with his teaching that 'Christ is the end of the law' (Romans 10.4). The Jamesian compromise, of the full Torah for Jewish Christians, and Kosher meat only for Gentile Christians, was itself rescinded. Christians now do not worry about eating Kosher meat. They have accepted Paul's teaching that 'There is neither Jew nor

Greek, slave nor free, male nor female, for you are all one in Christ Jesus' (Galatians 3.28). They have rejected Jesus' teaching that Torah should be kept to the last detail. They have rejected the teaching of Peter and James, the chief apostles and leaders of the earliest Church, that they should eat Kosher meat. Why?

The answer is of the utmost importance for biblical interpretation, and must be carefully considered. Jesus' teaching was taken to be in a restricted and now obsolete context – it was given to Jews before the destruction of the second Temple. Jesus' words could not be ignored, but a new context requires a spiritual interpretation (that is, we need not keep these rules literally, but we must strive for the attitudes which always underlay them, and constituted their inner meaning).

The apostolic teaching that the main food laws should be kept was gradually seen to be an unsatisfactory compromise, which there was little reason to continue. Once most of Torah has gone, the whole lot may as well be rescinded. The Torah could be seen as fulfilled, completed and brought to an end in Christ, and a clean break is in order – and such a break even helps to emphasize the fulfilment and completion of Torah in Jesus.

What is important is that neither of these moves was on the authority of Jesus or the apostles. They express later claims that a new context requires that for good reason a literal interpretation must be sublated (negated yet completed) by a spiritual interpretation. Once again we see clearly that modern Christian belief cannot reasonably be required to be identical with some particular stage of apostolic or biblical belief. Who decided this? It was the Church, the body of Christian believers, who, hoping that they were being guided by the Holy Spirit, but not without debate and argument, moved on to new interpretations of the biblical revelation.

Jesus as the end of the Law

Paul taught that the least of the commandments *should* be relaxed, thereby seeming directly to contradict the words of Jesus in Matthew 5.19. But a wider view sees that Jesus in fact insisted upon the spiritual meaning of Torah in its full rigour – to such an extent that only the hope of forgiveness and the grace of God could free humans from an oppressive sense of inevitable moral failure. It is possible, though I do not think it very plausible, that Jesus himself, in the crucial passage in Matthew 5.17–19, was speaking in a purely symbolic way. He says that the Law will remain in place 'till heaven and earth disappear . . . and everything is accomplished'. Perhaps he is using the symbols of the apocalypse here, and thinking of the end of the age of Israel and the accomplishing of his own task in his death and resurrection, after which Torah could be rescinded. The reason I find that implausible is the existence of a parallel passage in Luke's Gospel, which reads: 'It is easier for heaven and earth to disappear than for the least stroke of a pen to drop out of the Law' (Luke 16.17). It is very difficult to see that as apocalyptic prophecy.

If it were, however, we would not be disobeying Jesus in abandoning Torah. Some Christians might feel more comfortable with that. But the consequence for our interpretation is much the same. The first Christians all kept Torah, and only gradually, after much debate, began to abandon it. Finally, however, they did abandon it altogether, and at that point they had to give a symbolic interpretation to the commandments (they could not just ignore them), and see them as somehow sublated in the person of Christ.

Symbolic interpretations of apparently direct moral commands are frequent in the teaching of Jesus. 'If your right eye causes you to sin, gouge it out' (Matthew 5.29) sounds like a moral command. But anyone who took it literally would be considered deranged. The early theologian Origen is said to have castrated himself in obedience to this command. But that earned him the condemnation of the Church, not its approval! The symbolic interpretation would have to be something like: even seemingly trivial attitudes, which seem to do others no harm (like looking lustfully at a woman), may cut the heart off from God, and should be avoided. Certainly, looking at another's wife lustfully, or with a view to tempting her to have intercourse, undermines human relationships, and is therefore incompatible with true love of God.

This gives rise to a twofold problem. Are all commands to be interpreted symbolically? And how do we know what the symbolic interpretation really is? The Bible does not resolve these problems for us. It does not tell us which commands are symbolic. The command to gouge our eyes out obviously is, because it is so extreme. We cannot imagine anyone of supreme compassion and loving-kindness, as Jesus was, telling us to do that. But what about the command not to resist an evil person? (Matthew 5.39). Does that mean that if we see someone torturing a baby, we must let them carry on without trying to stop them? Early theologians, including most notably Augustine, wrestled with this question, and they had to come to a hard decision for themselves (Augustine decided you could defend others from evil, but not yourself). The Bible did not decide it for them. My own view on this issue is that we can defend ourselves and others, and our property, from unjust attack. But we must not be vindictive, and must always be concerned for the long-term good even of those who are evil. That is a difficult moral teaching to put into practice, but it is a long way from a literal interpretation of Jesus' words.

How are we deciding on an interpretation here? Well, we are taking the words seriously – we do not just cast them aside. But we are seeking to make them consistent with an understanding of what a love that cares for the good of all concerned, would require. For Jesus said, 'do to others what you would have them do to you, for this sums up the Law and the Prophets' (this is generally called 'the Golden Rule', Matthew 7.12). That sounds like a summary of his moral teaching, and a test we can apply to particular commands to see if they are to be taken symbolically, and what they might then mean. Personal judgement is still needed. I would want people to protect me if I was attacked, but what it is permissible for them to do is a matter for debate. Jesus' words prevent me from saying, 'Just blast the attacker out of existence; do not consider him at all.' But they do not tell me exactly what to do. The best we can do is to try to let our minds be formed by the person of Christ, and then decide as humanely and wisely as we can.

Virtually all Christians take Jesus' command to gouge right eyes out as symbolic. Most take his command not to resist evil people, or to give to *anyone* who asks, as symbolic. Some insist that his command not to swear on oath (Matthew 5.34) is to be taken literally, but again most think this is a symbolic expression recommending total truthfulness. Many Christians take literally Jesus' statement, 'anyone who marries [a] divorced woman commits adultery' (Matthew 5.32). This would make remarriage after divorce immoral. There are, however, very powerful reasons for not interpreting it in this sense.

First, in Jesus' time, a woman who was divorced at the whim of her husband was in a very difficult social situation. She would have to live with her parents, and was a virtual outcast. Now Jesus had a special care for the outcast, so it is hard to think he would have taught anything that made the situation of such people worse, by virtually forbidding remarriage.

Second, there is no way a prohibition of marriage to divorced people can be supported by the Golden Rule. I might well want someone to marry me if I am divorced, and care for the well-being of all concerned seems to suggest that remarriage is better than a life of solitude for someone who does not desire it.

Third, this is clearly not a literal statement in any case. Remarriage was perfectly legal in Jesus' society, and to marry a divorced woman does not destroy a marriage, as adultery might be held to do. There is no longer any marriage to destroy. So this is not literally adultery.

Fourth, the Jewish Law permits the divorce of wives for a number of reasons, and if Jesus began the Sermon by saying that the least letter of the Law had to be obeyed, he could hardly have been revoking that permission. Instead, he was pointing to the deeper spiritual principle it embodied, and encouraging his hearers to live up to it – but not revoking the Law.

So the statement must be symbolic. If so, its interpretation will depend upon its consistency with the Golden Rule, with the general character of Jesus as a wise and compassionate teacher, and upon our own wisdom, sensitivity and humanity.

The context of the remark is Jesus' comment on the prohibition of adultery. Adultery was conceived as taking another man's wife. Jesus' general technique in the Sermon on the Mount is to make these rules more rigorous, so we would expect him to say that tempting another man's wife to infidelity, or desiring her in a way that might lead to infidelity, is 'adultery in the heart'. And so he does. It is a natural extension of this thought to say that men who divorce their wives for trivial reasons treat them as though they were adulteresses ('makes her an adulteress'). Likewise, anyone who causes a man to divorce his wife in order to marry her himself (not anyone who marries an abandoned and divorced woman out of compassion for her situation) commits adultery. The wrong in each case is intentionally to destroy a marriage relationship, a relationship of love between two people. So the underlying moral teaching is that it is wrong to destroy relationships of loyalty and love. Such an interpretation is consistent with the principles of interpretation just outlined, and avoids the problems of inhumanity and insensitivity that would adhere to any literal prohibition of remarriage in the Jewish society of Jesus' day.

My conclusion is that virtually all the particular moral commands of Jesus are to be interpreted symbolically, and that their underlying meaning is always a spelling-out of particular instances falling under the Golden Rule, of loving your neighbour as yourself. As Paul writes, 'he who loves his fellow-man has fulfilled the law. The commandments . . . are summed up in this one rule: "Love your neighbour as yourself"' (Romans 13.8–9).

A more important point is that all these rules are sublated in the person of Christ, who is 'the end of the law' (Romans 10.4). That word 'end' has the double meaning of 'termination' and 'fulfilment or goal', and Jesus is both the termination and the fulfilling goal of Torah, and of all specific moral commands.

Jesus as the fulfilment of the Law

Jews see Torah, not as a set of inflexible laws, but as the living and dynamic presence of God to Israel. The commandments and ordinances are set in the context of the history of the Patriarchs, and this ensures that they cannot be lifted out of the text as abstract rules, but belong to a specific history of God interacting with the covenant people. In subsequent Rabbinic thought, the commands of Torah are subject to continued debate, argument and reinterpretation, as they are seen in new historical situations, and in the light of new perceptions of the purposes of Israel's God. They are like precedents for legal decision-making, not like inflexible rules that can never be amended.

Torah is sometimes personalized in Rabbinic thought, and identified with *chokmah*, the eternal wisdom of God upon which the world itself is founded, which is the archetype of creation and the continuing presence of God among the covenant people. When, in the prologue to John's Gospel, Jesus is identified with the *Logos* or 'Word' of God, he is identified with *chokmah*, the divine wisdom. Jesus is thus the living Torah, the Torah enfleshed, perfectly expressed in a human life. The inner meaning of Torah is complete obedience to the will of God, so that all life is sanctified and devoted to the divine presence. There is a Rabbinic saying that if ever Torah were perfectly followed, the Messiah would come. Christians believe precisely that in Jesus Torah was perfectly followed, and the Messiah did come, for he was the Messiah. For Christians, the Messiah is the one in whom Torah is brought to perfection in a human life.

Such a thing is humanly impossible, since 'all have sinned and fall short of the glory of God'. It is by a divine miracle that the human life of Jesus is free from sin, from all egoistic attachment, from greed, hatred and delusion. The miracle is that this life is so filled with the Spirit of God that it is inseparable from the divine in love. It is a miracle, an extraordinary act of God, but not an absurdity. All human lives are created so that their fulfilment lies in being channels of the divine Spirit. But humans have turned aside from this destiny through generations of attachment to egoistic desire, and without extraordinary divine help they cannot escape such attachment.

The raising of Jesus' humanity to unity with the divine is a natural human condition, though it has become impossible because of sin. In this respect human destiny is to become as Jesus was – Ephesians 3.19 prays that 'you may be filled to the measure of all the fulness of God', which is precisely what is said of Jesus – 'God was pleased to have all his fulness dwell in him' (Colossians 1.19). We are to become as Jesus was and is, when we attain to 'the whole measure of the fulness of Christ' (Ephesians 4.13).

This is a truly extraordinary thought, that we are to become like Christ. But is Jesus not our Lord and God, and so eternally and dimensionally unlike us? In John's Gospel he is seen as the eternal *Logos* made flesh. That *Logos* is said to be 'the true light that gives light to every man' (John 1.9), but in Jesus it actually came 'into the world'. It was left to later theologians to develop these rather cryptic hints, and state that we are to be of a similar nature to God (*homoi ousios*), to be filled with the divine fullness. But Jesus was of exactly the same nature as God (*homo ousios*); he *was* the divine fullness in human form.

The difference is that we are distinct individuals who, if and when we freely turn to God, can be filled with the divine life, so that we can say, 'I no longer I live, but Christ lives in me' (Galatians 2.20). We can distinguish our selves, which can turn and which have turned from God, and which can turn back to God again, from the Christ who lives out the divine life in us, so far as we are open to that life. The guiding principle of the Christian life is 'Christ in you, the hope of glory' (Colossians 1.27), the free subordination of self to the life of power and fulfilment which is the life of the risen Christ.

Jesus, so John's Gospel in particular seems to say, was not a distinct individual who could fall away from God, and whose life was to be filled by a power not his own which could bring it to fulfilment. Jesus was, from the first moment of his life and throughout it without any separation, the human form and expression of the wisdom of God. So it could be that in him Torah, the teaching of God-filled life by the personal presence of God, was fully embodied in a human person. Jesus' life and presence is now Torah, the teaching of God, the one who educates us in the divine life, who draws us towards the fullness of God.

Because Jesus lives within us, Torah is fully internalized in us, in so far as we share the mind of Christ (cf. 1 Corinthians 2.16, 'we have the mind of Christ'). What sublates Torah, for Christians, is the person of Jesus, the one who fully embodies divine wisdom and love, and who becomes our 'inner teacher' as our lives are shaped by his presence within us. Christians no longer appeal to external rules, not even if they are in the Bible. They rather seek to let Christ live more fully in them, allowing their minds to be shaped by the divine wisdom and love.

How can Jesus live within millions of his devotees, and how can we know that it is Jesus, and not some counterfeit, who 'lives within'? Obviously it is not the human person of Jesus who lives within. In a remarkable passage in Romans 8.9–11, Paul uses the expressions, 'the Spirit of God', 'the Spirit of Christ', 'Christ', and 'the Spirit of him who raised Jesus from the dead' immediately one after the other to refer to the One who gives us life by 'living in' us. We can readily see how the Spirit of God comes to be named the Spirit of Christ. The Spirit fills the life of Christ, shapes it into the fullness of the divine image, and frees it from the power of death. So the divine Spirit is known as the Spirit who takes the pattern of perfected humanity, embodies it fully and continuously in Jesus, and shapes it partially and intermittently in us.

That pattern itself, the archetype of humanity, is the eternal Word, who took human form in Jesus, but who is not limited to that form. Since the Word took form in Jesus, the Word has a character that is to be recognized as expressed in the gospel portraits of Jesus, so that it can be called simply 'Christ'. So it is possible to say 'Christ lives in you', meaning that the eternal Word which was enfleshed in Jesus is the archetype and pattern of our lives, and that Word is taking shape within us day by day. And we can also say, 'the Spirit lives in you', when referring to the dynamic power which shapes that pattern in us.

On one model of the relationship of God and humanity, God remains always other, different, transcendent and in personal relation to us. The will of God is expressed in the written and oral Torah, and humanity's proper vocation is to obey that law with reverence and devotion. The Christian gospel does not deny or mean to dishonour this view in any way. But it adds to it something of tremendous significance for Christians. God, known as dynamic Spirit and archetypal Word, is now seen as immanent within the human self. As such, the will of God becomes an inner power for creative life, and humanity's vocation is to let that power act freely and fully. 'Faith', in the profound sense of being inwardly empowered by the life of Christ, replaces 'obedience to law', a purely human striving to obey God's will.

Of course obedience to law requires faith, faith that God gave the Law, loyalty to God and hope for the triumph of God's purposes. But faith in Christ requires something more – it requires an inner turning of the heart to God, so that the divine Spirit, which was in Christ and which forms us in the pattern of Christ, might work in us what we cannot, might place the divine love itself within our hearts, as the true centre of our being.

This inner uniting of divine and human is the characteristic tone of Christian faith. For Christians it fulfils the promise of the prophet Jeremiah, that there should be a 'new covenant', of which God says, 'I will put my law in their minds and write it on their hearts' (Jeremiah 31.33). It is in that sense that 'Christ is the end of the law' (Romans 10.4). Written regulations are replaced by an inner shaping by the Spirit into the fullness of Christ.

'Christ in us' is the spiritual presence and power of the Word of God, experienced as a real transforming power within us, and known as Christ because it is in conformity with the gospel descriptions of Jesus, and because it comes to us within (or at least from) the community of the Church. The person of Jesus is important to this understanding in a twofold way. He provides the normative description of the historical form of the eternal Word of God, and he is the foundation of the Church, in which the Word continues to be mediated to believers.

The teachings of Jesus and moral decision-making

Because of this, it is important to seek to interpret the person of Jesus as depicted in the Gospels as well as we can. But we would also expect the Christ within to be a creative and renewing power. The inner Christ must be consistent with the gospel records of Jesus, but will hardly be constrained by them. Just as the judgements of Rabbis must interpret Torah, but may be new and creative, so Christian judgements must make a plausible claim to be made in the mind and spirit of the gospel Jesus, but will hardly be confined to the things Jesus did and said. It is obvious, for example, that Jesus said nothing about nuclear war, about genetic experimentation, about contraception, or about democracy. Particular moral decisions cannot be decided simply by appeal to gospel texts, but must nevertheless be defensible by appeal to the character and teaching of Jesus.

That is why it is very important to arrive at a reasonable interpretation of the teaching of Jesus. When he said that anyone who breaks even one of the least commandments is least in the Kingdom, Christians after the first generation have to deny that the teaching applies to them. Somehow, but quite definitely, this teaching was sublated. Perhaps it only applied to the people to whom Jesus was speaking at the time – Jews before the coming of the Spirit with power at Pentecost. That entails that some statements made by Jesus in the Gospels are not binding on later generations, if the context changes sufficiently (in this case, if the resurrection and the events of Pentecost, and the conversion of many Gentiles, render a literal obedience to Torah inappropriate). A written moral command, even if attributed to Jesus in the Gospels, cannot be assumed to be binding on us. We must ask if a change of context makes a symbolic interpretation more appropriate (in this case, a possible symbolic interpretation would be that we must love and obey God with all our hearts).

I have shown that the teaching of the Sermon on the Mount cannot be taken literally, in all its details, by anyone. The most consistent principle of interpretation is therefore to take it all symbolically, as containing a set of startlingly impractical statements that express underlying principles of compassion and neighbour-love in a memorable way. The Church gave up the written rules of Torah altogether, and so took the symbolic interpretation even further, accepting that the rules need no longer be kept, because acceptance of the mind of Christ sublated obedience to written rules. This conclusion was arrived at only after much argument, and in opposition to most of the senior apostles. That might seem a fairly radical conclusion, but it is securely based on biblical testimony. It is what the Bible really teaches!

The view of Paul could hardly be clearer: 'we serve in the new way of the Spirit, and not in the old way of the written code' (Romans 7.6). In one bold stroke the Torah is internalized and universalized. The written rules are abandoned, and emphasis is placed on being formed in the image of Christ by the power of the Spirit. Jews are no longer separated from Gentiles by Torah, but all humanity is challenged to receive the Spirit of God, and so be included in the new covenant of the heart. The new Israel becomes the potentially universal community of the Spirit of God. Unlike both orthodox Judaism and Islam, Christians have no written code, no Torah or Shari'a. It is the inwardly working Spirit who is to lead them gradually to new insights as, reflecting continually on the life of Jesus as their pattern and inspiration, they come to decisions about how to implement God's purpose in new contexts and historical situations.

It is therefore vitally important not to take the life or sayings of Jesus in the Gospels as a new written law, and it is obvious that if we should not take the moral teachings of Jesus literally (though we must always take them seriously!), then we should certainly not take any of the particular rules laid down by Paul or the apostles for their specific situation as new written laws. To do that would be to betray the hard-won insights of the New Testament. What we have to do is test all proposed

rules, whether in the Bible or not, against the one unshakeable principle of loving your neighbour as yourself, in the light of the exemplary
life of Jesus, the living Wisdom of God.

Morality and law

In the life of the Christian Churches, there has been a constant tendency
to lay down binding rules, a new Law, and require obedience to them.
This is deeply anti-Christian and anti-biblical. If Paul, or any other
apostle, says that women should be obedient to men – 'Wives, submit
to your husbands as to the Lord' (Ephesians 5.22), we are to remind
ourselves of his own saying, 'the letter kills, but the Spirit gives life' (2
Corinthians 3.6). We must ask if this recommendation is compatible
with loving one's (female) neighbour as oneself, and whether it is true
to the character of Jesus, who said that the true leader is one who
serves. The biblical teaching is that we must not simply accept the rule
on authority. We must make the test ourselves. That means there is
room for differing judgements and for disagreement. But no one can
stand up and say, 'This is the only possible decision', or even worse,
'This rule is in the Bible, so we must keep it.'

To me it is clear that full respect for all humans of whatever gender
or race requires that we do not subject one group in principle to
another, whatever their own feelings and capacities. And it is clear that
Jesus' life of forgiveness, reconciliation, compassion, and sensitivity to
the feelings and needs of others puts a question mark against all forms
of the human subordination of others. I believe most Christians have
come to see that the subjection of wives, or of women in general, is
incompatible with universal neighbour-love, whatever particular apostles might have said. For the apostles, as we have seen, were mistaken
and short-sighted on many matters – on the need to keep Torah, for
instance – and what they say needs to be measured against the deeper
principle of unrestricted love.

It has to be admitted that exhortations to subjection and submissiveness are to be found in many New Testament passages. Slaves are
to submit to their masters, the young are to submit to the old, citizens
are to submit to their rulers, and women are to submit to their husbands, or even to men in general. Submissiveness is present in the
New Testament, though it is countermanded by passages that enjoin
the equality of all in Christ. We need to be clear that there are
recommendations in the New Testament that seem restricted in their
moral outlook. And we need to be clear about exactly what it is in

New Testament teaching that decisively rejects and opposes them.

I have shown how limited understandings of Jesus' teachings abound in the New Testament, and the matter of submission is no exception. One of the most infamous passages is Romans 13, where Paul writes, 'Everyone must submit himself to the governing authorities, for there is no authority except that which God has established. The authorities that exist have been established by God' (Romans 13.1). This statement is breathtaking in its myopia. Almost the whole Bible rises up to contradict it, from the divine command to leave Egypt and disobey the King of Egypt (Exodus 6) through the records of the Maccabean revolt, to the characterization of Rome as the 'whore of Babylon' (cf. Revelation 14.8). All those rulers were far from being established by God. They were in revolt against God. Moreover, Christians in the Roman Empire soon began to disobey the Roman command to sacrifice to the Emperor, seeing that this would be idolatry.

It is not always right to submit to the authorities, and it is not true that all authorities have been established by God. Paul can only be writing to people whom he wishes to be seen as obedient members of the Roman Empire. Circumstances changed considerably after he wrote that letter, and we can hardly imagine him saying that, for instance, the Emperor Nero's rule was established by God.

This statement is grossly misleading if it is taken to ban any rebellion or resistance to political authority. Its force is to remind Christians that there is a duty of political obedience, and that it is a serious thing to contemplate civil disobedience. It would be disastrously wrong to take it as some sort of absolute rule, just because it is in the Bible.

How, then, do we determine the biblical attitude to political order? With great difficulty, and Christians have always disagreed on their political views. I think we have to say that what appear to be particular rules in the New Testament (like 'Do not resist evil' or 'submit to the governing authorities') are not absolute rules at all. They point to something important – the importance of not being vindictive or the duty of civil obedience in general, and in more or less normal or non-oppressive situations. But sometimes we ought to do the very opposite of what they say, resisting evil to help the innocent or disobeying commands to torture, for instance. The important principle is this: on very important moral matters, it is not enough to quote specific biblical rules. We have to do four things. First, we have to see the possibly limited circumstances in which the rule applies. Second, we have to see more general principles that underlie the rule. Third, we have to put the rule in the context of biblical teaching in general, especially the teaching that God requires unrestricted love, compassion and mercy. Fourth, we have to try to see how these principles can be applied in very different situations. On all these matters, we have to expect disagreement, as we seek to see what God requires in very complex and often new circumstances.

So there are some Christians who do teach that we should submit to the state under any circumstances. But they are a small minority. Most accept that the biblical teaching as a whole is one of being concerned for justice, and especially for the welfare of the weak and the oppressed. This often requires disobedience to unjust state authorities – though the limits of disobedience are disputed, and nearly all Christians agree that there has to be a very strong case for civil disobedience to be justified. In this, Christian moral thinking has moved well beyond obedience to every specific biblical rule. But it may reasonably claim to have moved closer to the general and authentic biblical teaching that there is a duty to preserve civil order, and also a duty to remedy gross injustice and to protect the innocent, when that can be done with good hope of success and without causing grievous harm.

The Bible on the subjection of slaves and women

A very similar situation obtains with the biblical teaching on slavery. Slavery is countenanced in the Old Testament, with specific rules about the possession of slaves. To the surprise of some, it is not condemned in the New Testament. At best there are some hints or indications that slavery is not ideal. In the letter to Philemon, the writer commends the slave Onesimus, who had run away, to his owner, on the ground that he will now be a much more useful slave (Philemon 11). But he does also suggest that 'you might have him back for good – no longer as a slave but better than a slave, as a dear brother' (Philemon 15–16). This suggests that relationships between slaves and their owners will be transformed by Christian faith, and therefore that perhaps slavery itself would be transformed or even abolished, ideally – but nowhere is there an explicit call for the freeing of slaves.

Similarly 1 Corinthians 7.23 declares, 'You were bought at a price; do not become slaves of men'. However it also counsels that slaves should remain slaves, unless they get the chance of freedom – and so that owners should continue to possess them, presumably.

The real driving force to abolish slavery comes from a much more general statement, repeated twice in the New Testament, that in Christ there 'is no Greek or Jew, circumcised or uncircumcised, barbarian, Scythian, slave or free' (Colossians 3.11), and that 'There is neither Jew nor Greek, slave nor free, male nor female, for you are all one in Christ Jesus' (Galatians 3.28).

The conclusion is not drawn in the New Testament that slavery is to be abolished. But the implication is fairly clear that there should be no social discrimination between slaves and freemen. To this extent slavery is incompatible with a Christian society – but it took hundreds of years for this to become clear to Christians. There is no explicit rule condemning it. We have to explore the implications of the apostolic teachings of the unity, equality and liberty of all in Christ, and draw out the social and political consequences of those teachings for ourselves.

The case is similar with the biblical teachings about relations between men and women. There are many places where the New Testament advocates that women should submit to men. 'I do not permit a woman to teach or to have authority over a man; she must be silent' (1 Timothy 2.12). The writer of this letter is supposed to be Paul, but this is a very different message from that given in Paul's first letter to the Corinthians, where he says that 'every woman who prays or prophesies with her head uncovered dishonours her head' (1 Corinthians 11.5). Whatever we think of the writer's peculiar notion that men must not wear hats in church or have long hair, while women must cover their hair 'because of the angels', at least it is obvious that this Paul permits women to pray and prophesy, and does not bid them to be silent. Not only that, but in Romans 16 Paul refers to Phoebe, a deaconess, and to *Junian* (that is, the feminine name Junia), who is described as an apostle. In Rome women undertook some form of ministry in the church, and it is not true that women had no authority over men in that church.

The important point is that we cannot accept both of these recommendations – we cannot both tell women to be silent and tell them to wear a veil when prophesying. Which should we accept, and why should we accept either? The reason for not accepting either is that they seem to be wholly arbitrary matters of social convention, not to say of male prejudice. There is no good reason why one should replace (sublate) the other. Neither seems to offer profound insight into the true nature of freedom in Christ. They rather seem to display a rather startling lack of freedom from sheer social convention, and in fact from two conflicting social conventions in different places.

The statements already quoted about there being 'no slave or free, male or female' in Christ, suggest that it would be better to abandon all such divisive conventions. The statement about the unity of slaves and free was eventually seen to imply that slaves should be treated as free men. The statement about the unity of male and female implies equally strongly that men and women should be treated in the same way, except where there is good reason to the contrary. Regrettably, the apostles were slow to see these implications – but they were slow to see many things, and it is our job to pursue implications of Christian liberty that previous generations have overlooked.

Moral rules and human relationships

There is no doubt that freedom from the regulations of the law is a crucial Christian teaching. Paul, as we have noted, writes that 'the letter kills, but the Spirit gives life' (2 Corinthians 3.6). We have seen that one of the earliest battles in the Church was the battle to achieve freedom from Torah, the Jewish Law. That battle was won, in principle, but the victory was not carried through. One early Christian document, the *Didache*, or *The Teaching of the Twelve Apostles*, recommends that Christians should not fast with the hypocrites, on the second and fifth days of the week. Instead, Christians should fast on the fourth and sixth days of the week! This is a good example of how some early Christians (almost certainly not the apostles!) were eager to set up new rules, and completely misunderstood the Pauline teaching that the written Law had come to an end in Christ.

There have been some Christians who have argued that only the ritual laws were to be abandoned in the Church – laws about sacrifices or prohibition of unclean foods. The moral laws, they say, remain intact. There is absolutely no biblical warrant for such a view. It is contrary to the whole spirit of Jewish law to divide Torah into parts, ritual, hygienic and moral, and then say that some parts are more important than others. If you keep Torah, you keep the whole thing. If you abandon it, you abandon the whole thing. So you abandon moral rules as well – rules like those concerning the ownership of slaves, or stoning to death for adultery (Deuteronomy 22).

Paul saw the danger that Christians might think that, being free from the written moral law, they could do anything they liked. Therefore he insists that they are still bound by what he calls 'Christ's law' (1 Corinthians 9.21). But what is that law? It is not a written code. Paul says, 'The entire law is summed up in a single command: "Love your neighbour as yourself"' (Galatians 5.14). Particular moral rules are ways of working out what it is to love our neighbour. They are not to be treated as unchangeable divine commands. They are rather laws devised in the freedom of Christian life to help us to live that life more effectively.

The ultimate test is whether moral rules enable us to 'live by the Spirit' rather than to gratify the desires of the sinful nature (Galatians 5.16). Paul classifies the 'acts of the sinful nature' as 'sexual immorality, impurity and debauchery; idolatry and witchcraft; hatred, discord, jealousy, fits of rage, selfish ambition, dissentions, factions and envy; drunkenness, orgies, and the like' (Galatians 5.19–20). It would be ridiculous to take these words as a list of moral rules prohibiting specific practices, when they are written by the very person who says that written rules kill. Nevertheless, they give a good idea of the sorts of things Paul thought express or encourage indulgence in self-centred passion. They fall into three main groups. First there are three general and rather unspecific sorts of excessive sensuality – *porneia* is adultery, or unspecified sexual sin, *akatharsia* is lack of cleanliness, and probably also has a reference to unusual sexual practices, and *aselgeia* is lewdness. These are sins connected with sexual conduct, but they are very unspecific, and have a general reference to sexual acts that dishonour human persons and human dignity or break human relationships. That seems to be the reason they are classified as wrong by Paul – the impact of these practices on personal relationships of integrity, respect, trust and loyalty.

The second group is concerned with religion – idolatry and witchcraft are practices that worship something else in place of God, or try to control God for your own purposes. It is important not to see Hindus, for example, as idolatrous, just because they bow down before images. What we need to know is whether they are replacing the worship of God with the worship of powers of greed and ambition. Also many who call themselves witches have no intention of controlling God by magic. They merely wish to encourage a sense of unity with nature. So it is necessary to see just what Paul is condemning when he uses these terms, and not to simply transfer the terms to different practices today, and use them to condemn fairly harmless – even if one thinks misguided – practices.

The third group comprises a set of dispositions that impair or destroy human relationships and cause the self to disintegrate. This is by far the largest group of named 'sins', with no less than ten vices named by Paul, showing the great importance he places on building up and maintaining loyal and loving relationships between people, and controlling the self so that it is always in a position to serve God fully and consciously.

Paul contrasts these with the 'fruit of the Spirit . . . love, joy, peace, patience, kindness, goodness, faithfulness, gentleness and self-control'

(Galatians 5.22). These are all personal dispositions regarding our relations to other people, and this shows that 'the way of the Spirit' is primarily a way of relating to others in love and respect. What matters above all, the New Testament teaches, is not specific rules in themselves, whatever their consequences, but finding ways of building up, strengthening and securing loving relationships between people.

The love commandment

There must be moral rules and conventions, but they must always be tested against the primary commandment of love. 'Since you died with Christ to the basic principles of this world, why, as though you still belonged to it, do you submit to its rules?' (Colossians 2.20). The point is that no rule should be accepted just because it is found in a written text, even less because it is a social convention that has been followed for a long time. Rules are meant to build up relationships of loyalty, respect and trust, and if they do not do so, they can, and sometimes should, be changed.

A very good example of a written rule that should be changed is the injunction, 'Wives . . . be submissive to your husbands' (1 Peter 3.1). That rule in fact undermines the proper respect due to women, making them in effect slaves of their husbands, and it makes impossible a relationship of mutual companionship which is so important in marriage. Assuming that Peter wrote this letter, we have to say that, just as he was wrong in refusing to eat with Gentiles at Antioch (Galatians 2.11), so he was wrong when he assumed that all women, however able, should submit to their husbands, however weak and unreliable.

Once we see that the apostles were sometimes wrong, being over-influenced by the social pressures and conventions of their day, we are free to begin to look with a new eye at the social pressures and conventions of our own society, and begin to challenge them wherever they conflict with the true biblical teaching of the summing up of all rules in the principle of 'love of neighbour', of the universal extent of who our neighbours are, and of a primary concern, not for obedience to rules, but for building up human relationships of love, loyalty, respect and trust. We have the strongest biblical authority for testing all alleged moral rules against these three fundamental biblical principles. 'It is for freedom that Christ has set us free. Stand firm then, and do not let yourselves be burdened again by a yoke of slavery' (Galatians 5.1) – even if that yoke is imposed by the Church itself!

People often overlook the true biblical teaching about marriage and sexual relationships. They impose on the Bible standards of their own which are not to be found there, and they accept as binding specific rules which happen to suit them, while completely ignoring many other biblical rules that they do not like. In other words, they pick and choose what they like, and what they provide is not a biblical morality at all, but a combination of social convention and prejudice, which they support by carefully selected and edited parts of the Bible.

Biblical teaching on sexual relationships is very different from present Christian views, though it is recommended that bishops should only have one wife (1 Timothy 3.2). The Patriarchs and David and Solomon had many wives, and are never criticized for that. Not only that. Concubines are permitted, together with stoning to death for adultery (Deuteronomy 22). The death penalty is also enjoined for homosexual relations (Leviticus 18), for adultery (Deuteronomy 22), for disobedience to parents (Deuteronomy 21), and for sexual relations with one of your father's wives (Leviticus 18). Marriage to your dead brother's wife is, under certain circumstances, compulsory (Deuteronomy 25).

These are all parts of Torah, which Jesus said should be obeyed to the letter. In Jewish tradition they had all been interpreted in a relatively liberal sense by the time of Jesus, but that only reinforces the fact that biblical rules, even of the law of God, can be and should be reinterpreted in new social situations. Most people today would say that these are rather primitive rules. The basic trouble with them is that they do not grant full honour and respect to women, and the penalties are much too cruel by the standards of a Christian love that is always concerned for the ultimate well-being even of offenders.

Monogamy is justifiable on the grounds that it allows for a fully mutual respect, loyalty and trust between two people, and safeguards the security of children.

These are indeed important biblical principles, but the rule of monogamy in its present Christian form needs to be worked out by reflection on the biblical teaching, by the reinterpretation of many specific biblical rules, and by a sensitive application to particular cases of Jesus' teaching of universal respect, love and compassion. Fundamentalists make a great fuss about same-sex love, but if they are consistent they should use the same principles about that as they do about monogamous marriage.

In other words, we should not hesitate to change specific rules where they seem to make respect and love harder, and where they fail to show compassion and understanding. Of course there are rules forbidding homosexuality in the Bible – that is not in question. The question is

whether those rules should be taken any more seriously than the rule
that you must marry your dead brother's wife. Most people reinterpret
the rule straight away by ignoring the stated penalty – of death by stoning. It seems clear that if two people of the same sex genuinely love each
other, and wish to commit themselves to a relationship of life-long
loyalty and trust, this preserves all the basic biblical moral principles.
Biblical condemnations of homosexual practice can be consigned to the
morally primitive past, along with all the biblical rules about slavery,
the possession of concubines, stoning to death, the right of private
vengeance (Deuteronomy 19) and the obligation of capital punishment
(Exodus 21).

We do not need to debate the issue of the biblical attitude to homosexuality at all, once we have seen how many biblical moral rules we
reject. The reason we reject them is that they are in conflict with the
three great fundamental biblical moral principles. These are:

1. The principle of unrestricted neighbour love, which states that we
   should treat all human beings with the same concern that we treat
   ourselves.
2. The principle of unrestricted compassion, stating that we must
   always have in mind the ultimate good of others, even when we are
   compelled to restrain or punish them.
3. The principle of freedom from law to walk in the Spirit, which
   reminds us that all written laws are to be tested by whether they
   encourage relationships of loyalty, trust, honesty and friendship.

We do need to explore with great sensitivity the extent to which and the
ways in which same-sex love, for example, can be expressed in conformity with the love of others and of God. But we do not need to
worry about the fact that explicit condemnations of it are found in the
Bible, because the Bible teaches that we can reject any written rule that
is in conflict with the love of Christ, for 'Christ is the end of the law'
(Romans 10.4).

The first-generation Christian Church moved from millennialism to
a much more sophisticated understanding of how each moment of time
is taken into eternity, as a prototype of the final fulfilment of all things
in God. So it also moved from a rigorist commitment to Torah and
separatism to a recognition that the Christian life is one of letting the
Spirit of God transform the self inwardly so that the nature of Christ,
of unrestricted love, is fully formed within it.

If the first-generation Church is any sort of pattern for the modern

Church, it is a pattern of radical and creative change, of a readiness to question all written rules, and to move to new understandings of what faith requires, under the direction of the Spirit of God, both responding to and transforming the new historical contexts in which the gospel of new life in Christ is proclaimed.

Christian life is not a matter of obedience to rules, either of the Bible or of the Church. It is a life that is to be formed on the pattern of Christ, by the inner working of the Spirit. That pattern is clear, but it is a pattern of attitudes and dispositions, not of rules and prescriptions. It, and not the words of any Creed, is the final test of the authenticity of Christian faith.

Why have Christians been so slow to see that the gospel of Christian freedom entails the freedom from all written laws, even if they are written in the Bible itself? Perhaps because they are afraid of freedom, of the freedom that Christ brings. They want to be told what to do, they want to be certain it is right, they want God to tell them something clear and definite. But the only consequence is that they have to ignore huge amounts of the Bible, and the most important parts at that. Christians in general – and I am not speaking specifically of fundamentalists here – do not want to be told what the Bible actually tells them, that they must challenge moral conventions, practise sacrificial self-giving, and care for the poorest people on earth as they would care for themselves. They want a few simple rules that happen to fit a middle-class and comfortable lifestyle, and if they have to ignore most of the Bible to do it, they will.

I want to make it quite clear that I do not think fundamentalists are any worse than other Christians in this respect. My fundamentalist friends are, in fact, much more morally zealous than most middle-of-the-road believers. But sometimes their moral zeal is, I have come to think, misplaced. For there are some moral rules in the Bible, even in the New Testament, that conflict with the basic Christian principle of unrestricted love. Because fundamentalists believe that they should obey these rules, they are forced, often despite themselves, to undermine possibilities of greater love and understanding, particularly in regard to gender and sexual conduct.

What I have tried to demonstrate is that it is not possible to obey all the rules of the Bible, and that it would be wrong to try to do so, since one of the chief 'rules' is that you should not obey written rules, for you are free from the moral law! So in fact what is happening is that a few rules are selected, while others are rejected (always the rules against lending at interest, enjoining stoning to death, or permitting polygamy

and slavery, often the rule against divorce, sometimes the rule prohibiting women speaking in church, or enjoining capital punishment).

The tragedy of fundamentalism is that it is so utterly unbiblical. It
insists on the literal truth of a few selected passages, neglecting or twisting the interpretation of many others. A truly Bible-based faith would
see that fallibility and diversity, development and poetic vision, are
basic characteristics of the Bible. It testifies to the fallibility of the
human understanding of divine revelation and the many different
human perspectives on divine revelation, even as it corrects that understanding and moves us on to new imaginative visions of the divine.
What the Bible teaches, at least to Christians, is that we should take
responsibility for our own moral decisions, always being motivated by
the basic Christian principles of the self-giving, agapistic love and the
new and joyous life of freedom that is to be found in Christ Jesus. That
is biblical morality, and we should never try to disguise it by hiding
behind a few written rules that often show the limitations of past moral
perceptions that the Spirit calls us to leave behind.

♦ Conclusion ♦

Fundamentalism and the Future of Christianity

Fundamentalist Christians have many vitally important things right about God's revelation in Jesus. They uphold unflinchingly the sovereignty of God over all human life. They witness to deep personal relationship with Jesus Christ. They call for selfless loyalty to the will of the creator God. In a world that is confused and confusing, morally uncertain and spiritually adrift, they speak with confidence about new life with God available through Jesus Christ. All these are immensely good things.

But fundamentalism has some decided peculiarities. The main peculiarity is that what they *say* is fundamental really is not. What is really fundamental for them, as for most Christians, is new, eternal life in God, companionship with Jesus Christ, and the inner working of the Holy Spirit. It is something real and experiential, a vital living relationship with God. But what they *say* is fundamental is something intellectual, academic and abstract – a doctrine of the verbal inerrancy of the Bible, and of its interpretation in as literalistic a way as possible. They add to this an extremely abstract 'theory of atonement' – the substitutionary theory – that developed very late in Christian history, and that they impose on the Bible by ignoring much of what the Bible teaches, by misrepresenting the biblical doctrine of sacrifice, and by interpreting much of the rest of the Bible in a surprisingly literalistic way. They then make what is a terrible spiritual mistake of confusing the fact that Jesus Christ is the only Saviour of all (of 'the world') with the claim that Jesus only saves those who explicitly believe in him – which fatally undermines any belief in a God of unrestricted love, and so turns the good news of the gospel into the bad news of damnation for almost everyone. They take biblical passages about creation and the final ending of the universe in such a crudely literal way that they are bound to come into a quite unnecessary conflict with ordinary scientific knowledge. Worse, this means that they miss the inner spiritual meaning of those passages, and the importance of metaphor and symbolism in bringing disciples to greater spiritual perception and self-awareness. And when it comes to morality, they choose to take a few texts as literally binding, when they blithely disregard others, and completely miss Paul's teaching on the triumph of grace over law.

I have tried to set out what the Bible teaches on a number of issues that fundamentalists get wrong. What fundamentalists say about the coming in glory of Christ, about the Sermon on the Mount, about the possibility of universal salvation, and about the resurrection and life after death seems to me to be pretty obviously wrong. On all these subjects the Bible actually teaches the opposite of what fundamentalists say. When it comes to specific topics in morality, like issues of gender and sexuality, of politics and medical advances, my main point has been that the Bible challenges us to think through these things for ourselves, giving guidelines but not issuing definitive commands. I would expect disagreement on some of these issues. But that disagreement is not about what the Bible teaches. It is about what we conscientiously decide when we seek to apply biblical principles to hard moral issues. That disagreement is something we find within the pages of the Bible, something we should expect, and something we have to work through prayerfully and charitably.

So I will end where I began, by distinguishing evangelicalism from fundamentalism. Evangelicals have been a major reforming influence on Christian faith. They have made the reading of the Bible by the laity in the vernacular important to Christian life and prayer. They have successfully criticized some of the exclusive and authoritarian practices of traditional Christian Churches. And they have made a living experience of Christ the centre of Christian faith.

Fundamentalists, however, subtly pervert these evangelical insights. They impose an authoritarian interpretation of the Bible that is as dogmatic as any medieval Catholic theology, and usually less informed. They make their faith even more exclusive than that of those Catholics who claimed that there is no salvation outside the Church. And they make intellectual assent to 'sound' doctrines a more important test of Christian faith than life in the Spirit.

The greatest tragedy of fundamentalism, however, is that it gets the Bible wrong. Fundamentalists read back into the Bible a sort of literalism that could only have existed after the sixteenth-century growth of science, which suggested that only literal truths are real truths. They impose on it a millenarian belief that became outdated in the second Christian generation, that ignores all scientific knowledge about the universe, and that betrays a deep fear of science and reason. In this respect, they betray the long Christian tradition that always saw the universe as the work of the divine Wisdom (and thus as supremely reasonable), and that gave birth to science as rational investigation into the handiwork of divine reason. And they distort the basic nature of Christian revelation, which is in the person of Jesus and in relationship to that person, and not primarily in the words of any book and in intellectual submission to those words.

The Christian Church is growing fast in many parts of the world today. Very many new Christians are evangelicals, or are influenced by evangelical teachings. But many new Christians, particularly in Africa and Asia, are tempted beyond evangelicalism to adopt fundamentalist views of the Bible. This is because they have been taught by some missionaries to read the Bible very selectively, to take much of it (which is written metaphorically) literally, and to ignore those sections that undermine fundamentalist views.

What is important for these new and vital forms of Christianity is that they come to a genuinely Bible-based faith, seeing what the Bible really says about the revelation of God and about the transformation of the moral law in Jesus. They need to distinguish what the Bible teaches from what fundamentalists teach, and to see fundamentalism as a product of the worst aspects of the European and Western Enlightenment, which sees literal truth as the only sort of truth, and which confuses conventional Western social and moral views with the freedom of the gospel.

Christianity is contracting in Europe and North America, and that, too, is because of the impact of fundamentalism. Fundamentalists have managed to convince many people that the real Christian message is a literalistic one about the violent end of the world and the miraculous salvation of a few people with fantastic beliefs. Consequently, the majority of Western people have turned away from Christianity, as irrelevant to their hopes and concerns. So in the West as in the rest of the world it is important to distinguish Bible teaching and evangelicalism from fundamentalism, and expose the errors of fundamentalist interpretation.

Christianity is about the entrance of eternity into time, in order that time might be transfigured into eternity. The person of Jesus is the central revelation and realization of this truth. The Bible is the normative witness to it, and a profound spiritual resource for evoking a sense of the eternal in time. When more people see this, and realize what the Bible really teaches, fundamentalism will be seen for what it is, a twentieth-century Western literalistic millenarian philosophy imposed on the Bible without regard for scholarship or tradition. It is a corruption of the evangelical faith in the saving experience of Christ above acceptance of doctrines, the priority of the person of Christ over all written laws, the centrality of the Bible as always pointing to the personal Lordship of Christ, the need to critically examine all human teachings and interpretations, and the glorious freedom in the Spirit of the Christian man and woman. When evangelicals rediscover their own heritage, and read the Bible carefully, fundamentalism will fade away.

Index